Real-World Testimonials

"Whether you are a manager or just starting your transformation to Agile or looking to improve it, you will find practical advice rooted in good research and wide experience."
—*Shaheeda Nizar, Engineering Leader, Google*

"Makes the core concepts of cutting-edge Agile development accessible and relevant to leaders, while providing a business/value-centric view."
—*John Reynders, Vice President, R&D Strategy, Program Management and Data Sciences, Alexion Pharmaceuticals*

"This book makes clear that Agile is a set of practices determined by outcomes that are important to your business, not merely a prescriptive set of rituals to be performed."
—*Glenn Goodrich, VP, Product Development Practice, Skookum*

"Its 28 key principles are an excellent 'cheat sheet' of arguably the most valuable lessons learned in software product development over the last four decades. The book brings these principles into sharp focus by weaving together theory and practice and using lucid language and visuals."
—*Xander Botha, Technical Director, Demonware*

"Makes clear that Agile can (with the right approach) be surprisingly effective in contexts that have historically assumed sequential development, such as when predictability is critical or in a regulatory context."
—*Charles Davies, CTO, TomTom*

"Uniquely easy to read for technical and non-technical audiences, bridging the gap to a common understanding of Agile."
—*Sunil Kripalani, Chief Digital Officer, OptumRx*

"Even Agile experts will find food for thought in this book that will reinvigorate their use of Agile methodologies."
—*Stefan Landvogt, Principal Software Engineer, Microsoft*

"Many idealistic Agile approaches tend to fail in complex real-life situations. This book is a good guiding light through the maze of Agile adoption, describing what to look for (Inspect) and what to do about what you find (Adapt)."
—*Ilhan Dilber, Director of Quality and Testing, CareFirst*

"Refreshingly, this book avoids Agile dogma and explains how to use Agile practices suited to the needs of your business."
—*Brian Donaldson, President, Quadrus*

"Predictability is often (mistakenly) seen as a trade-off to Agile instead of something Agile itself provides. The techniques outlined here are excellent suggestions that debunk that myth."
—*Lisa Forsyth, Senior Director, Smashing Ideas*

"Succinct, practical, and tightly focused on delivering what the title promises, this book is especially valuable for software leaders who want to make their Agile processes more effective. It will also be very useful to leaders just starting or considering moving to Agile."
—*David Wight, Consultant, Calaveras Group*

"A holistic overview of how to effectively implement agile and improve over time so that agile moves beyond just the adoption phase. Many books focus on how to get started, but few share the knowledge and specific tools to keep going."
—*Eric Upchurch, Principal Software Architect, Synaptech*

"Brings together all aspects of creating modern software-intensive systems—technical, managerial, organizational, cultural, and human—into an easy-to-understand, coherent, and actionable whole based on real experience."
—*Giovanni Asproni, Principal Consultant, Zuhlke Engineering Ltd*

"Great advice on how to tackle the larger organizational aspects required to make Agile work, such as the Agile boundary, change management models, portfolio management, and predictability vs. control."
—*Hiranya Samarasekera, VP of Engineering-Sysco LABS*

"Concise and impactful presentation that offers something of value to every individual and company—primarily where software is a key component of what they do—and many of the concepts apply in a general sense for just about any business."
—*Barbara Talley, Director, Business Systems Analysts, Epsilon*

"An authoritative source of information, best practices, challenges, actions, and further sources of knowledge. This book is a go-to resource for myself and my team. I sometimes struggle to explain Agile practices and how to make them effective; this book does so brilliantly."
—*Graham Haythornthwaite, VP of Technology, Impero Software*

"*More Effective Agile* teaches you how to look at Agile as a set of tools to selectively bring to bear when the situation calls for it, rather than as an all-or-nothing proposition."
—*Timo Kissel, SVP Engineering, Circle Media*

"This is an excellent book that finally answers the question 'Why use Agile?'"
—*Don Shafer, Chief Safety, Security, Health and Environment Officer, Athens Group*

"For those getting started with Agile, go straight to the 'More Effective Agile Adoptions' section. I have seen far too many organizations go 'all Agile' without putting in the proper foundation to make it succeed."
—*Kevin Taylor, Sr. Cloud Architect, Amazon*

"This is a tremendous book, filled with extremely useful information that even seasoned practitioners can learn from. This is the missing handbook for applying Agile practices pragmatically."
—*Manny Gatlin, VP of Professional Services, Bad Rabbit*

"Cuts through the hype to tell me what works and what others have found useful, including soft issues around culture, people, and teams, as well as process and architecture. The depth of coverage is surprising given the size of the book!"
—*Mike Blackstock, CTO, Sense Tecnic Systems*

"An honest look at this 20-year-old methodology, and probably the first book that directly addresses managers and tells them what to do."
—*Sumant Kumar, Development Director (Engineering), Innovative Business Solutions Organization, SAP*

"I appreciated the discussions on what motivates individuals and teams along with leadership traits that help in any environment. We often take for granted the human element and focus only on the procedural."
—*Dennis Rubsam, Senior Director, Seagate*

"Leaders coming from a traditional project management culture often struggle to grasp Agile concepts. For them, *More Effective Agile* will be revealing."
—*Paul van Hagen, Platform Architect and Software Excellence Manager, Shell Global Solutions International B.V.*

"Provides key insights not only into how to build an effective Agile team but also into how an organization's leadership should relate to its development teams to ensure success."
—*Tom Spitzer, VP Engineering, EC Wise*

"A much-needed update in the fast-changing world of software development, where across disparate industries there is an increasing urgency to deliver more, faster."
—*Kenneth Liu, Senior Director, Program Management, Symantec*

"Provides valuable insights and lessons for all types of software development practitioners—Business Leaders, Product Owners, Analysts, Software Engineers, and Testers."
—*Melvin Brandman, Chief Technology Advisor–Human Capital and Benefits, Willis Towers Watson*

"For leaders of existing Agile projects who want to improve or leaders who are adopting Agile, this book provides a comprehensive reference covering all aspects of Agile leadership."
—*Brad Moore, Vice President Engineering, Quartet Health*

"A very valuable digest of principles that are proven to level up Agile teams. A lot of valuable experience—not just information—is packed into this single resource."
—*Dewey Hou, VP Product Development, TechSmith Corporation*

"*More Effective Agile* is a great mirror for Agile implementation—hold your processes up to it to see both positives and negatives."
—*Matt Schouten, Senior Director of Product Development, Herzog Technologies*

"I wish I had this book five years ago when I was rolling out the Agile adoption at our company. It clarifies (and predicts) many of the problems we experienced."
—*Mark Apgar, Manager Product Design, Tsunami Tsolutions*

"Most companies probably think they have an 'Agile' development process, but they may be missing a lot of key pieces that could make their process better. McConnell draws from research on software development and his own experience at Construx and distills that knowledge into one concise resource."
—*Steve Perrin, Senior Development Manager, Zillow*

"Addresses many of the issues we have struggled through over the years—would have been most helpful if it was available when we started our journey. The Suggested Leadership Actions are wonderful."
—*Barry Saylor, VP, Software Development, Micro Encoder Inc.*

"*More Effective Agile* represents the culmination of 20 years' experience with agile adoptions. Just as *Code Complete* became the definitive handbook for software developers in the 1990s, *More Effective Agile* will become the definitive handbook for agile leaders in the upcoming decade."
—*Tom Kerr, Embedded Software Development Manager, ZOLL Medical*

More Effective Agile

More Effective Agile

A Roadmap for Software Leaders

Steve McConnell

Construx
P R E S S

Published by

Construx Press
10900 NE 8ᵗʰ Street, Suite 1300
Bellevue, WA 98004
www.construx.com

Construx Press books are available through most bookstores. For copies for your team, contact us at press@construx.com for discounts.

Library of Congress Cataloging-in-Publication Data

McConnell, Steven C.

More Effective Agile: A Roadmap for Software Leaders / Steve McConnell. —1st ed.

p. cm.

Includes bibliographical references and index.

ISBN 978-1-7335182-0-8 (hard cover), 978-1-7335182-1-5 (paper-back) 978-1-7335182-2 (ebk)

1. Agile software development. 2. Computer software—development. 3. Management. I. Title.

QA76.76.D47M39 2019
005.1 –dc22   2019904601

First Edition

1 2 3 4 5 6 7 8 9 10

Contents at a Glance

i

MORE EFFECTIVE WORK

MORE EFFECTIVE ORGANIZATIONS

CLOSING

Detailed Contents

MORE EFFECTIVE TEAMS

MORE EFFECTIVE WORK

CLOSING

More Effective Agile

INTRODUCTION TO
MORE EFFECTIVE AGILE

Part I of this book describes foundational concepts for Agile software development. Parts II–IV then dive into specific suggestions.

The concepts introduced in Part I are referenced extensively throughout the rest of the book, so if you jump ahead to Parts II–IV, keep in mind that those discussions depend on ideas presented in Part I.

If you'd like to start with a big-picture overview, skip to Part V, "Closing," and read "Enjoy the Fruits of Your Labor" and "Summary of Key Principles."

CHAPTER ONE

Introduction

In the early 2000s, software leaders raised significant questions about Agile development. Leaders were concerned about Agile's ability to support quality, predictability, large projects, measured improvements, and work in regulated industries. Their concerns were well-founded at the time: Agile's initial promises were inflated, many Agile adoptions were disappointing, and achieving results often took longer than planned.

The software industry has needed time and experience to distinguish ineffective missteps of early Agile from genuine advances. In more recent years, the software industry has improved some of Agile's early practices, added new practices, and learned to avoid a few practices. Today, the use of modern Agile development offers the opportunity to improve quality, predictability, productivity, and throughput all at the same time.

For more than 20 years, my company, Construx Software, has worked with organizations that develop software systems ranging from mobile games to medical devices. We have helped hundreds of organizations be successful with Sequential development, and over the past 15 years we have experienced increasingly good results from Agile development. We have seen organizations significantly reduce cycle times, increase productivity, improve quality, improve customer responsiveness, and increase transparency by using Agile practices.

Much of the Agile literature has focused on high-flying, high-growth companies in new markets, such as Netflix, Amazon, Etsy, Spotify, and other similar companies. But what if your company makes software that's less leading edge? What about companies that make software for scientific instruments, office machines, medical devices, consumer electronics, heavy machinery, or process control equipment? We've found that modern Agile practices—applied with a focus on what's best for the specific business—provide advantages for these kinds of software too.

Why Effective Agile Matters

Companies want more effective software development for its own sake. They also want more effective software development because software enables so many other business functions. The *State of DevOps Report* found that, "Firms with high-performing IT organizations were twice as likely to exceed their profitability, market share, and productivity goals" (Puppet Labs, 2014). High-performing companies were twice as likely to meet or exceed their goals for customer satisfaction, quality and quantity of work, operating efficiency, and other objectives.

Selective, well-informed use of modern Agile practices offers a proven path toward more effective software development and all the benefits that go with it.

Unfortunately, most organizations are not realizing the potential of Agile practices because most implementations of Agile practices are not effective. For example, Scrum is the most common Agile practice and it can be incredibly powerful, yet we have most often seen it implemented in ways that fail to realize its benefits. The diagram below compares the average Scrum team my company has seen to a healthy Scrum team.

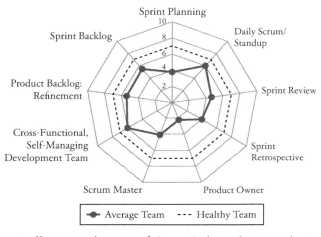

We typically see only one of Scrum's key elements being applied effectively (daily scrum/standup), and even that's far from universal. The rest of Scrum's elements are applied sporadically or not at all. (The scoring used in this diagram is described in detail in Chapter 4, "More Effective Agile Beginnings: Scrum.")

A poor implementation of a potentially good practice is not the only source of Agile failure. The term "Agile" has become an umbrella term that covers myriad practices, principles, and theories. We have seen Agile implementations fail because organizations are not aligned on what they mean by "Agile."

Under that large Agile umbrella, some practices work much better than others, and we've seen some organizations fail because they choose practices that are just not effective.

Organizations can achieve markedly better performance, and this book describes how to do that.

Who This Book Is For

This book is for C-level executives, VPs, Directors, managers, and other leaders of software teams and organizations who want to ensure effective Agile adoptions. If you have a technical background but do not have deep experience in modern Agile practices, this book is for you. If you have a *nontechnical* background and just want a working knowledge of Agile practices, this book is also for you (it's OK to skip the technical parts). And if you learned a lot about Agile practices 10–15 years ago but haven't updated your knowledge of modern Agile since then, this book is for you.

Most important, if your organization has adopted Agile development and you are not satisfied with the results, this book is for you.

How This Book Is Different From Other Agile Books

This book is not about how to do Agile "correctly"—it's about how to get the most value from the Agile practices that make sense for your business.

This book addresses the topics that businesses care about but that Agile purists often neglect: common challenges with Agile implementations, how to implement Agile in only part of your organization, Agile's support for predictability, the best ways to use Agile on geographically distributed teams, and using Agile in regulated industries, just to name a few of the neglected topics this book describes.

Most books about Agile development are written by evangelists. They're advocating a specific Agile practice, or they're promoting Agile overall. I am not an Agile evangelist. I'm an advocate for "things that work," and I'm an opponent of "things that over-promise with no evidence." This book does not treat Agile as a movement that requires an elevated state of consciousness, but as a collection of specific management and technical practices whose effects and interactions can be understood in business and technical terms.

I could not have written this book in the early 2000s because the software world had not accumulated enough on-the-ground experience with Agile development to know with any confidence what was working and what wasn't. Today, we have learned that some of the practices that were the most publicized then did not turn out to be very effective, while other practices that were less publicized then have emerged as the reliable workhorses of effective modern Agile implementations. This book sorts out which is which.

Agile enthusiasts might criticize this book as not representing the leading edge of Agile development, but that is precisely the point—this book focuses on practices that have proven to work. The history of Agile development is rich with ideas that one or two enthusiasts used successfully in a handful of organizations but that were ultimately not found to be generally useful. This book does not dwell on those limited-use practices.

This book provides a roadmap to modern Agile practices that work—and a few cautions about Agile practices and ideas to avoid. This book is not an Agile tutorial but a guide to help software leaders separate the signal from the noise.

How This Book Is Organized

This book begins with *background and context*, moves to *individuals and teams*, then to the *work practices* used by the individuals and teams, then to the *organizations* within which the teams employ the work practices, and last to *summary and perspective*.

The book's part openers provide guidance to help you decide whether to read each part and in what order to read them.

Let Me Know What You Think

The contents of this book would not have been possible without extensive peer review. The initial manuscript was thoroughly reviewed by my staff at Construx Software. I asked for outside volunteers to review the next draft, and more than 300 software leaders contributed more than 10,000 review comments. Their generous help has greatly benefited this edition.

What is your reaction to this book? Does it match your experience? Did it help you with any issues you are facing? I welcome your comments at any of the coordinates below.

Bellevue, Washington
July 4, 2019

 stevemcc@construx.com

 Linkedin.com/in/stevemcc

 SteveMcConnellConstrux

 @Stevemconstrux

 MoreEffectiveAgile.com

CHAPTER TWO

What's Really Different About Agile?

⌇

Most Agile books with a chapter title like "What's Really Different About Agile?" would immediately dive into historical descriptions of the 2001 Agile Manifesto and its related 20-year-old Agile Principles.

These documents served important and useful purposes 20 years ago, but Agile practices have continued to mature since then, and neither of these historic references accurately characterize the most valuable aspects of Agile today.

So, what is different about Agile today? The Agile movement historically contrasted itself with waterfall development. The claim was that waterfall development tried to do 100% of its planning up front, 100% of its requirements work up front, 100% of its design up front, and so on. This was an accurate characterization of literal "waterfall" development, but it described a mode of development that was never actually in widespread use. Various kinds of *phased development* were common.

True waterfall development existed mainly in early US Department of Defense projects, and that early crude implementation had already been superseded by more sophisticated lifecycles by the time the Agile Manifesto was written.[1]

The most meaningful contrast with Agile development today is *Sequential development*. Mischaracterizations aside, the contrasts are as shown in Table 2-1.

Short release cycles vs. long release cycles

Teams using Agile practices develop working software in cycles measured in days or weeks. Teams using Sequential practices measure their development cycles in months or quarters.

End-to-end development work performed in small batches vs. large batches

Agile development emphasizes complete development—including detailed requirements, design, coding, testing, and documentation—in small batches, meaning a small number of features or requirements at a time. Sequential development emphasizes moving an entire project's worth of requirements, design, coding, and testing through the development pipeline at the same time in large batches.

Just-in-time planning vs. up-front planning

Agile development typically does only a little planning up front and leaves most of the detailed planning to be done just in time. Well-done Sequential development also does a lot of its planning just in time, but Sequential practices such as earned value

---

[1] The waterfall software development standard for US Department of Defense projects, MIL-STD-2167A, was superseded by a non-waterfall standard, MIL-STD-498 at the end of 1994.

project management put a stronger emphasis on planning in more detail up front.

Table 2-1 Different Emphases Between Sequential Development and Agile Development

Sequential Development	Agile Development
Long release cycles	Short release cycles
Most end-to-end development work performed in large batches across long release cycles	Most end-to-end development work performed in small batches within short release cycles
Detailed up-front planning	High-level up-front planning with just-in-time detailed planning
Detailed up-front requirements	High-level up-front requirements with just-in-time detailed requirements
Up-front design	Emergent design
Test at the end, often as separate activity	Continuous, automated testing, integrated into development
Infrequent structured collaboration	Frequent structured collaboration
Overall approach is idealistic, prearranged, and control-oriented	Overall approach is empirical, responsive, and improvement-oriented

Just-in-time requirements vs. up-front requirements

Agile development focuses on doing as little requirements work as possible up front (emphasizing breadth rather than details); it delays the vast majority of detailed requirements work until it is needed after the project is underway. Sequential development defines most requirements details up front.

Requirements is an area in which modern Agile practices have moved beyond the ideas that were associated with Agile development in the early 2000s. I'll discuss those changes in Chapter 13, "More Effective Agile Requirements Creation," and Chapter 14, "More Effective Agile Requirements Prioritization."

Emergent design vs. up-front design

As with planning and requirements, Agile defers detailed elaboration of design work until it is needed, with minimal emphasis on up-front architecture. Sequential development emphasizes developing a greater level of detail up front.

The acknowledgment of value in *some* up-front design and architecture work is another area in which modern Agile has moved beyond the early Agile philosophy of the 2000s.

Continuous, automated testing integrated with development vs. separate test at the end

Agile development emphasizes testing as something that is done concurrently with coding, sometimes preceding coding. It is performed by integrated development teams that include both developers and test specialists. Sequential development treats testing as an activity that is done separately from development and typically after development has occurred. Agile development emphasizes automating tests so that tests can be run more often, by more people

Frequent structured collaboration vs. infrequent structured collaboration

Agile development emphasizes frequent, structured collaboration. These collaborations are often short (15-minute daily standup meetings), but they are structured into the day-by-day, week-by-week rhythm of Agile work. Sequential development certainly does not prevent collaboration, but it doesn't particularly encourage it, either.

Empirical, responsive, improvement-oriented vs. idealistic, prearranged, control-oriented

Agile teams emphasize an empirical approach. They focus on learning from real-world experience. Sequential teams try to learn from experience too, but they place greater emphasis on defining a plan and imposing order on reality, rather than observing reality and constantly adapting to it.

What Agile Development and Sequential Development Have in Common

Comparisons of Agile and Sequential development tend to compare good Agile to bad Sequential, or vice versa. This is not fair or useful. Well-run projects emphasize good management, a high level of customer collaboration, and high-quality requirements, design, coding, and testing—regardless of whether the projects use Agile or Sequential approaches.

Sequential development at its best can work well. However, if you study the differences described in Table 2-1 and reflect on your own projects, you'll see some hints about why Agile works better than Sequential development in many cases.

What Is the Source of Agile's Benefits?

The benefits of Agile development do not arise from a mystical application of the term "Agile." They come from easily explainable effects of the Agile emphases listed in Table 2-1.

Short release cycles allow for more timely and less expensive correction of defects, less time invested in dead ends, more immediate customer feedback, quicker course corrections, and shorter paths to increased revenue and operational savings.

End-to-end development work performed in small batches provides benefits for similar reasons—tighter feedback loops, allowing errors to be detected and corrected more quickly, at lower cost.

Just-in-time planning results in less time spent creating detailed plans that are later ignored or thrown away.

Just-in-time requirements results in less work invested in up-front requirements that are eventually discarded when requirements change.

Emergent design results in less work invested in designing up-front solutions for requirements that later change, not to mention designs that don't work out as well in the details as planned. Up-front design can be powerful, but up-front design for speculative requirements is error-prone and wasteful.

Continuous automated testing, integrated into the development teams tightens the feedback loop between the time a defect is inserted and the time it's detected, contributing to lower-cost defect corrections and a strong focus on initial code quality.

Frequent, structured collaboration reduces the communication mistakes that can contribute significantly to defects in requirements, design, and other activities.

A focus on an empirical, responsive improvement model helps teams learn more quickly from experience and improve over time.

Different organizations will focus on different Agile emphases. An organization that develops safety-critical software will typically not adopt emergent design. Emergent design might save money, but safety considerations are more important.

Similarly, an organization that incurs a high cost each time it releases its software—perhaps because the software is embedded in a difficult-to-access device or due to regulatory overhead—will not choose to release often. The feedback obtained from frequent releases might save some organizations money, but it might cost other organizations more than it saves.

Once you move beyond the thinking that "Agile" is an indivisible concept that must be applied *all-or-nothing*, you become free to adopt Agile practices individually. You start to realize that some Agile practices are more useful than others—and some are more useful *in your specific circumstances*. If your organization needs to support business agility, modern Agile software practices are a natural fit. If your organization needs to support quality, predictability, productivity, or some other not-obviously-Agile attribute, modern Agile software practices are also valuable.

The Agile Boundary

Most organizations cannot achieve end-to-end agility. Your organization might not see any benefit from Agile HR or Agile procurement. Even if you commit to Agile for your whole organization, you might find that your customers or your suppliers are less Agile than you are.

It is useful to understand where the boundary is between Agile and non-Agile parts of your organization—both the current boundary and the desired boundary.

If you're a C-level executive, the area inside the Agile boundary could include your entire organization. If you're the top technical leader in your organization, it could include the entire technical organization. If you're a lower-level leader in your organization, the area inside the Agile boundary might include only your teams. Take a look at Figure 2-1 on the next page for an example.

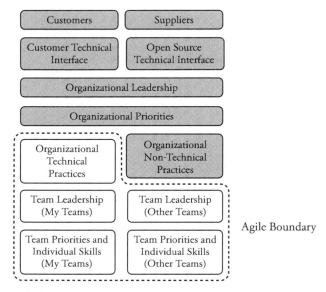

Figure 2-1

Example of an Agile boundary. In this example, Agile practices are limited to the technical organization.

Misunderstanding of the Agile boundary can cause misaligned expectations and other problems. Consider these scenarios:

* Agile software development and non-Agile regulations
* Agile sales and non-Agile software development
* Agile software development and non-Agile enterprise customers

Every organization has a boundary. How thoroughly do you want to implement Agile in your organization? What will best serve your business?

Suggested Leadership Actions

Inspect

- Reflect on the degree to which you've previously considered Agile to be an all-or-nothing proposition. To what degree has that affected your approach to improving management and technical practices?
- Talk to at least three technical leaders in your organization. Ask them what they mean by "Agile." Ask them what specific practices they are referring to. To what degree do your technical leaders agree on what Agile means? Do they agree on what is not Agile?
- Talk to non-technical leaders about what Agile means to them. How do they perceive the boundary or interface between their work and your software teams?
- Review your project portfolio in terms of the emphases described in Table 2-1. Rate your projects on each factor with 1 being entirely Sequential and 5 being entirely Agile.

Adapt

- Write down a preliminary approach to drawing the "Agile boundary" in your organization.
- Write a list of questions to answer as you read the rest of this book.

Additional Resources

Stellman, Andrew and Jennifer Green. 2013. *Learning Agile: Understanding Scrum, XP, Lean, and Kanban.* This book is a good introduction to Agile concepts from a pro-Agile point of view.

Meyer, Bertrand, 2014. *Agile! The Good, the Hype and the Ugly.* This book begins with an entertaining critique of excesses of the Agile movement and identifies the most useful principles and practices associated with Agile development.

Responding to the Challenges of Complexity and Uncertainty

⌒

Software projects have long struggled with the question of how to deal with complexity, which has been the source of many challenges, including low quality, late projects, and outright failure.

This chapter presents a framework for understanding uncertainty and complexity known as *Cynefin*. It describes how Cynefin applies to Sequential and Agile software problems. The chapter then presents a model for making decisions in the face of uncertainty and complexity known as *OODA*. It describes cases in which OODA decision making provides advantages over the typical Sequential decision-making approaches.

Cynefin

The Cynefin framework (pronounced kuh-NEV-in) was created by David Snowden at IBM in the late 1990s (Kurtz, 2003).

It has continued to be evolved by Snowden and others since then (Snowden, 2007). Snowden describes Cynefin as a "sense-making framework." It helps in understanding the kinds of tactics that will be useful depending on a situation's complexity and uncertainty.

The Cynefin framework consists of five domains. Each domain has its own attributes and suggested responses. The domains are illustrated in Figure 3-1.

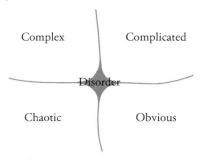

Figure 3-1
The Cynefin framework is a useful sense-making framework that can be applied to software development.

Cynefin is a Welsh word that means "habitat" or "neighborhood." The domains are not considered to be categories; rather they are considered to be clusters of meanings, which is the source of the "habitat" emphasis in the name.

The Complex and Complicated domains are the most relevant to software development. All five domains are described in the following sections to provide context.

Obvious Domain

In the Obvious domain, problems are well understood and solutions are self-evident. Literally everyone agrees on the one correct answer. The relationship between cause and effect is simple and direct. This is the realm of pattern application: programmed, proceduralized, rote behavior.

The approach to Obvious problems is described in the framework as

sense • categorize • respond

Examples of problems in the Obvious domain include:

- Taking an order at a restaurant
- Processing a loan payment
- Filling a car with gasoline

At the detailed level, software teams encounter numerous Obvious problems, such as, "This *if* statement should check for 0 instead of 1."

At the project level, it's difficult to find examples of Obvious problems, as defined in Cynefin. When's the last time you saw a problem of any size in software that had only one correct answer and for which everyone agreed on the solution? There's good research in software that says when different designers are presented with the same design problem, they will create solutions that vary by a factor of 10 in the code volume needed to implement their designs (McConnell, 2004). In my experience, this difference exists even in seemingly straightforward tasks such as, "Create this short report." This is about as different from "one correct solution" as you can get. So, beyond a "hello world" program, I don't believe that Obvious problems exist in software development. As far as software development in the large is concerned, I believe you can safely ignore the Obvious domain.

Complicated Domain

In the Complicated domain, you know the general shape of the problem, what questions to ask, and how to obtain answers.

Also, multiple correct answers exist. The relationship between cause and effect is complicated—you have to analyze, investigate, and apply expert knowledge to understand the relationship between cause and effect. Not everyone can see or understand the cause/effect relationships, which makes Complicated the domain of experts.

The approach to Complicated problems is described in the framework as

sense • analyze • respond

This approach contrasts with the approach in the Obvious domain in that the middle step requires *analysis* rather than simply *classifying* the problem and choosing the one correct response.

Examples of problems in the Complicated domain include:

- Diagnose an engine knock sound
- Prepare a gourmet meal
- Write a database query to obtain a certain result
- Fix a bug in a production system that resulted from an incomplete update
- Prioritize user requirements for version 4.1 of a mature system

What these examples have in common is that first you formulate an understanding of the problem and an approach to the problem, and then you move in a straightforward way toward solving the problem.

Numerous software development activities and projects fall into the Complicated domain. Historically, this has been the realm of Sequential development.

If the project is mostly in Cynefin's Complicated realm, a linear, sequential approach that relies heavily on up-front planning and analysis can work. Challenges arise with this approach when the problems cannot be well defined.

Complex Domain

The defining characteristic of the Complex domain is that the relationship between cause and effect is not immediately apparent, even to experts. In contrast to the Complicated domain, you don't know all the questions to ask—part of the challenge is discovering the questions. No amount of advance analysis will solve the problem, and experimentation is required to progress toward a solution. In fact, some amount of failure is part of the process, and decisions will often need to be made on the basis of incomplete data.

For Complex problems, the relationship between cause and effect is knowable only in hindsight—certain elements of the problem are emergent. However, with enough experimentation, the relationship between cause and effect can become known well enough to support practical decision making. Snowden says that Complex problems are the realm of collaboration, patience, and allowing solutions to emerge.

The recommended approach to Complex problems is described in Cynefin as

probe • sense • respond

This contrasts with Complicated problems in that you can't analyze your way out of the problem. You have to probe first. Eventually, analysis will become relevant, but not immediately.

Examples of problems in the Complex domain include:

- Buying a gift for someone who is difficult to shop for—you give the gift knowing that you'll need to exchange it!

- Fixing a bug in a production system in which diagnostic tools make the bug disappear during debugging but not in production
- Eliciting user requirements for a brand-new system
- Creating software that runs on underlying hardware that's still evolving
- Updating your software while competitors are updating their software

Many software development activities and projects fall into the Complex domain, and this is the realm of Agile and iterative development. If the project is mostly in the Complex realm, a workable approach will need to build in experimentation and probing before the problem can even be fully defined.

In my view, Sequential development's failure to do well on Complex projects is a substantial part of what gave rise to Agile development.

In some cases, you can probe a predominately Complex project in enough detail to turn it into a Complicated project. The remainder of the project can then be conducted using approaches that are appropriate for Complicated projects. In other cases, a Complex project retains significant Complex elements throughout its project lifecycle. An attempt to convert the project to Complicated wastes time that would be better spent completing the project using approaches appropriate for Complex projects.

Chaotic Domain

The Chaotic domain departs a bit from the pattern you might expect based on the first three domains. In the Chaotic domain, the relationship between cause and effect is turbulent and in flux. There's no discoverable relationship between cause and effect even with repeated experimentation, even in hindsight.

You don't know the questions to ask, and probes and experiments do not produce consistent responses.

The domain also includes a time-pressure element not present in the other domains.

Cynefin defines the Chaotic domain as the domain of decisive, action-oriented leadership. The recommended approach is to impose order on chaos and to do it quickly:

act ● *sense* ● *respond*

Examples of Chaotic problems include:

- Providing natural-disaster relief while the disaster is still happening
- Stopping a food fight in a high school cafeteria
- Fixing a bug in a production system by rolling back to a previous version because no amount of analysis or probing has found the cause of the bug
- Defining a feature set in an intensely political environment, where requirements emerge and change because of the ambitions of powerful stakeholders

Finding project-size examples of Chaotic problems in software is difficult or impossible. The bug-fix example has the "no time to analyze, just act" element, but it isn't a project-size example. The feature-set example is a project-size example, but it doesn't have the extreme time-pressure element, which means it isn't a representative example of a Chaotic problem in Cynefin terms.

Disorder Domain

The middle of the Cynefin diagram is described as Disorder, the realm in which you lack clarity about which domain applies to your problem. Cynefin's recommended approach to Disorder is to decompose the problem into its elements and then assess which domain each element is in.

Cynefin provides a way to identify these different elements and treat each appropriately. You approach requirements, design, and planning work one way in the Complex domain and a different way in the Complicated domain. No single approach works everywhere.

Most software project-size problems are not tidily contained in one domain, so keep in mind that the domains are "neighborhoods"—collections of meanings that cluster together. Different elements of a problem or system can exhibit different attributes; some might be Complicated while others are Complex.

Cynefin and Software Challenges

Cynefin is an interesting and useful sense-making framework, and all five domains apply to problems outside of software. As shown in Figure 3-2, however, the Chaotic and Obvious domains don't apply at the whole-project level for the reasons I've described. That means, for practical purposes, software projects should orient themselves as being mostly in the Complicated, Complex, or Disorder domain (and Disorder will ultimately resolve to Complicated, Complex, or a combination of the two).

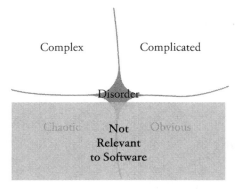

Figure 3-2
The relationship between Cynefin's domains and software challenges.

Considering that you have only two choices of domains in Cynefin, it's useful to ask the question, "What if I guess wrong about my project's domain?"

As Figure 3-3 illustrates, the more uncertainty you have on your project, the more advantageous a Complex (Agile) approach will be over a Complicated (Sequential) approach.

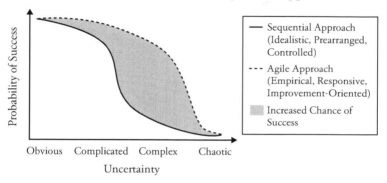

Figure 3-3

Probability of success on different kinds of problems with Sequential vs. Agile approaches.

If you believe your project is mostly Complex and it turns out to be only Complicated, you will have spent time on probing and experimentation that you didn't need to. The apparent penalty for guessing wrong in this case is a less efficient project, but that's arguable because the experiments you performed probably increased your understanding of your project and improved how you approached it.

If you believe your project is mostly Complicated and it turns out to be mostly Complex, you will have spent time analyzing, planning, and probably at least partially executing a project that you didn't understand as well as you thought you did. If you're one month into a six-month project when you discover your mission was actually something different, a complete restart of the project might be necessary. If you're five months into a six-month project, the project could be cancelled outright.

The consequence of guessing wrong is lower for guessing a project is Complex than for guessing it's Complicated. The safe money, therefore, goes into treating a project as Complex, and using Agile practices, unless you can be absolutely sure that it's Complicated, in which case a Sequential approach can work.

Succeeding on Complex Projects: OODA

A useful model for dealing with Complex projects is OODA. As illustrated in Figure 3-4, "OODA" stands for Observe, Orient, Decide, Act and is normally described as the "OODA loop."

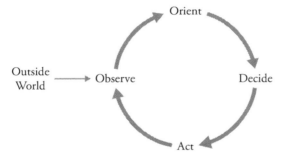

Figure 3-4
The basic OODA loop contains four steps that begin with observation.

OODA originated out of US Air Force Colonel John Boyd's frustration with US Air Force dogfighting results. He invented the OODA loop as a way to accelerate decision making, make decisions faster than the enemy, and invalidate the enemy's decision making. OODA is a methodical approach to establishing context, formulating a plan, performing work, observing results, and incorporating learnings into the next cycle.

Observe

The OODA loop begins with "Observe." Observe the current situation, observe outside information that's relevant, observe any aspects of the situation that are unfolding (emergent), and observe how the unfolding aspects of the situation interact with the environment. Because OODA places a strong emphasis on observation, you can view OODA as an empirical approach—an approach that focuses on observation and experience.

Orient

In the "Orient" step, you relate the observations to your situation. Boyd stated that we relate them to our "genetic heritage, cultural tradition, previous experience, and unfolding circumstances" (Adolph 2006). Put more simply, you decide what the information means to you, and you identify the options that are available in response.

The "Orient" step provides the opportunity to challenge your assumptions, adjust for cultural and company-cultural blind spots, and, in general, de-bias data and information. As you Orient, you shift priorities based on your increasing understanding. This allows you to realize the significance of details that others have overlooked. Apple's iPhone is a classic example. The rest of the wireless handset industry was focused on camera megapixels, RF signal quality, and battery life. Apple oriented in a completely different way, focusing on creating a mobile information appliance with a ground-breaking UX. The iPhone was inferior in almost every respect *as a traditional mobile phone*, but that didn't matter because Apple had oriented toward solving a different problem that was ultimately more important.

Decide

In the "Decide" step, you make a decision based on the options you identified in the "Orient" step. In a military context, you often decide to do something that disrupts your adversary's plans—called "getting inside the opponent's OODA loop." This is sometimes interpreted as operating faster than your opponent, but, more accurately, it's operating at a different tempo. A baseball pitcher who throws a change-up (slow pitch) when the batter is expecting a fast ball is effectively getting inside the opponent's OODA loop by operating more slowly. Another way to think of this is making your opponent play your game instead of theirs (which is what Apple did with the iPhone).

Act

Finally, you "Act" by implementing the decision. And then you jump back to "Observe" so that you can see the impact of your action ("unfolding circumstances") and begin the loop again.

Beyond Basic OODA

Despite the basic OODA loop appearing to be a linear cycle, the full OODA loop features implicit guidance and control, as shown in Figure 3-5.

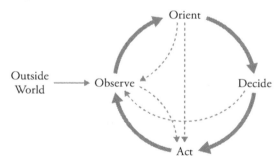

Figure 3-5
The full OODA loop. Any step can shortcut straight to Act or back to Observe, as indicated by dashed lines.

You don't need to proceed through the full OODA loop to pull your hand away from a hot stove; you move straight from

Observe to Act. If you encounter a recognized pattern in Observe or Orient, you can proceed straight to Act ("it's raining, so I'll drive instead of walk").

Whereas another decision-making approach might require you to proceed through all its steps for thoroughness's sake, OODA emphasizes decision-making speed, which allows you to out-decide your opponent.

OODA vs. Sequential Development

The software problems that companies are addressing today have many cross-cutting, emergent characteristics that are not naturally addressed by Sequential approaches. Agile practices provide a better fit for these problems, with better risk management and softer failure modes.

A key difference between OODA and the Sequential approach (summarized in Table 3-1) is that OODA focuses on observing the environment and reacting to it whereas Sequential focuses on controlling the environment.

Table 3-1 Different Emphases Between Sequential and OODA (Agile) Approaches

Sequential	OODA (Agile)
Initial focus on planning	Initial focus on observation
Emphasizes the long term	Emphasizes the short term
Predictive	Responsive
Idealistic	Empirical
Views uncertainty as risk	Views uncertainty as opportunity
Control-oriented	Improvement-oriented
Can perform well on Complicated problems	Can perform well on Complex problems as well as Complicated problems

Sequential engages in big planning up front, big design up front, and so on. OODA (Agile) performs most of its work just in time, including planning, requirements, design, and implementation. Agile development does not try to anticipate as much as Sequential does. Sequential can be seen as more predictive, OODA as more reactive.

Sequential and Agile development both consider the long term and the short term, but they have opposite emphases. Sequential development has a long-term plan, and it fits short-term work within the long-term plan. Agile development emphasizes short-term work; it maintains awareness of longer-term plans for the purpose of providing context to the short term.

Sequential development views uncertainty as risk—as something you need to reduce or eliminate. OODA views uncertainty as opportunity—something you can exploit to gain an advantage over your opponent.

The overall difference between Sequential and Agile development can be summed up as the use of planning, predicting, and control on the one hand and observation, response, and improvement on the other.

Key Principle: Inspect and Adapt

I find the phrase "Inspect and Adapt" a useful shorthand for OODA and also for an appropriate, effective focus in Agile development. Agile teams should avoid being idealistic about their practices and instead adjust their practices based on empirical observations about what has been proved to work. Agile teams should regularly Inspect and Adapt *everything*—plans, designs, code quality, tests, processes, team interactions, organizational interactions—every factor that can make a difference in a team's effectiveness. This is not a license to adapt without inspecting. Changes should be based on experience.

As you saw in the previous chapter, the "Suggested Leadership Actions" at the end of each chapter emphasize the value of this principle.

Suggested Leadership Actions

Inspect

- Review your current projects. Which elements of your projects would you describe as Complex, and which would you describe as Complicated?

- Review a recent challenged project. Did your teams treat important aspects of the project as though they were Complicated or Complex? Does it appear that any of those projects' challenges might have arisen from a Complex project being misclassified as Complicated (or vice versa)?

- To what degree are your projects using Inspect and Adapt? When and where else could you use Inspect and Adapt?

- In OODA terms, *Observe* who your "opponent" is (specific competitor, market share, profit goal, bureaucracy, etc.).

- *Observe* 3–5 areas of uncertainty that you could potentially exploit to gain advantage over your opponent.

Adapt

- Create a list of projects that your organization should be treating as Complex rather than Complicated. Work with your project teams to begin treating them that way.

- *Orient* using the areas of uncertainty in ways that will provide advantages over your opponent.

- *Decide* how to take advantage of your insights into uncertainty and then *Act*.

Additional Resources

Snowden, David J. and Mary E. Boone. 2007. A Leader's Framework for Decision Making. *Harvard Business Review.* November 2007. This is a readable introduction to Cynefin that goes into more detail than the description I've provided in this chapter.

Boehm, Barry W. 1988. A Spiral Model of Software Development and Enhancement. *IEEE Computer,* May 1988. In Cynefin terms, this paper proposes an approach to projects in which each project is initially treated as Complex. Issues are probed until the project's complete set of challenges is understood well enough to treat the project as Complicated. At that point, the project is completed as a Sequential project.

Adolph, Steve. 2006. What Lessons Can the Agile Community Learn from a Maverick Fighter Pilot? *Proceedings of the Agile 2006 Conference.* This is a summary of OODA presented in an Agile-specific context.

Boyd, John R. 2007. *Patterns of Conflict.* January 2007. This is a re-creation of a briefing presented by Col. John Boyd.

Coram, Robert. 2002. *Boyd: The Fighter Pilot Who Changed the Art of War.* This is an in-depth biography of Col. John Boyd.

Richards, Chet. 2004. *Certain to Win: The Strategy of John Boyd, Applied to Business.* This book is a readable description of the origin of OODA and its application to business decision making.

PART II

MORE EFFECTIVE TEAMS

This part of the book describes issues related to individuals and how collections of individuals are combined into teams. It describes the most common Agile team structure, Scrum. It then discusses Agile teams in general, Agile team culture, geographically distributed teams, and the individual and interaction skills that support effective Agile work.

If you're more interested in specific work practices than team dynamics, skip to Part III, "More Effective Work." If you're more interested in top leadership issues, skip to Part IV, "More Effective Organizations."

More Effective Agile Beginnings: Scrum

The primary challenge in the software industry for the 35 years I've been working in it, and probably longer, has been avoiding "code-and-fix development"—writing code without forethought or planning, and then debugging it until it works. This ineffective development mode results in teams spending more than half their effort correcting defects they created earlier (McConnell 2004).

In the 1980s and 1990s, developers would say they were doing structured programming, but many were really doing code-and-fix and missing all the benefits of structured programming. In the 1990s and 2000s, developers would say they were doing object-oriented programming, but many were still doing code-and-fix and suffering the consequences. In the 2000s and 2010s, developers and teams are saying they're doing Agile development, but even with decades of history to warn them, many are still doing code-and-fix. The more things change, the more they stay the same!

A challenge created by Agile development is that it is explicitly short-term-oriented and code-focused, which makes it more difficult to tell whether teams are using Agile development practices effectively or are doing code-and-fix. A wall full of sticky notes doesn't necessarily mean a team is taking an organized, effective approach to its work. Where Sequential approaches fail in bureaucracy, Agile approaches fail in anarchy.

One part of the mission of more effective Agile is protecting against Agile theater—teams using Agile cosmetics as a cover for code-and-fix.

Scrum is a good place to start.

Key Principle: Start with Scrum

If you do not already have an Agile implementation—or if you have an Agile implementation that is less effective than you want it to be—I recommend that you begin at the beginning. In Agile, that means Scrum. Scrum is the most prescriptive of the common Agile approaches. It has the largest ecosystem of books, training offerings, and tools. And there's evidence that it works. David F. Rico's comprehensive "study of studies" analysis found that the average ROI for Scrum implementations was 580% (Rico, 2009). The *State of Scrum 2017–2018* report found that 84% of Agile adoptions included Scrum (Scrum Alliance, 2017).

What Is Scrum?

Scrum is a lightweight but structured and disciplined workflow management approach for teams. Scrum doesn't dictate specific technical practices. It defines how the work will flow through a team, and it dictates some specific roles and work-coordination practices that the team will use.

Scrum Basics

If you're familiar with Scrum basics, feel free to skip this section and move on to this chapter's "Common Failure Modes in Scrum" section or, if the failure modes are also familiar, to "Success Factors in Scrum." The most canonical description of Scrum is normally considered to be *The Scrum Guide* (Schwaber, 2017). My company's experience with Scrum mostly matches what's described in the *Guide*, so the following description follows the November 2017 version of the *Guide*, except where noted.

Scrum is often summarized as having events (also known as meetings or ceremonies), roles, and artifacts that are bound together with a set of rules.

Scrum begins, conceptually, with a "product backlog," which is created by the Product Owner (the person responsible for requirements in Scrum). The product backlog is a set of requirements, requirements-in-progress, features, functions, stories, enhancements, and fixes that the Scrum team might possibly deliver. Rather than providing a complete list of every possible requirement, the product backlog focuses on those requirements that are most important, that are most urgent, and that offer the highest ROI (return on investment).

The Scrum team performs its work in "sprints," which are time-based iterations of 1–4 weeks. Sprints of 1–3 weeks usually work best. We have found that risks increase with longer sprints and improvement opportunities are more limited. Two-week sprints are by far the most common.

The terminology related to cadences can be a little confusing.

"Sprint" refers to a development iteration, which is nominally on a 1–3-week cadence.

"Deployment" refers to delivery to the user or customer, which can range from hourly in an online environment to yearly or longer for software embedded in hardware devices. Development work can be organized on a 1–3-week cadence regardless of whether deliveries are measured in hours, months, or years.

The meaning of "release" varies across contexts but most often refers to a larger scope of work than a sprint—a longer length of time or a larger collection of cohesive functionality.

Figure 4-1 summarizes the flow of work on a Scrum project.

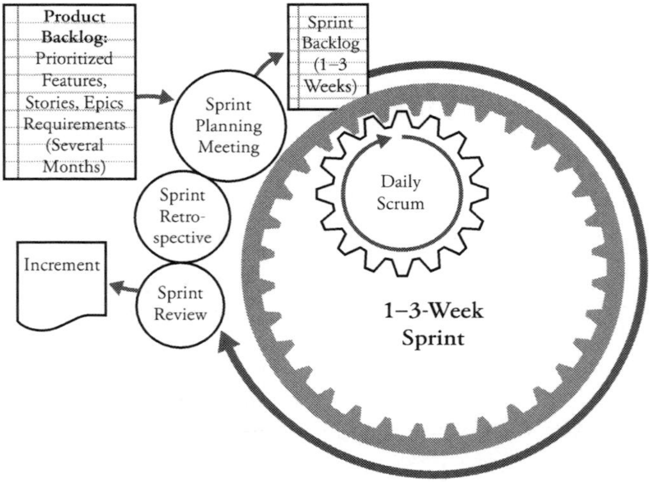

Figure 4-1
The flow of work through Scrum at a glance.

Each sprint begins with a "sprint planning meeting," during which the Scrum team reviews the product backlog, selects a subset of the work to put into a sprint backlog, commits to deliver the items in the sprint backlog by the end of the sprint, and makes other plans needed to conduct the sprint.

The team also defines a "sprint goal" that concisely captures the focus of the sprint. If work during a sprint unfolds in a way that surprises the team, the sprint goal provides a principled basis for renegotiating details of the sprint after work is underway.

The whole team works on design during sprint planning, which is effective because the team is cross-functional and has every discipline needed to make good decisions about design.

The team does not enter the sprint planning meeting "cold." The team refines requirements and design in enough detail prior to the sprint planning meeting to support an efficient meeting.

The functionality that the team delivers at the end of each sprint is called an "increment." In normal conversation, an "increment" would refer to only the additional functionality delivered in each sprint. In Scrum, however, "increment" refers to the aggregate of functionality developed to date.

During the sprint itself, the sprint backlog is considered to be a closed box. Requirements clarifications occur throughout the sprint, but no one can add, remove, or modify requirements that would imperil the sprint goal unless the Product Owner agrees to cancel the sprint and start the cycle over. In practice, few sprints are cancelled; sprint goals and details are sometimes changed by mutual agreement when priorities change.

During the sprint, the team meets for a "daily scrum" (also known as a "daily standup"), which is held each day except the first and last day of the sprint. Time-boxed to 15 minutes and focused on inspecting progress toward the sprint goal, the meeting is usually limited to answering "the three questions":

* What did you do yesterday?
* What will you do today?
* What is blocking progress?

Any discussion other than these three questions is normally deferred until after the standup, although some teams use a more discussion-oriented approach.

The current *Scrum Guide* has deprecated the role of the three questions, but I think they provide important structure and help prevent poorly run meetings.

The Scrum team follows the basic rhythm of daily scrum, daily work, daily scrum, daily work, rinse and repeat for the entire sprint.

The team will often use a "sprint burndown chart" such as the one shown in Figure 4-2 to track its progress during each sprint.

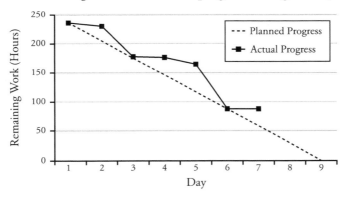

Figure 4-2

An example of a sprint burndown chart showing planned vs. actual hours remaining. The sprint burndown is usually based on task hours rather than stories.

Sprint burndown charts are based on task estimates and show hours remaining for incomplete tasks rather than hours spent on completed tasks. If a task was planned to consume 8 hours and actually took 15 hours, the graph shows remaining work being reduced by only the planned 8 hours. (This is essentially the same as earned value management.) If the team's plans for the sprint are optimistic, the sprint burndown will show that the remaining hours are not burning down as quickly as they should be.

Some teams track their progress during each sprint using story points rather than hours. (Story points are a means of measuring size and complexity of work items.) The purpose of the sprint burndown is to support tracking progress daily. If the team usually completes at least one story each day, a story-based burndown will show progress daily and tracking progress using stories will be appropriate. If the team usually completes a story only every two or three days, or if it completes most of its stories toward the end of its sprints, stories will not provide daily progress tracking and hours will be a more useful measure.

When the organization values longer-term predictability, we also recommend that teams use a "release burndown chart" to track overall progress toward the current release. The release burndown nominally shows the total number of story points planned for the release, rate of progress to date, and a projection of when the release will be completed.

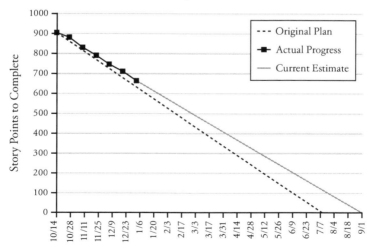

Figure 4-3
An example of a nominal release burndown chart.

More informative and elaborate burndowns are possible. They can be presented as burndowns or as burnups. They can show the history of the release's build-up of functionality, reductions in functionality, ranges of projected completion dates, and so on. Figure 4-4 shows an example of a more elaborate burnup.

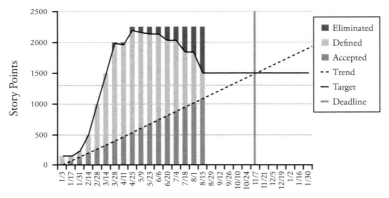

Figure 4-4

An example of a more elaborate release burnup chart.

Chapter 20, "More Effective Agile Predictability," contains a deeper discussion of how to support predictability on Agile projects.

Throughout the sprint, the team maintains high quality in its work. By the end of the sprint, the work must be at a "releasable" level of quality that meets the team's "Definition of Done" (described later in this chapter). The team does not need to actually release the software at the end of each sprint, but the quality must be good enough to support releasing what's been implemented each sprint, eventually, without further changes.

At the end of the sprint, the Scrum team demonstrates the tangible results of its work in a meeting called a "sprint review" or a "sprint demo." The team invites project stakeholders to share perspectives and provide feedback. The Product Owner accepts or rejects items based upon the agreed-upon acceptance criteria as well as stakeholder feedback, though this should be worked out well before the sprint review. The team uses feedback obtained during the sprint review to improve the product as well as its processes and practices.

The final event of each sprint is a "sprint retrospective," at which the team reviews successes and failures of the sprint. This is the team's opportunity to use Inspect and Adapt to improve the process it's using to develop software. The team reviews any previous changes made and decides whether to continue with each change or reverse it. The team also agrees on new process changes to implement during the next sprint.

Scrum Roles

Scrum defines three roles to support project workflow.

The "Product Owner" (or PO) is the interface between the Scrum team on the one hand and the business management, customers, and other stakeholders on the other. The PO has primary responsibility for defining the product backlog and prioritizing items in the product backlog, with the overarching responsibility of defining the product in a way that maximizes the value delivered by the Scrum team. The Product Owner regularly refines the product backlog with the team so that it contains about two sprints' worth of refined (fully defined) backlog items beyond the current sprint's backlog.

The "Scrum Master" is responsible for the Scrum implementation. The Scrum Master helps the team and larger organization understand Scrum theory, practice, and general approach. The Scrum Master manages the process, enforces the process if necessary, removes impediments, and coaches and supports the rest of the Scrum team. The Scrum Master can be a technical contributor on the team as long as sufficient time is allocated to perform the Scrum Master role.

The "Development Team" consists of the cross-functional individual contributors who directly do the work to implement the backlog items.

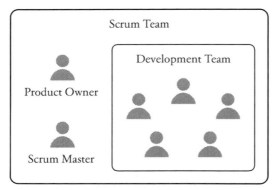

Figure 4-5

The organization of a Scrum team. Sometimes the Scrum Master is part of the Development Team and sometimes not.

The overall Scrum team usually consists of 3–9 individuals on the Development Team, plus the Scrum Master and Product Owner.

Note that the Scrum roles are *roles*—they are not necessarily job titles. As one senior leader said to me, "Our job titles are not based on Scrum roles. We don't want our HR practices to be dependent on our technical methodologies."

Common Failure Modes in Scrum

My company has seen many more ineffective Scrum implementations than effective ones. Most ineffective implementations are "Scrum-but," meaning, "We're doing Scrum, *but* we aren't using some of its key practices." Examples include, "We're doing Scrum, *but* we aren't doing daily standups." Or "We're doing Scrum, *but* we aren't holding retrospectives." Or "We're doing Scrum, *but* we haven't been able to fill the Product Owner role." Ineffective Scrum implementations have usually removed at least one essential attribute of Scrum. Here's my favorite example: "We looked at Scrum but found that most of the practices wouldn't work in our organization. We're doing Scrum, but the main practice we use is daily standups, and we do those on Fridays."

Unlike the enormous umbrella of Agile practices generally, Scrum is a minimal process for managing workflow. Because it is already minimal, there really isn't any part of Scrum that you can remove and still achieve the benefits of Scrum.

> *"Perfection is achieved, not when there is nothing more to add, but when there is nothing left to take away."*
> *—Antoine de Saint-Exupery*

If your organization has adopted Scrum and you aren't realizing significant benefits, the first question to ask is, "Have you really adopted Scrum, or have you adopted only parts of Scrum?"

An advanced Scrum implementation might eventually remove specific parts of Scrum by applying Inspect and Adapt to their Scrum process with rigor. But that is an advanced activity, not a beginner activity. Beginners will do better if they adopt Scrum *by the book*.

The following sections describe the most common challenges we see with Scrum implementations.

Ineffective Product Owner

For decades before Agile development existed, the most commonly reported source of project challenges and failures was poor requirements. It should not be a surprise that post-Agile the most problematic role on Scrum projects is the one that's responsible for requirements.

Problems with Product Owners take several forms:

- No Product Owner—the role is expected to be filled by individuals on the Scrum team.

- The PO is spread too thin—the Scrum team is starved for requirements. A PO can support 1–2 teams, rarely more than that.

- The PO doesn't adequately understand the business— this results in low-quality requirements being fed to the Scrum team or requirements that are prioritized poorly.

- The PO does not understand how to specify software requirements—this is another way that low-quality requirements are fed to the Scrum team.

- The PO doesn't understand the Development team's technical challenges—and does not effectively prioritize technically oriented work or forces a just-get-it-done approach that leads to accumulation of technical debt.

- The PO is not co-located with the rest of the Scrum team—the rest of the team cannot get timely answers to requirements questions.

- The PO is not empowered to make product decisions.

- The PO's agenda differs from the business's—the PO sends the team in directions the business later rejects.

- The PO does not represent typical users—for example, the PO is a power user and is too detailed.

- The PO refuses to abide by Scrum rules—this forces changes in requirements mid-sprint or otherwise disrupts the Scrum project.

Many of these problems arise from businesses not taking the PO role as seriously as they take the Development Team and Scrum Master roles. Businesses should treat the Product Owner as the highest-leverage role on a Scrum team and prioritize filling the role accordingly. With appropriate training, former business analysts, customer support staff, and testers can make excellent POs. Keys to a high-performing PO are discussed in Chapter 14, "More Effective Requirements Prioritization."

Insufficient Product Backlog Refinement

The product backlog is used to feed work to the Development Team in Scrum. The Product Owner is responsible for the product backlog, and backlog refinement needs to be an ongoing activity so that the team is never starved for work.

Backlog refinement (also sometimes called "backlog grooming") includes fleshing out stories in sufficient detail to support implementation of the stories, splitting stories that are too large to fit into one sprint into smaller stories, adding new stories, updating the relative priorities of different backlog items, estimating or re-estimating stories, and so on. In general, refining the backlog consists of filling in the details the Scrum team will need to begin implementing a sprint's worth of backlog items at the next sprint. A "Definition of Ready" is useful and is discussed in Chapter 13, "More Effective Agile Requirements Creation."

Insufficient backlog refinement can cause a number of problems for the Scrum team. A well-refined product backlog is such a decisive issue for Agile projects that it is discussed at much greater length in Chapters 13 and 14.

Backlog refinement is nominally a whole-team activity. But because the Product Owner is responsible for the product backlog, if a project falls prey to the preceding pitfall of inadequately staffing the Product Owner role, it will typically fall prey to poor backlog refinement too.

Stories Too Large

In support of driving work to a releasable state by the end of each sprint, stories should be completeable within a single sprint. There aren't any hard-and-fast rules in this area, but here are two useful guidelines:

- The team should decompose its stories so that no single story consumes more than half the team for half the sprint; most stories should be smaller.
- The team should aim to complete 6–12 stories each sprint (assuming recommended team size)

The overall objective is to have the team completing stories throughout the sprint—not just on the last couple of days, but all along the way.

Daily Scrums Not Held Daily

Daily scrums can become repetitive, and so some teams evolve toward holding them three times a week—sometimes even just one time per week. However, it is important to hold the daily scrums *daily* to give team members the opportunity to coordinate work, ask for help, and hold each other accountable.

The most common reason we hear for holding daily scrums less than daily is, "The meetings take too long." This is a clear identification of a problem! The meetings are supposed to be time-boxed to 15 minutes. Stay focused on the three questions, and they can be completed in that amount of time. The solution to overly long daily scrums is not to reduce the number of meetings; it's to keep the meetings time-boxed and focused on the three questions. More details on the daily scrums are provided later in this chapter.

Overly Long Sprints

The current best practice is 1–3-week sprints, with most teams gravitating toward 2 weeks. When sprints are longer than 3 weeks, too much space opens up for planning mistakes, overly optimistic sprint commitments, procrastination, and so on.

Emphasis on Horizontal Slices Rather than Vertical Slices

The term "vertical slice" refers to end-to-end functionality across the full technology stack. The term "horizontal slice" refers to an enabling capability that doesn't directly produce demonstrable business-level functionality. Performing work in vertical slices supports tighter feedback loops and earlier delivery of business value. Horizontal vs. vertical slicing is an important topic that is discussed in more detail in Chapter 9, "More Effective Agile Projects."

Separate Development Teams and Test Teams

A common holdover from Sequential development is separate development and test teams. This structure deprives the Scrum team of the cross-functional expertise that it needs to operate effectively.

Unclear Definition of Done

One important support for maintaining high quality is a rigorous "Definition of Done" (commonly abbreviated as DoD in Agile discussions). This helps to ensure that when an individual or team declares an item to be "done," the team and organization can be truly sure that no more work remains for that item. The DoD is effectively the exit criteria that define the standard that work must meet to be released into production or into the next downstream integration or testing phase. This is discussed in more detail in Chapter 11, "More Effective Agile Quality."

Not Driving to a Releasable Level of Quality Each Sprint

One of the consequences of excessive schedule pressure is that teams and individuals will place the appearance of progress above actual progress. Because quality is less visible than basic functionality, teams under pressure sometimes emphasize quantity over quality. They might implement the functionality contained in their sprint backlog but not perform the testing, create automated tests, or otherwise assure that the software has been developed to a releasable level of quality. This leads to work being declared "done" while some tasks are still incomplete.

We have found that the more successful Agile teams do not wait for the end of the sprint to achieve releasable quality: they drive each story to production quality before moving to the next one.

Retrospectives Not Held

When teams feel overwhelmed by the amount of work they're responsible for, they often skip retrospectives. This is a huge mistake! The vicious cycle of over-commitment and burnout will continue unless you give yourself an opportunity to learn from the planning and commitment mistakes that led to that cycle in the first place.

Agile development depends on the Inspect and Adapt cycle, and Scrum gives your teams regular opportunities to do that.

Lessons from Retrospectives Not Implemented in the Next Sprint

The final failure mode we see most commonly is holding the sprint retrospective but not actually implementing lessons learned in the next sprint. Lessons accumulate to be implemented "later," or retrospectives become a gripe session rather than one that's truly focused on taking corrective action.

Don't live with your problems—do something about them. Most of the problems we've seen affecting teams' ability to deliver are addressable by the teams. Support your teams in taking corrective actions through retrospectives, and you'll be amazed at how quickly they improve. Retrospectives are discussed in more detail in Chapter 19, "More Effective Agile Process Improvement."

"Scrum And"

You don't need more than Scrum to start. Some teams try to pile on additional practices unnecessarily. One company we worked with told us, "We had good success with Scrum with the first team that used it, but after that we couldn't find another team that was willing to do pair programming or that could figure out how to do continuous integration in our legacy environment." Neither pair programming nor continuous integration are required by Scrum. After that organization realized its teams could adopt Scrum without adopting pair programming or continuous integration it was able to expand its use of Scrum.

Ineffective Scrum Master

The person most responsible for avoiding these failure modes is the Scrum Master. The problems with Scrum Masters parallel a few of the problems with POs:

* No Scrum Master—the team is expected to apply Scrum without an identified Scrum Master.
* The Scrum Master is spread too thin, supporting too many teams.
* A Scrum Master in a dual Scrum Master/developer role prioritizes personal development work over Scrum work.
* The Scrum Master does not understand Scrum well enough to coach the team and other project stakeholders.

It might seem obvious that the Scrum Master is critical to an effective Scrum implementation, but we've often seen organizations shortchange this role. Many of the problems described in this section can be avoided by an effective Scrum Master.

What the Scrum Failure Modes Have in Common

The failure modes I've just described are all variations on the theme of "Scrum-but." The first order of business for a team or organization adopting Agile development is to ensure that it is making high-fidelity use of Scrum.

Most of these failure modes have another attribute in common: the failure to consistently use high-discipline practices. A high-discipline practice is a practice that people tend to drift away from unless there's social or structural support in place to make sure the practice occurs.

The Scrum Master is responsible for ensuring the team uses the high-discipline practices in Scrum (as well as the other practices). The meetings in Scrum—sprint planning, daily scrum, sprint review, and sprint retrospective—provide both social and structural support for the high-discipline practices.

Success Factors in Scrum

Each of the failure modes can be converted to a success factor, which results in a list like this:

- Have an effective Product Owner.
- Refine the backlog.
- Keep stories small.
- Hold daily scrums daily.
- Limit sprints to 1–3 weeks.
- Organize work into vertical slices.
- Integrate test, testers, and QA into the Development Team.
- Create a clear Definition of Done.

- Drive to a releasable level of quality each sprint.
- Hold retrospectives every sprint.
- Apply the lessons learned from each retrospective soon.
- Have an effective Scrum Master.

More details on these topics are provided in later chapters.

A Successful Sprint

A successful sprint will support the main goal of Scrum, which is to deliver a product of the highest possible value. At the sprint level, this includes the following:

- The sprint delivers a usable, valuable increment (aggregate functionality) of the product that fully meets the Definition of Done.
- The sprint's increment increases in value compared to the previous sprint.
- The Scrum team improves its process when compared to the previous sprint.
- The Scrum team learns something about itself, its business, its product, or its customers.
- The Scrum team's motivation is as good or better than it was at the end of the last sprint.

Time Allocation for a Typical Sprint

This chapter has discussed the full range of activities that occur in Scrum, and it would be easy to conclude that not very much software development occurs in Scrum. Table 4-1 shows a representative example of how effort is allocated for developers on a Scrum team for a 2-week sprint.

Table 4-1 Example Effort Allocation During a Sprint

Sprint Planning Parameters	
Sprint duration (business days)	10
Ideal hours per day (project-focused hours)	× 6
Total ideal hours, per developer, per sprint	= 60

Scrum Activities, Per Sprint, Per Developer	Hours
Development work, including test	48
Daily scrums (standups)	2
Product backlog refinement (5%)	3
Sprint planning	4
Sprint review	2
Sprint retrospective	1
Total	60

In the table, "ideal hours" refers to the number of project-focused hours (what's available after corporate overhead). Ideal hours of 5–6 hours per day is typical for a large, established company. Small companies can average 6–7 hours, and start-up companies sometimes average more than that.

Of the 60 ideal hours available per sprint, about 20% go into planning and process improvement and about 80% is available for development work.

Issues Transitioning to Scrum

Teams need to learn how to address practical implementation issues—geographic distribution, legacy systems, product support, challenges filling new roles, and so on.

During an initial Scrum implementation, a team can feel that it's slowing down. In reality, the team is more quickly encountering work that it should have been doing more frequently in the first place (work that used to stack up at the end in Sequential projects or was just not visible). As the team becomes more skilled working incrementally, it will feel its speed increasing.

A Scrum Scorecard

For the sake of assessing fidelity of Scrum implementations, we have found it useful to score Scrum projects on the most important Scrum success factors. Figure 4-6 shows the example of a Scrum star diagram that was presented in Chapter 1.

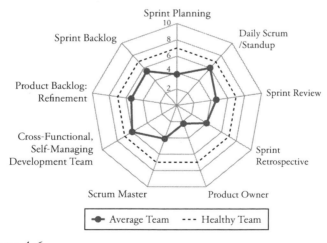

Figure 4-6

A diagnostic tool that shows a Scrum team's performance according to key Scrum success factors.

The diagram uses this key:

0   Not Used
2   Used infrequently and ineffectively
4   Used occasionally with mixed effectiveness
7   Used consistently and effectively
10 Optimizing

The gray line reflects the average practice my company has seen through consulting and training with slightly more than 1,000 Scrum teams since 2010, biased toward what we have observed in the past two years.

The dashed line shows a healthy team. As I mentioned earlier, the average Scrum team we see is not making very good use of Scrum! A healthy, effective Scrum team will have scores of 7 or higher for all of the success factors.

Inspect and Adapt in Scrum: Daily Scrum

Over time, an effective team will Inspect and Adapt its implementation of Scrum. Initial implementation should be by the book, with adaptations arising from on-the-ground experience.

The most common area that teams customize is the daily scrum, probably because it's conducted the most often and offers the most frequent opportunity for reflection and improvement.

We've seen teams customize the three questions in many ways. Here are some ways teams have changed the first question:

- What did you do yesterday? (nominal question)
- What did you *accomplish* yesterday?
- What did you *complete according to the DoD* yesterday?
- How did you *make progress toward the sprint goal* yesterday?
- How did you *move the sprint plan forward* yesterday?

Teams refine the way in which the daily scrum is conducted. Some teams put the three questions on a monitor to keep the meeting from straying away from them. Some teams use a talking stick to limit off-track discussions. Some teams move away from the three questions to a more discussion-oriented approach. Changes like these are healthy as long as the team monitors whether each change results in improvement.

Other Considerations

One hallmark of Agile development has been a proliferation of named practices. Each practice was invented for a reason by an intelligent consultant or practitioner, and each worked well at least one time, in at least one organization. Each of these practices has its advocates.

The focus of this book is on proven practices that have worked broadly for many organizations. From this point forward in the book, the "Other Considerations" sections will describe selected practices that you might have heard of but that, in my company's experience, do not rise to the level of proven, broadly applicable practices.

Extreme Programming (XP)

Much of the initial focus of Agile development was on Extreme Programming (XP) (Beck, 2000), (Beck, 2005), which was a specific set of technical practices, processes, and disciplines that embodied early Agile principles. Early attention on XP was, as advertised, extreme, but longer-term use of XP as a holistic development approach did not pan out. At a time when XP version 1 was described as requiring use of all 12 practices, even the projects touted as exemplar projects used only about half the practices (Grenning, 2001), (Schuh, 2001), (Poole, 2001).

The emphasis on full-fledged use of XP has dwindled since the early 2000s. XP's contribution today is as the source of technical practices that are integral to modern Agile development, including continuous integration, refactoring, test-driven development, and continuous testing.

Kanban

Kanban is a system for scheduling and managing work as it moves through stages of development. Kanban emphasizes pulling work into later stages rather than pushing it from earlier stages. Kanban provides support for visualizing work, reducing work in progress, and maximizing flow through a system.

In Cynefin terms, Kanban works well for Complicated work where prioritization and throughput are the primary concerns, whereas Scrum works better for Complex work because it focuses on small, iterative steps toward a general goal. Either can be a good foundation for process improvement.

Kanban can be more appropriate than Scrum for small teams (1–4 people) or for work that is more production-oriented than project-oriented.

Scrum teams often evolve toward incorporating Kanban into their Scrum implementations as their use of Agile practices matures, and some organizations have had success with using Kanban as a larger-scale project portfolio management tool.

Some groups and teams have been successful starting their Agile implementations with Kanban. But Scrum is more structured, more prescriptive, and more team-oriented, so it is usually the most useful place to begin Agile development.

Kanban is described in a little more detail in Chapter 19, "More Effective Agile Process Improvement."

Suggested Leadership Actions

Inspect

* Interview your teams about their use of Scrum. Have them score themselves according to the Scrum scorecard. How effectively are they using Scrum?
* Review the Scrum failure modes in this chapter with your key team members, and identify areas for improvement.
* Review staffing for the Scrum Master role on your teams. Are your Scrum Masters effective at helping your teams execute Scrum practices, including the high-discipline practices associated with Scrum's failure modes?

Adapt

* Insist that your teams use by-the-book Scrum—unless they can show you a quantitative, measured basis for doing something different. (Chapter 19, "More Effective Agile Process Improvement," goes into more detail about measuring Agile process changes.)
* If your Scrum Masters are not effective, develop them or replace them.

Additional Resources

Schwaber, Ken and Jeff Sutherland. 2017. *The Scrum Guide: The Definitive Guide to Scrum: The Rules of the Game.* 2017. This terse guide to Scrum is considered by many to be the definitive description of the practice.

Rubin, Kenneth, 2012. *Essential Scrum: A Practical Guide to the Most Popular Agile Process.* This is a comprehensive guide to Scrum that addresses common issues related to Scrum adoptions.

Lacey, Mitch, 2016. *The Scrum Field Guide: Agile Advice for Your First Year and Beyond, 2d Ed.* This guide to implementing Scrum focuses on nuts-and-bolts practical issues that arise in Scrum implementations.

Cohn, Mike. 2010. *Succeeding with Agile: Software Development Using Scrum.* This is another good alternative to (Rubin 2012) or (Lacey 2016).

Sutherland, Jeff, 2014. *Scrum: The Art of Doing Twice the Work in Half the Time.* This business-oriented book presents the story of Scrum.

Stuart, Jenny, et al. "Six Things Every Software Executive Should Know about Scrum." Construx White Paper, July 2018. This is a short overview of Scrum aimed at executives.

Stuart, Jenny, et al. "Staffing Scrum Roles," Construx White Paper, August 2017. This paper describes common issues encountered in staffing Scrum roles.

More Effective Agile Team Structure

⟜

The fundamental unit of productivity in Agile development is the team—not high-performing individuals, but high-performing teams. This is a key concept, and we have seen many organizations sabotage their Agile adoptions from the outset by not understanding what is needed for Agile teams to succeed and not supporting them in the ways they need to be supported.

This chapter discusses structural issues related to Agile teams, and the next chapter describes Agile team culture.

Key Principle: Build Cross-Functional Teams

The *2018 Accelerate: State of DevOps* report found that, "High-performing teams are twice as likely to be developing and delivering software in a single, *cross-functional team* ... we found that low performers were twice as likely to be developing and delivering software in *separate, silo'd teams* than elite performers" [emphasis added] (DORA, 2018).

An effective Agile team includes the functions or disciplines needed for the team to work independently (that is, be largely self-managed). For work in Cynefin's Complex domain, much of the team's work will consist of *probe • sense • respond*. If the team must go outside itself each time it probes or senses, it will not have a timely ability to respond. The team must be able to make decisions on its own about most of its work, including decisions about product details (requirements), technical details, and process details. The bulk of people writing production code should also be creating the bulk of automated test code and sorting out requirements details. Such a team can move quickly in a complex environment and still support the business's needs reliably.

A self-managed, cross-functional team normally requires at least the following specializations:

- Developers from different layers of the application (front end, back end, etc.) and with different expertise (architecture, user experience, security, etc.)
- Testers from different layers of the application
- Technical writers
- Experts in the development process being used (Scrum Master)
- Subject matter experts
- Business experts who bring business understanding, vision, and ROI to the team (Product Owner)

It's difficult to assemble a team that possesses the full set of skills needed while staying within the recommended team size of 5–9. Multiple roles need to be played by the same people, and most organizations need to help their staff develop additional skills. Chapter 8, "More Effective Individuals and Interactions," describes practices for doing that.

Beyond skills, a high-functioning cross-functional team must have both the *ability* and the *authority* to make binding decisions in a timely way.

Ability to Make Decisions

The ability to make decisions is strongly affected by how the team is composed. Does the team include all the expertise needed to make effective decisions? Does it include expertise in architecture, quality, usability, the product, the customer, and the business? Or does it have to go outside the team to find expertise in these areas?

A team that lacks expertise in any of these areas will not have the ability to be an effective cross-functional team. The team will often encounter areas in which it does not have the expertise to make a decision. It will then need to reach out to other parts of the organization to access that expertise. This inserts numerous delays. The team will not always know who to reach out to, and it will take time to identify the right person. The outside person will not always be available immediately. It will take time to describe the team's context to that person. If the team needs feedback on its interpretation of the outside person's input, that feedback might be subject to many of the same delays. Both the team and the outside person will make assumptions, some of which will turn out to be mistaken, and those mistakes will take still more time to find and correct.

Every team needs to reach outside itself occasionally, but a team that includes all the expertise needed to make most decisions locally can close issues in minutes that would take days if the expertise were not within the team. The team should be set up so that it can close as many issues as possible on its own.

A team of 5–9 cannot have an infinite number of specialists. A common adaptation is to embed less-than-full-time specialists in subjects such as UX or architecture for a few sprints at a time.

Willingness to staff Agile teams with the expertise needed to make most of its decisions locally is a make-or-break issue for Agile adoptions.

Authority to Make Decisions Within Its Scope

The authority to make decisions comes partly from having all key stakeholders represented on the team and partly from having appropriate permission from the organization. For the team to be effective, it needs the ability to make *binding decisions—* decisions that cannot be undone by others in the organization.

The absence of adequate authority gives rise to several dynamics, all of them counterproductive:

- The team will spend too much time reworking decisions that have been overturned by others in the organization.
- The team will operate at an overly deliberate pace caused by constantly looking over its shoulder in anticipation of having its decisions second-guessed or overturned.
- The team will insert wait states as it seeks approval for decisions from others in the organization.

Authority and ability must be considered together. It is not effective for an organization to grant authority to make decisions if it does not also create the circumstances that give the team the ability to make decisions. If all stakeholder interests are truly represented within the team, any decision will be considered from all relevant points of view. This doesn't mean the team will never make mistakes. It means the team will have a sound basis for making decisions and the rest of the organization will have a sound basis for trusting the team's decisions.

An organizational unwillingness to delegate the authority to make binding decisions to the team is another kiss of death for Agile teams and Agile implementations.

Standing Up Self-Managed Teams

Truly self-managed teams can't just be instantiated; they must be grown. Teams aren't always ready to self-manage on Day 1. Part of a leader's job is to understand their teams' maturity and provide leadership, management, and coaching to help their teams develop the ability to self-manage.

The Role of Mistakes

Like any other kinds of team, self-managed Agile teams will make mistakes. That will be OK if the organization has established an effective learning culture. For one thing, the team will learn from its mistakes and improve. For another, knowing that the organization trusts the team enough to let them make mistakes is a powerful motivator.

Test-Staff Organization

The organization of testing staff has been a moving target throughout my entire career. Once upon a time, testers were integrated into development teams and reported to the development manager. That was found to be problematic because the development managers would pressure testers to, "Stop finding so many defects"—which resulted in customers finding them instead.

For several years after that phase, testers were separated into their own group, often sat in a different area, and didn't report to the development manager. They reported through a different reporting structure that usually didn't converge with the reporting structure for developers until the level of Director or VP. This structure created new problems, including an antagonistic relationship between development and testing. This antagonism was exacerbated by a "tester as gatekeeper" mentality, in which testers implicitly or explicitly had responsibility for blocking poor-quality releases. The separation of development and test responsibility created a dynamic in which developers abdicated responsibility for testing their own code.

In the next evolutionary phase of organization of testing staff, testers continued to report separately but were seated with developers to support a more collaborative relationship. Developers would give testers private builds to test, testers would write test cases and share them with developers, and developers would run their code against the test cases and fix many defects before they officially checked in their code. This arrangement worked pretty well for its time in minimizing the gap between defect insertion and defect detection.

Key Principle: Integrate Testers into the Development Teams

Today, two factors influence the approach to test organization: the rise of Agile development, and the rise of automated testing.

Agile development emphasizes developers testing their own work, a positive and important step that minimizes the gap between defect insertion and detection. Unfortunately, this has led some organizations to eliminate testing as a specialization altogether. That step is misguided. Software testing is an incredibly deep knowledge area. Without understanding fundamental test concepts, most developers fixate on test tools but don't apply fundamental test practices, much less advanced practices.

Test specialists still have several roles to play:

- Taking primary responsibility for test automation

- Creating and maintaining more sophisticated types of testing, such as stress tests, performance tests, load tests, and so on
- Applying more sophisticated test practices than developers do, such as input domain coverage, equivalence class analysis, boundary value coverage, state chart coverage, risk-based testing, and so on
- Creating tests that would not be created by developers testing their own code due to blind spots

Developer testing is the foundation for testing in Agile development, but test specialists still add value. In organizations that have discontinued the role of tester, we see staff members formerly classified as testers primarily focusing on integration tests, load tests, and other cross-cutting kinds of tests. We also see them shouldering a higher percentage of the test automation work than their more development-oriented team members. The Agile slang phrase "Three Amigos" includes test as one of the three amigos (along with development and business). The org chart might not recognize test specialists, but on the ground they still exist. This is an implicit recognition of the value that test specialists provide.

As discussed in Chapter 5, "More Effective Agile Team Structure," effective Agile development depends on creating cross-functional teams, which includes testing. Testers should work side by side with developers throughout the software development and delivery process.

Organization of Production Support

I can't recall any company we've worked with that has been 100% satisfied with how it organizes production support. Companies try some or all of these patterns:

- The people who built a system provide all production support.
- A separate team provides all production support.
- A separate team provides first- and second-level support; the engineering organization supports third-level issues.

The last approach is most common, and it is approached in multiple ways. One way is that third-level support is provided by a separate support team (which is more technical than the first- and second-level support team). That team's primary responsibility is production support. Another way that third-level support is provided is by staff who originally built the system, even though they have mostly transitioned to working on other systems.

Within development teams that are handling escalated support issues as a secondary responsibility (that is, they are supporting systems they worked on previously), support is organized in a variety of ways:

- Escalated support issues are allocated to each team member on a round-robin basis as they arrive.
- Escalated support issues are all handled by one team member; that responsibility rotates daily or weekly.
- Escalated support issues are assigned to the team member most qualified to resolve the issue.

Most companies try several of these patterns over time and conclude that none is completely free of problems. The goal is to find the dog with the fewest fleas rather than hoping to find a perfect solution.

Production Support on Scrum Teams

In terms of production support issues that are specific to Agile development, the challenge is handling support issues without disrupting Scrum's sprints. Teams need to anticipate and plan for the time they will spend on escalated support issues. Here are some guidelines:

Plan support time into sprints. If production support takes 20% of a team's ongoing effort, sprint planning should assume only 80% time is available for sprint-related work.

Set a policy for the kind of work that is allowed to interrupt a sprint. Differentiate between regular work that can go into the product backlog for a future sprint vs. issues that are both urgent enough and important enough to intrude on the sprint. A specific definition is most useful, such as "Priority 1, Severity 1, SLA-related defects are allowed to take precedence over the sprint goal."

Use retrospectives to refine production support planning. Velocity-based sprint planning and sprint retrospectives can help a team measure the amount of time that should be allowed for this work each sprint. As the team reviews challenges it encountered in meeting its sprint goal, it should review the amount of time allocated for production support vs. the amount of time actually spent and make future plans accordingly.

Allow the production support structure to vary from team to team. Different teams will have different numbers of issues escalated to them, the new work they're doing will vary in priority and urgency, and team members will have different levels of experience and ability to handle support issues with prior systems. All these factors suggest that different teams will best handle support issues in different ways.

Agile Teams as Black Boxes

The Agile practice of Scrum explicitly treats the Scrum team as a "black box." If you are an organizational leader, you are allowed to see the inputs to your teams and the outputs from your teams, but you are not supposed to be very concerned with the inner workings of the teams.

In Scrum, this idea is implemented by saying that the team takes on a defined amount of work (the sprint goal) at the beginning of each sprint. The team commits to deliver the work—no matter what—by the end of the sprint. Then, for the duration of the sprint, the team is treated as a black box—no one gets to see inside, and no one gets to put more work into the box during the sprint. At the end of the sprint, the team delivers the functionality it committed to at the beginning. Sprints are short, which means managers don't have to wait long to check whether a team is meeting its commitments.

This description of the team as a black box has been exaggerated somewhat to make a point, but the essence is important. Based on hundreds of conversations with managers and other leaders, I believe that treating teams as black boxes leads to healthier, more effective management. Managers should not be reviewing minute technical or process details. They should be focused on making sure the team has clear direction, and they should hold the team accountable for performing to that direction. They do not need to be aware of moment-to-moment decisions or mistakes in how the team is proceeding toward its goals. Being overly concerned with details is antithetical to a number of key principles, including decriminalizing mistakes and maximizing the team's autonomy.

Appropriate "black box" concerns for a leader include clearing roadblocks (impediments), shielding the teams from avoidable disruption during the sprint, coaching teams through conflict resolution, addressing priority conflicts among projects, supporting staff development, hiring new team members, streamlining organizational bureaucracy, and encouraging the team to reflect on its experience and learn from it.

Is Your Organization Willing to Create Agile Teams?

An Agile anti-pattern is adopting Scrum without creating truly self-managed teams. If management pays lip service to self-management while continuing to direct and control the team at the detailed level, the Agile implementation will fail. Organizations should not adopt Agile unless they are willing to, ready to, and committed to establishing and supporting self-managed teams.

Other Considerations

Geographically Distributed Teams

Geographic distribution creates challenges for effective teams. These are discussed in detail in Chapter 7, "More Effective Distributed Agile Teams."

Open Office Floor Plans

A feature of some Agile adoptions has been to shift from offices or cubes to an open floor plan to support a higher level of collaboration. I do not recommend this.

Counter to expectations, a Harvard study found that open floor plans reduced face-to-face communication by about 70% compared to cubes (Jarrett, 2018). Research for several years has found that open floor plans reduce employee satisfaction, increase stress, reduce job performance, reduce creativity, damage concentration, reduce attention spans, and decrease motivation (Konnikova, 2014).

Some teams might prefer open floor plans (which is fine for them), but most do not. Indeed, backlash against open floor plans has been intense (Jarrett, 2013). One recent article's headline stated, "It's Official: Open-Plan Offices Are Now the Dumbest Management Fad of All Time" (James, 2018).

In my 1996 book, *Rapid Development*, I summarized research at that time that found that the highest levels of productivity were achieved in private or semi-private (two-person) offices (McConnell, 1996). Current research indicates that that finding has not changed.

I recommend the following, in order of effectiveness:

- Private or semi-private offices with open work spaces for team work
- Teams clustered in cubes with open work spaces for team work and with concentration rooms (tiny offices) available for temporary use by individuals
- Cubes with concentration rooms
- Open work bay with concentration rooms

With any floor plan other than the first one, I have seen near-universal use of headphones and increased frequency of working from home—both are symptomatic of staff not being able to concentrate sufficiently at the office to do their jobs well.

Suggested Leadership Actions

Inspect

- Review the composition of your teams. Do your teams contain the expertise needed to make the vast majority of decisions within the teams?
- Interview your team members to understand your teams' *de facto* test organization (as opposed to what's shown on the org chart). Are your teams effectively self-contained and doing their own testing, with or without embedded test specialists?

Adapt

- Based on the review of your team's composition above, create a gap analysis that describes the skills that need to be developed in order for your teams to become self-managed.
- Create a plan to revise the composition of your teams and/or develop missing skills so that each team can make its own decisions and develop toward becoming truly self-managing.
- Make a plan to ensure the test function is incorporated as an integral part of your development teams.

Additional Resources

Aghina, Wouter, et al. 2019. *How to select and develop individuals for successful agile teams: A practical guide.* McKinsey & Company. This white paper studies the value of diversity on Agile teams. It includes diversity based on the five-factor personality model and based on a work values model that includes Agile-focused values.

CHAPTER SIX

More Effective Agile Team Culture

~

Agile organizations find an interplay between Agile team structure and team culture. The shift to self-managing teams requires a shift in team culture that complements and supports the teams' ability to self-manage.

This chapter describes team-level elements of Agile culture. Chapter 17, "More Effective Agile Organizational Culture," provides further perspective on Agile culture at the organizational level.

Key Principle: Motivate Teams Through Autonomy, Mastery, Purpose

Most productivity studies have found that productivity depends more on motivation than any other factor (Boehm, 1981). For software development work, the only kind of motivation that matters is *internal* motivation. A company is essentially renting space in people's brains, paying its employees to think about what they want them to think about. External motivation doesn't work because you can't compel someone to think about something; you can only set up the circumstances in which they will think about your problem because they want to.

In his 2009 book, *Drive*, Daniel Pink proposed a theory of internal motivation based on the factors of Autonomy, Mastery, and Purpose. Pink's motivation theory dovetails with the support that Agile teams need to be effective.

Autonomy

"Autonomy" refers to the ability to direct your own life and work—what you do, when you do it, and who you do it with. Autonomy is related to trust. If a person believes their organization doesn't trust them to make decisions, they won't believe they have real autonomy. The work you do to develop cross-functional Agile teams with the ability and authority to make their own decisions also supports their sense of Autonomy.

Mastery

"Mastery" refers to the desire to learn and improve. It is not the idea of reaching a defined standard of competence, but the idea of constantly getting *better*. This is especially important for technical staff. As I pointed out many years ago in my book *Rapid Development* (McConnell, 1996), the opportunity for growth has been found to be a stronger motivator for developers than advancement, recognition, salary, status, level of responsibility, and other factors that you might assume matter more. Agile's focus on learning from experience will support your teams' sense of Mastery.

Table 6-1 Practices Supporting or Undermining Autonomy

How to Support Autonomy	How to Undermine
Lead by setting direction (aligning with the broader organizational vision and mission)	Leaders concern themselves with details of how the work is performed
Commit to a direction	Change direction frequently
Include all skills on the team necessary to act independently	Withhold expertise from the team that it needs in order to work independently
	Do not create real teams; just groups of highly matrixed individuals
Allow teams to experiment with change to their practices based on their retrospectives	Insist upon predefined processes, regardless of the team's experience
Allow teams to pull work at a pace they determine for themselves	Dictate the rate at which work is pushed to the teams
Feed requirements through the agreed-upon requirements process	Push requirements directly to the team or to individual team members
Keep high-performing teams intact; move work to people	Frequently break up and reconfigure teams; move people to work
Allow teams to make mistakes and learn from them	Criminalize mistakes and penalize teams for them

Purpose

"Purpose" refers to understanding why what you're working on matters. What is the big picture? How is the thing you're working on bigger and more important than yourself? How does it support your company or the world at large? Agile's focus on direct contact with customers will support your team's sense of Purpose. Agile's emphasis on shared team responsibility and accountability promotes a sense of camaraderie that also supports your team's sense of Purpose.

Table 6-2 Practices Supporting or Undermining Mastery

How to Support Mastery	How to Undermine
Allow time for retrospectives	Discourage retrospectives
Encourage changes to be made each sprint for sake of learning and improvement	Disallow changes, or require a bulky change-approval process
Allow technical staff to explore new technology areas	Restrict technical staff's work to immediate business needs
Allow time for training and professional development	Demand that all time be allocated to short-term project goals; don't allow time for training
Support innovation days	Discourage experimentation
Support deliberate practice such as coding katas	Insist on strict task focus; do not allow time for individual improvement
Allow staff members to move into new areas	Require staff members to stay in the area in which they have the most experience

The Virtuous Combination of Autonomy, Mastery, and Purpose

Daniel Pink's research has found that a team that works on its own, understands why it's doing its work, and is steadily improving will also be highly motivated. The factors that create an effective team also create a motivated team, and in this virtuous interaction effectiveness and motivation support each other.

Table 6-3 Practices Supporting or Undermining Purpose

How to Support Purpose	How to Undermine
Provide technical staff with regular contact with actual customers	Restrict technical staff from interacting directly with customers
Provide technical staff with frequent contact with internal business staff	"Silo" the technical teams and business staff so that they rarely interact
Regularly communicate the big picture surrounding the team's work	Communicate the big picture only at infrequent all-company meetings
Ensure communications are grounded in reality	Communicate cliched information that is disconnected from reality
Describe the real-world impact of the team's work: "Our defibrillator saved xyz lives last year"	Insist that big-picture issues are the domain of leadership, and the team doesn't have a "need to know"
Emphasize the value of high-quality work to the organization	Discuss only immediate financial benefit to the company and/or short-term delivery goals

Key Principle: Develop a Growth Mindset

The idea of "more effective" Agile is a constantly moving target. No matter how effective you are this year, you can be *more effective* next year. For growth to take place, however, teams must be allowed to spend time improving. Some of that improvement should happen in the regular cycle of sprint retrospectives and sprint planning, and some improvement should occur during the sprints.

Becoming more effective requires a Growth Mindset—a mindset of "we can get better over time"—which not all leaders have.

Some software leaders look at software projects as having only the basic inputs and outputs shown here:

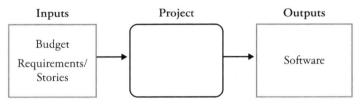

In this view, the only purpose of a project is to create software, and the only relevant output of a project is the software itself.

A more holistic view of a project's inputs and outputs considers the capability of the team before and after the project. A project that's exclusively task-focused—which usually includes a dose of schedule pressure—can produce inputs and outputs like this:

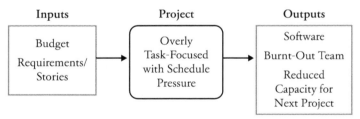

If the leader isn't focused on growing the team, it's easy to run a project in a way that produces a worn-out team that has *less capacity* than it had at the beginning of the project. The same logic applies to sprints and releases. Some Scrum teams experience "sprint fatigue" when sprints are not run at a sustainable pace.

The delta between how teams start their projects and how they end their projects significantly influences the effectiveness of the organization. In many organizations, every project is a rush. Projects focus exclusively on the tasks immediately in front of them, and there's never time for the individuals or teams to get better at what they do. Indeed, constant schedule pressure literally makes them worse at what they do—in terms of their feelings of Autonomy and Mastery and, ultimately, in terms of their motivation.

This leads to a predictable set of dynamics in which teams experience burnout, the best team members leave for other organizations, and organizational capacity degrades over time.

An organization committed to being more effective will take a more comprehensive, Growth-Mindset view of the purpose of its software projects. Of course, one purpose of the project is to produce working software, but another purpose is to enhance the capabilities of the team that produces the software: *"We can get better over time, and we will allow time to do that."*

A Growth Mindset produces several benefits to the organization:

* Increased individual energy level
* Improved individual and team motivation
* Higher team cohesion
* Increased company loyalty (better retention)
* Expanded technical and nontechnical skills—better code and higher quality

A company that realizes how much benefit a Growth Mindset makes possible will conduct its projects like this:

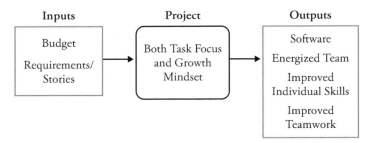

The traditional Agile mantra of "sustainable pace" is one necessary element of more effective Agile, but that implies merely that teams won't burn out, not that they will continually get better. A commitment to a Growth Mindset takes the foundation established by working at a sustainable pace and leverages it to provide additional benefits to the organization and to its individuals.

Growing team capacity is one of the central responsibilities of a software leader. A systematic approach to developing staff capability is described in Chapter 8, "More Effective Individuals and Interactions."

Key Principle: Develop Business Focus

There are no silver bullets in software development, but one business-oriented practice is close, and far too few organizations employ it. The practice is simple, and its benefits greatly outweigh any implementation difficulties.

What is this near-silver bullet? It is simply putting every single developer in direct contact with actual customers, the actual users of their system.

Some businesses resist putting developers in contact with users because they fear that the great unwashed masses of developers are, well, literally unwashed. They treat the Product Owner (or

Sales, or Business Analyst) as a shield between developers and users. This is a mistake and a significant lost opportunity.

For a developer, experiencing direct contact with users is often a life-changing experience. A developer who previously argued for technical purity (whatever that is) and viewed users mainly as an annoying source of illogical feature requests becomes a vigorous advocate for ease of use and user satisfaction.

Business leaders who expose developers to real users invariably report that the benefits from understanding the user perspective far outweigh any risks they were concerned about. Technical staff members develop an understanding of how their work is used in the field, how much their users depend on it, what frustrates users, and how much impact their work can have when it really addresses their users' needs. There is a strong interplay between exposing developers to users and the "Purpose" part of Autonomy, Mastery, and Purpose. This practice delivers both product-quality benefits and motivational benefits.

Here are ways you can connect developers to users:

- Have developers listen to support calls for a few hours at a time, periodically.
- Have developers field support calls for a few hours.
- Send developers to observe users using their software in the field.
- Have developers observe users in a UX lab through a one-way glass or TV monitor.
- Have developers accompany sales staff on customer visits or listen in on sales calls.

These practices are not treated as rewards or penalties but as part of maintaining a healthy business. They apply to senior developers, junior developers, newly on-boarded developers—everyone.

It's important that user contact be implemented as an ongoing program, not just a one-time experience. Otherwise, developers can become overly fixated on issues they observed in one user interaction. Ongoing exposure is needed to provide them with a balanced view of user issues.

The Product Owner role is the weak link in the chain in many organizations. While developing a business mindset in the technical staff is not a replacement for a good PO, it can soften the failure mode of having a less-than-perfect PO.

Putting developers in direct contact with users is an incredibly simple idea that is practiced far too seldom, yet it yields significant results whenever it's done.

Other Considerations

Personal Interaction Skills

People's ability to work well in teams is affected by their personal interaction skills. This factor is discussed in more detail in Chapter 8.

Personal Orientations and Roles

Teams tend to perform best when they have a balance of personal orientations and roles. Belbin's Team Roles theory provides an interesting and useful way to assess the presence of roles on teams. The theory includes an assessment of how each person behaves on a team, how likely a group of people is to work well together, and how to select candidates to fill each role. Belbin's roles include Company Worker, Chairman, Plant, Shaper, Resource Investigator, Team Worker, Co-ordinator, Monitor/Evaluator, and Completer/Finisher.

Research on IT teams shows a high correlation between having a balance of team roles and team performance (Twardochleb, 2017).

Suggested Leadership Actions

Inspect

* Review the lists in Tables 6-1, 6-2, and 6-3. How do your personal interactions rate according to the entries in those tables?

* How does the rest of your organization rate according to the lists in Tables 6-1, 6-2, and 6-3?

* Have your teams score their own motivation and morale at the beginning and end of each project or release cycle. Do the numbers show that the teams are working at a sustainable pace and growing, or are they burning out?

Adapt

* Change your own actions, as needed, to provide your teams with Autonomy.

* Implement other changes based on your review of Tables 6-1, 6-2, and 6-3.

* Create a plan to ensure that your teams are healthier at the ends of their projects and have developed more capabilities than they had at the beginnings. Communicate to your teams that you want them to spend a little bit of time learning each cycle.

* Create a plan to put your technical staff into direct contact with your customers.

Additional Resources

Pink, Daniel H. 2009. *Drive: The Surprising Truth About What Motivates Us.* This popular business book advanced the theory of motivation based on Autonomy, Mastery, and Purpose described in this chapter.

McConnell, Steve. 1996. *Rapid Development: Taming Wild Software Schedules.* Several chapters in this book discuss motivation explicitly or implicitly.

Twardochleb, Michal. 2017. "Optimal selection of team members according to Belbin's theory." *Scientific Journals of the Maritime University of Szczecin.* September 15, 2017. This academic paper summarizes Belbin's Team Roles theory and applies it to student projects. Twardochleb found that the absence of even one role led to teams being unable to complete their tasks.

Dweck, Carol S. 2006. *Mindset: The New Psychology of Success.* This is the classic description of the Growth Mindset and includes discussions of how the Growth Mindset applies to students, parents, leaders, romantic partners, and other roles.

CHAPTER SEVEN

More Effective Distributed Agile Teams

In more than 20 years of working with companies that have established geographically distributed development teams, we have seen only a small number of examples in which productivity was comparable to a team that was co-located. We have not seen any indication that geographically distributed Agile teams will ever be as effective as co-located teams. However, distributed teams are a fact of life for most large companies today, so this chapter describes how to make them work as well as possible.

Key Principle: Tighten Feedback Loops

One principle of effective software development is to tighten feedback loops as much as possible. Many of the details in this book can be inferred from that principle. Why do we want a Product Owner within the Agile team? To tighten the feedback loops related to requirements. Why do we use cross-functional teams? To tighten the feedback loop needed for decision making. Why do we define and deliver requirements in small batches? To tighten the feedback loop from requirements definition to executable, demonstrable software. Why do we perform test-first development? To tighten the feedback loop between code and test.

Tight feedback loops become all-the-more important when working in Cynefin's Complex domain, because the work cannot be mapped out in advance; it must be discovered through numerous *probe • sense • respond* cycles. Those cycles are a type of feedback loop that should be as tight as possible.

Geographically distributed teams have the effect of loosening feedback loops. That slows decision making, increases error rates, increases rework, reduces throughput, and ultimately delays projects. Any communication that can't occur face to face inserts more potential for miscommunication, which loosens the feedback loop. Time-zone differences insert delayed responses, which has the same effect. Work done in larger batches before being sent offshore, such as during the time an onshore Product Owner visits the offshore team to support face-to-face communication, again loosens the feedback loops. Add differences in language, national culture, site culture, and the time-zone fatigue that accumulates from participating in remote meetings at awkward hours, and the feedback loop loosens and mistakes increase even more.

We worked with a company at which the offshore team was significantly underperforming the onshore team. When we brought some of the offshore individuals onshore, their productivity increased dramatically for the short time they were working onshore, but it fell again when they returned home. This demonstrates that the performance problem was not because of the individuals involved—the communications gap and delays caused by 12,000 miles of separation made it impossible for the offshore team to perform effectively.

Loose feedback loops are the biggest problem I see with distributed teams. These appear in a number of forms, illustrated in Figure 7-1, all of which I'm inclined to call classic mistakes:

* Development at one location; test at another
* Product ownership at one location; development at another
* Work on shared functionality that's split 50/50 across two sites

None of these configurations work well—each creates a situation in which people who need to communicate with one another frequently are delayed in their communications.

Figure 7-1
Examples of how not to allocate responsibilities across a distributed team.

In the early 2000s, companies put development and test at different sites to support a follow-the-sun methodology—test could detect bugs while dev was sleeping, and turnaround time would decrease. While logical, what happened instead was that dev would not understand a defect report, or test wouldn't understand a change made by dev, and a back-and-forth communication cycle that would have taken a couple hours with a co-located team took a day and a half instead.

The best practice in this area is to establish teams that can operate as autonomously as possible at each location, as shown in Figure 7-2. In software terms, think of the teams as having high cohesion and loose coupling.

Figure 7-2
Example of how to allocate responsibilities across a distributed team.

It is also not an accident that the best practice for distributed teams is the same as the best practice for Agile teams in general: establish self-directed cross-functional teams that have both the ability and the authority to make binding decisions locally.

Toward Successful Distributed Agile Teams

Succeeding with distributed teams requires the following:

- Schedule routine face-to-face communication.
- Increase logistical support for distributed teams.
- Leverage Autonomy, Mastery, and Purpose.
- Respect Conway's Law.
- Treat Agile teams as black boxes.
- Maintain high quality.
- Be aware of cultural differences.
- Inspect and Adapt.

Schedule Routine Face-to-Face Communication

Most problems with multi-site development are not technical; they're interpersonal communication problems. Geographic distance, time-zone offsets, language differences, national-culture differences, site-culture differences, and site-status differences make communication less reliable and more difficult.

Periodic in-person communication is important. As one senior leader of a global company said to me, "The half-life of trust is 6 weeks." When you see mistakes begin to increase, it's time to put people on airplanes, have them play games together, eat together, and develop human connections.

Aim to have a percentage of staff members traveling from site to site approximately every 6 weeks, with a goal of 100% of team members visiting other sites over a period of years.

Increase Logistical Support for Distributed Teams

If you want to be successful with distributed teams, you need to invest money, effort, and time to support that style of work.

Scheduled communications. Establish mandatory meetings that everyone must attend. Rotate the inconvenient times across sites so that no single site incurs all the time-zone fatigue. Provide effective tools for remote meetings and the network bandwidth to support the tools. Insist on good meeting practices: create agendas, define deliverables, stay on topic, end on time, and so on.

Ad hoc communications. Support cross-site communications that arise spontaneously. Provide each staff member with communication technology: high-quality microphone, web cam, and adequate network bandwidth. Provide tools for text-based, time-sensitive, streamed communication as well as online forums (Slack, Microsoft Teams, and so on).

Remote proxies. Designate people at remote sites as proxy PO or proxy engineering manager. When the team can't get an answer from the remote PO or engineering manager, they can reach out to the proxy. The proxies have regular one-on-one discussions with their remote counterparts so they can stay in sync.

Staff transfers. Consider moving staff permanently or on a long-term basis. Because of the international composition of many software teams, it is not uncommon to find team members who want to return to their home countries. A little-known fact is that Microsoft populated its first Indian site with Indian nationals who had already worked at Microsoft's Redmond campus. This helped with establishing company culture and deep knowledge at the Indian location.

Onboarding and training. Schedule new staff to visit the site remote to them as an onboarding activity. Provide mentors to coach new staff on effective multi-site work practices.

Leverage Autonomy, Mastery, and Purpose

Some companies distribute teams evenly across multiple sites, with each site having equal status. More commonly, companies that have multiple sites create status discrepancies among their sites: onshore vs. offshore, in-house vs. outsourced, parent company vs. acquired company, and main site vs. satellite sites. They allocate different kinds of work to secondary sites, including less important work, and they allow those sites less latitude.

The differences in status and lower Autonomy limits each site's motivation. I have found that secondary teams tend to be self-aware and candid about their status and level of responsibility. Managers of secondary teams frequently report that their teams ask for more Autonomy and self-direction, ask for opportunities to grow (Mastery), and want to understand the bigger picture of the work they're doing (Purpose).

To be successful with multi-site development, Agile or otherwise, find ways to provide each location with work it can perform autonomously and allow each site to grow professionally.

Actively communicate why each site's work is important to the organization or the world at large.

Respect Conway's Law

Conway's Law, loosely speaking, says that the technical structure of a system reflects the structure of the human organization that built the system (Conway, 1968).[2] This structure includes the formal management structure and the informal interpersonal network structure. The interplay between these structures is significant on geographically distributed work.

Conway's Law is a two-way street: the technical design also influences the human organization design. If the team is distributed across three sites but the technical architecture doesn't support work in three independent areas, the teams will struggle because they will have technical dependencies on one anothers' work that span geographic boundaries.

If a team has been geographically distributed for years, the technical architecture probably already reflects the team's structure. If your team is transitioning to becoming geographically distributed, compare the technical architecture and the human organization and look for mismatches.

Treat Agile Teams as Black Boxes

As with co-located teams, the management discipline of treating teams as black boxes supports managers acting more as leaders who set direction than as managers who are overly concerned with details. Manage inputs to your teams and outputs from

---

[2] Conway's exact language is this: "Organizations which design systems (in the broad sense used here) are constrained to produce designs which are copies of the communication structures of these organizations."

your teams. Avoid focusing on the details of how your teams perform their work.

Maintain High Quality

The Agile discipline of keeping the software close to releasable at all times helps prevent teams at different geographies from diverging too much from one another.

Part of treating each team as a black box is assuring that the output that comes out of the box is high quality. The practice of keeping a code base at a releasable level of quality is a high-discipline practice that even co-located teams struggle with.

Teams' natural tendency when they are distributed is to converge to a releasable state less often. This is a mistake. Geographically distributed teams are at risk of going in different directions without realizing it, which means, for the sake of risk management, that they should converge more often rather than less. To ensure they're converging effectively, distributed teams should pay special attention to their Definition of Done.

The effort required to keep the software at a releasable level of quality highlights the costs of geographic distribution. If a distributed team finds that it's spending an inordinate amount of time in its frequent convergences to a releasable level of quality, the solution is not to converge less often. That increases the risk that the team won't be able to converge at all! The solution is to modify practices to streamline the work required to converge reliably and frequently. In some cases, highlighting the convergence effort might lead to a decision to reduce the number of development sites.

Be Aware of Cultural Differences

Common differences across cultures include:

- Willingness to communicate bad news, including even answering "no" to simple questions
- Response to authority
- The ethos of individual vs. team accomplishment
- Work-hour expectations, and prioritization of work vs. personal life

Much has been written about this, so if you aren't aware of these issues, go read about them.

Inspect and Adapt

Developing with geographically distributed teams is difficult. The challenges will vary based on how many sites you have, where the sites are located, your software's architecture, how the work is allocated across sites, and the capabilities of the specific teams and individuals at each location.

For geographic distribution to work, teams must engage in regular retrospectives to candidly assess what's working, what's taking more time than it should, and whether issues related to working in a distributed team are causing problems or inefficiencies. Cultural differences can create challenges for retrospectives, and extra work might be required to encourage frank discussions.

The organization should also support system-level retrospectives that focus specifically on streamlining issues related to multi-site development. The teams must then use those insights to make changes that address the difficulties they're identifying—and the teams must be empowered to make those changes. If they are not empowered, the organization risks low effectiveness from geographically distributed development.

Poor execution of distributed development can demotivate staff both at primary and secondary sites, leading to lower morale and higher turnover.

Many organizations—perhaps even most organizations—fail to achieve the objectives that led them to establish geographically distributed teams. You have to do a lot of things right to be successful with distributed teams, and this is not an area where you should take shortcuts.

Key Principle: Fix the System, Not the Individual

Geographically distributed development increases miscommunication, which in turn increases errors. Geographically distributed teams spend more of their time fixing defects than a co-located team would—because of both increased defect counts and increased defect-resolution times caused by distance between the teams. Increased error rates tend to increase stress, which increases the tendency to point fingers and assign blame.

To be successful with a geographically distributed team, it's important to emphasize the principle of decriminalizing errors. Treat errors as *system* problems, not personnel problems. Ask this question: What is it about our system that allowed this error to occur? This is a good practice in general, but it's especially important in a geographically distributed environment.

Other Considerations

If you experience inefficiencies with your distributed teams because they're not able to make decisions locally, determine whether you're experiencing similar challenges with your teams at your primary sites. It's possible that you are experiencing similar inefficiencies—they're just less visible because it's easier for the primary-site team to compensate for their lack of Autonomy by working with people who are geographically closer to them.

Suggested Leadership Actions

Inspect

* How tight are the feedback loops with your distributed teams? Are you committing any of the classic mistakes listed in this chapter?
* Review your sites' differences in language, national culture, and site culture. Estimate the impact of those differences on communication mistakes.
* Are your teams organized in such a way that each team can have Autonomy, Mastery, and Purpose?
* Are your distributed teams highly disciplined about converging to a releasable level of quality often—*at least as often* as they would if they were co-located?
* Have you systematized your distributed teams' use of Inspect and Adapt so that they can learn how to work more effectively in their challenging configuration?

Adapt

* Reorganize your teams and communication patterns, if necessary, to tighten feedback loops.
* Develop a plan to improve communication and understanding across sites.
* Make a plan for supporting your distributed teams in having Autonomy, Mastery, and Purpose.
* Communicate the importance of maintaining a releasable level of quality at all times to your teams, and make sure they are using an appropriate Definition of Done.
* Empower your teams to make changes based on the findings of their retrospectives.

Additional Resources

Most of the information in this chapter summarizes my company's direct experience. As such, additional resources are limited.

Conway, Melvin E. 1968. How do Committees Invent? *Datamation.* April 1968. This is the original paper on Conway's Law.

Hooker, John, 2003. *Working Across Cultures.* Stanford University Press. This book describes general considerations in working across cultures and includes specific commentary on China, India, the United States, and other countries.

Stuart, Jenny, et al. "Succeeding with Geographically Distributed Scrum," Construx White Paper, March 2018. This white paper provides suggestions for distributed teams specific to Scrum. It brings in much of the same experience that I've described in this chapter.

More Effective Individuals and Interactions

∽

The Agile Manifesto stated that Agile values individuals and interactions over processes and tools. But Agile to date has focused much more extensively on processes than individuals, and its focus on individuals has been limited to the interactions around certain structured collaborations.

The principle "Develop a Growth Mindset" contributes to a general tendency to learn, but if that tendency is not developed into more than a general aspiration, the learning will be ad hoc and will not add up to much. If you agree with the idea that a team should finish each project stronger than it started, you need to allow time for that learning and you need a plan for it.

This chapter presents a systematic approach to technical staff learning and covers the areas of learning that are either most important or most often lacking in technical staff. Because of the broad, overview approach of this chapter, I've provided extensive "Additional Resources" at the end of the chapter.

The Potential of Focusing on Individuals

Maximizing individual effectiveness should be the cornerstone of any program intended to increase organizational effectiveness. Researchers for decades have found that productivity among individuals with similar levels of experience varies by at least a factor of 10 (McConnell, 2011). They have also found that productivity among teams working in the same industries also varies by a factor of 10 or more (McConnell, 2019).

To some degree differences in personal effectiveness are probably born, and to some degree they are made. Netflix's cloud architect, Adrian Cockroft, was once asked where he got his amazing people. He told the Fortune 500 leader, "I hired them from you!" (Forsgren, 2018). The point, of course, is that good performers don't become good performers overnight. They develop over time, which means an organization that wants to be effective has the opportunity to support its staff in that development. As the recent internet meme said:

CFO: What happens if we invest in our staff and they leave?
CEO: What happens if we don't invest in them and they stay?

Supporting your staff's development is synergistic in numerous respects. The first and foremost reason to support staff development is that it increases staff members' ability to contribute to your organization. There's also synergy between the Inspect and Adapt Growth Mindset at the project level and a personal Growth Mindset at the professional development level. Finally, supporting staff development taps into the motivational power of Mastery.

As Forsgren, Humble, and Kim report in their far-reaching study of high-performing technology organizations:

> *"In today's fast-moving and competitive world, the best thing you can do for your products, your company, and your people is to institute a culture of experimentation and learning, and invest in the technical and management capabilities that enable it."*
> *(Forsgren, 2018)*

Forsgren, Humble, and Kim also reported that a climate for learning was one of the three factors that were highly correlated with software delivery performance.

In some organizations a tension exists between new learning and application of prior learning. A common pattern is that staff want to move into new areas to maximize learning, but the organization wants them to stay in their current areas to apply expertise already acquired. Transferring across areas is so difficult that the most motivated staff members move to other companies to pursue their professional development.

The organization that wants to develop effective individuals will provide clear guidance about how to progress from junior engineer to senior engineer, how to move from development into management, how to grow from technical lead to architect, and so on.

Key Principle: Increase Team Capacity by Building Individual Capacity

Most software professionals' career progression can be described as pinball—bouncing project by project from one technology to another, from one methodology to another. Professional experience of any kind is valuable, but this pattern is a prescription for ad hoc accumulation of scattered experiences rather than a systematic program for building cohesive expertise and capability over time.

Increase Role Density

Cross-functional Agile teams depend on having technical staff who perform well in their own specializations and who can extend into other areas as needed. "Role density" refers to how many different roles a person is capable of performing. Compare the differences in role density here:

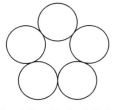 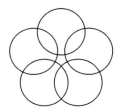

Specialists Trained Only
for Their Specialties
(Low Role Density)

Specialists Cross-Trained
for Other Specialties
(High Role Density)

⊙ Role Coverage

Which team is more vulnerable to staff turnover? Which is more flexible in how work is allocated? Which is more adaptable?

A software organization that wants to be more effective will support its software staff by ensuring that their professional development experiences *add up to something*—which in turn allows them to achieve higher levels of Mastery.

Develop Three Kinds of Professional Capability

Technical organizations tend to fixate on technology knowledge as the type of knowledge most important to a software professional, but this is short-sighted. A highly competent software professional will have strong capability in three kinds of knowledge:

* Technology knowledge—knowledge of specific technologies, such as programming languages and tools.

- Software development practices—knowledge of practices in areas including design, coding, test, requirements, and management.
- Domain knowledge—domain knowledge of the specific business or scientific area where the professional works.

Technical individuals need these different kinds of knowledge to different degrees. A software developer needs deep knowledge of technology and software development practice, with a lesser emphasis on the business or scientific domain. A product owner needs deep knowledge of the domain, and lesser knowledge of technology and software development practices. Specifics can be defined on a role-by-role basis.

Structure a Career Pathing Program Using the Professional Development Ladder

Twenty years ago my company and I recognized that career pathing for software professionals was poorly defined and poorly supported, so we developed a detailed Professional Development Ladder (PDL) to provide both overall direction and detailed support for professional development of software staff. We have continued to maintain, update, and evolve the PDL since then, and we make many of the PDL materials freely available for software professionals and their organizations to use for career pathing.

Construx's PDL supports long-term career pathing for a variety of software staff, including developers, testers, Scrum Masters, Product Owners, architects, business analysts, technical managers, and other common software positions. The PDL provides direction and structure while still allowing the interests of individuals to guide their specific career paths.

The PDL is comprised of four building blocks:

- Standards-based software development knowledge areas, including requirements, design, test, quality, management, and so on
- Defined capability levels—introductory, competence, and leadership
- Professional development activities—including training, reading, and defined experience—needed to attain capability in each knowledge area
- Role-specific career paths that are built using the knowledge areas, capability levels, and professional development activities described above

The heart of Construx's Professional Development Ladder is an 11x3 Professional Development Matrix (PDM) that is produced when the 11 knowledge areas and 3 capability levels are combined (McConnell, 2018). This is illustrated in Figure 8-1.

	Knowledge Area										
Capability Level	Configuration Management	Construction	Design	Foundations	Maintenance	Management	Models and Methods	Process	Quality	Requirements	Testing
Introductory	●	●	●	●	●	●	●	●	●	●	●
Competence	●	●	●								●
Leadership		●									

Figure 8-1
The 11x3 Professional Development Matrix.

In the example shown in the figure, boxes containing circles represent the capabilities that the PDL recommends for a person to perform as a Senior Developer. For example, a Senior Developer needs to attain Leadership capability in Construction, and Competence capability in Configuration Management, Design, and Testing. For each circle in the PDM, the

PDL materials provide a specific list of reading, training, and directed experience needed to attain that level of capability.

The Professional Development Matrix appears simple, but it is surprisingly powerful. Career goals can be defined in terms of which boxes are checked in the matrix. Career progression can be defined by charting a path through highlighted sections of the matrix. Professional development activities can be defined in terms of which cells they support in the PDM.

The matrix arising from the combination of the 11 standards-based knowledge areas and the 3 defined capability levels provides a framework for career development that is simultaneously highly structured and highly flexible and customizable. Most important, it offers each software professional a clear path toward steadily increasing levels of Mastery.

For more information on details of the PDL, including when professional development occurs, suggestions for supporting professional development, and other implementation questions, see my white paper *Career Pathing for Software Professionals* (McConnell 2018).

More Effective Interactions (Teams)

While every team can improve if individuals improve their software development capabilities, many teams struggle because of poor interactions. Agile development requires face-to-face collaboration, so frictionless interactions are more important in Agile development than they were in Sequential development. After working with leaders at many companies over the past 20 years, I believe the following interaction soft skills are most helpful to Agile team members.

Emotional Intelligence

If you've ever seen two developers engage in an email flame war over technical minutia, you've seen evidence of the need for greater emotional intelligence on software teams.

For leaders, the value of emotional intelligence has been well-documented. Daniel Goleman reported in the Harvard Business Review that 90% of the difference between star performers and average performers can be attributed to emotional intelligence (abbreviated as EQ) (Goleman, 2004). A study of 500 executive search candidates found that EQ was a significantly better predictor of placement success than intelligence or experience (Cherniss, 1999).

Technical contributors can benefit from increasing awareness of their own emotional states and emotional states in others, improving emotional self-regulation, and managing relationships with others.

I find the Yale Center for Emotional Intelligence's RULER Model to be a useful resource in this area (Yale, 2019). RULER stands for:

- Recognizing emotions in self and others
- Understanding the causes and consequences of emotions
- Labeling emotions accurately
- Expressing emotions appropriately
- Regulating emotions effectively

The RULER model was originally developed for work with adolescents and was subsequently adapted for use with adults, especially adults working in groups.

Communicating with Different Personality Types

Sales staff intuitively understand that people communicate in different ways and adapt their communications appropriately.

Technical staff often need explicit instruction and encouragement to adapt their communication style to suit their audience.

A study of personality types helps technical staff understand that different people emphasize different kinds of factors in their decision making (e.g., data vs. people's feelings). They express themselves differently, and they react differently under stress. Labeling the variations, seeing how the variations apply to others, and self-assessing is often an eye-opening experience for technical staff members.

I find the Social Styles model to be an intuitive tool for understanding personality types (Mulqueen, 2014). Social Styles is based on observable behaviors; you don't need to know someone's test results to understand how to interact with them. DISC, Myers Briggs, and Color Codes are similarly useful.

The value of appreciating differences in social styles is most obvious in improving interactions among different types of staff. As shown in Figure 8-2 (on the next page), according to the Social Styles model, technical staff tend to be on the Analytical side, sales staff tend to be Expressive, and management tend to be Drivers. (These are all generalizations with numerous exceptions, of course.)

Learning about social styles can help technical staff communicate more effectively with sales, it can help them do a better job of managing up in the organization, and it can help improve communications among different personality types within a team. Some technical staff view adjusting their communication style to match the person they're communicating with as somehow dishonest. This can become a self-imposed career limitation. Training in communication styles can be enlightening and can help overcome that limitation.

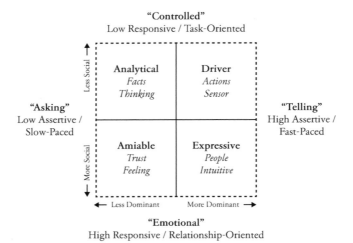

Figure 8-2
Overview of the Social Style model.

The scientific validity of these popular models has been questioned. If you're interested in the most scientific approach, look up the Big Five Personality Traits/OCEAN model. For practical purposes, I subscribe to the idea that, "All models are wrong; some models are useful." And I find the Social Styles model to be especially useful.

Crucial Conversations

Structured approaches can provide good support for people who don't have an intuitive sense of how to perform a task. The Crucial Conversations approach to having difficult conversations is an effective model that applies in the following circumstances (Patterson, 2002):

* Stakes are high
* Opinions vary
* Emotions run strong

In technical contexts, crucial conversations can arise in situations ranging from needing to confront a staff member about a performance issue, deciding on a design approach, presenting bad news to a key stakeholder, and many other circumstances.

Communication with Executives

Understanding the different personality types provides a useful foundation for improved communication in general and better communication with executives in particular.

As one of the manuscript reviewers of this book wrote, "Your head is entirely full of your issue, and you have all day to resolve it. Your boss has seven minutes available, and enough free working memory for three bullet points."

Identifying the executive's personality type (according to the Social Styles model), understanding the executive's decision-making style, and anticipating how the executive is likely to react under stress can all help technical staff prepare for successful communication.

Stages of Team Development

Although the Tuckman model of group development is almost a cliché in management circles, because software work is so often performed in teams and because teams in many organizations change often, it's useful for team members to understand Tuckman's four phases: forming, storming, norming, and performing, as shown in Figure 8-3 (on the next page).

I've found that teams that are in the forming or storming phases are relieved to learn that what they're experiencing is normal. Furthermore, that realization helps them move toward norming and performing more quickly.

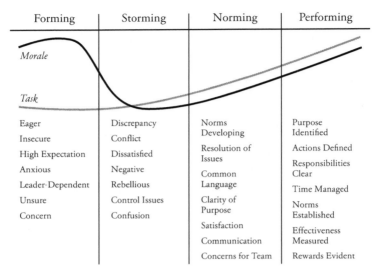

Forming	Storming	Norming	Performing
Morale			
Task			
Eager	Discrepancy	Norms Developing	Purpose Identified
Insecure	Conflict	Resolution of Issues	Actions Defined
High Expectation	Dissatisfied	Common Language	Responsibilities Clear
Anxious	Negative	Clarity of Purpose	Time Managed
Leader-Dependent	Rebellious	Satisfaction	Norms Established
Unsure	Control Issues	Communication	Effectiveness Measured
Concern	Confusion	Concerns for Team	Rewards Evident

Figure 8-3

The Tuckman Model's stages of team formation.

Leaders should also understand that this progression is normal and expected. They should also be aware that one cost of disassembling and reassembling teams is the time it takes for teams to progress through the stages again to get to performing.

Streamlined Decision-Making Models

Software teams need to make numerous decisions about requirements priorities, design approaches, work assignments, process changes—the list is endless. Knowing a few team-oriented decision-making models is useful. I have had success using streamlined decision-making practices including thumb voting/Roman voting, fist of five, dot voting, and decision leader decides.

Conducting Effective Meetings

Scrum's standard meetings are well-structured—the meeting roles, purpose, and basic agenda are all defined by Scrum, which keeps the meetings on track and ensures good use of time.

In many organizations, other kinds of meetings are huge time-killers. For general meetings, it's useful to provide guidance in conducting meetings effectively. At a minimum this should include standard advice: have a clear purpose for the meeting, set clearly defined expectations about what decision or other deliverable the meeting will produce, err on the side of scheduling the meeting to be shorter rather than longer, invite only people who are necessary to support the meeting's deliverable, declare the meeting to be over as soon as it has met its objective, and so on. A good resource in this area is *How to Make Meetings Work* (Doyle, 1993).

Win-win Mindset for Interactions

Developing a mindset that focuses on how to help others be successful creates a virtuous dynamic within a team. The best model I know for this is Rotary International's Four-Way Test (Rotary International):

- Is it the truth?
- Is it fair to all concerned?
- Will it build goodwill and better friendships?
- Will it be beneficial to all concerned?

Any decision or interaction that passes the Four-Way Test is likely to lead to a stronger team overall.

General Personal Interaction Skills

Any person can benefit from periodically reviewing their general personal interaction skills. Dale Carnegie's *How to Win Friends and Influence People* is as good a guide to effective interactions as it was when the research for it was conducted almost 100 years ago (Carnegie, 1936).

Suggested Leadership Actions

Inspect

- Reflect on your organization's approach to maximizing individual capability. Does the approach include ongoing development after each person is hired?
- Review the time allowed by your organization for professional development. Considering the amount of time allowed, realistically, how much professional development can occur?
- Interview your staff. How important are well-defined opportunities for professional growth to them? How satisfied are they with the current support they're receiving from the organization?
- Review the non-technical-related interactions in your organization. How effectively does your staff conduct meetings, work together, communicate to executives, and demonstrate other soft skills?
- Reflect on the conflicts you see within your teams, technical or otherwise. How would you score the emotional intelligence level (EQ) of your staff?

Adapt

- Create a plan to allocate time regularly for professional development.
- Through the use of Construx's PDL (or some other approach), ensure that each person on your staff has a defined program for professional growth that is meaningful to them.
- Create a plan for improving the interpersonal skills of the people on your teams, including learning about personality types, communicating throughout the organization, resolving conflict, and developing win-win outcomes.

Additional Resources

Carnegie, Dale. 1936. *How to Win Friends and Influence People.* If it has been a few years since you last read this book, make a point of reading it again. You'll be surprised how relevant the lessons are despite their age.

Doyle, Michael and David Strauss. 1993. *How to Make Meetings Work!* This is a classic discussion of running effective meetings.

Fisher, Roger and William Ury. 2011. *Getting to Yes: Negotiating Agreement Without Giving In, 3rd Ed.* This is the classic text on achieving win-win outcomes. Although nominally about negotiation, it's really about group problem solving.

Goleman, Daniel, 2005. *Emotional Intelligence, 10th Anniversary Edition.* This is the book that made the original argument for EQ (emotional intelligence) mattering as much as IQ.

Lencioni, Patrick. 2002. *The Five Dysfunctions of a Team.* This short business book is written in the form of a parable that chronicles the life of a team in disarray, followed by a model for creating and maintaining healthy teams.

Lipmanowicz, Henri and Keith McCandless. 2013. *The Surprising Power of Liberating Structures.* This innovative book describes numerous patterns or "liberating structures" for how groups interact.

McConnell, Steve and Jenny Stuart. 2018. *Career Pathing for Software Professionals.* [Online] This white paper describes the background and structure of Construx's Professional Development Ladder (PDL). Companion implementation papers describe career paths that lead to Architect, QA Manager, Product Owner, Quality Manager, and Technical Manager.

Patterson, Kerry, et al. 2002. *Crucial Conversations: Tools for talking when the stakes are high.* This is a highly readable book that makes a compelling case for the world being a better place if everyone had the skills to engage in crucial conversations.

Rotary International, 2019. *The Four-Way Test.* [Online] An online search will yield numerous descriptions of the history and present-day application of the Four-Way Test. The Wikipedia article is as good a summary as any.

TRACOM Group, 2019. [Online] TRACOM's website contains many materials on the Social Style model (no 's'), including overview descriptions of the model, reports on the validity of the model, and comparison of Social Style to other popular models such as Myers-Briggs.

Wilson Learning, 2019. [Online] Wilson Learnings website contains several articles on the Social Styles model (with an 's'), mostly discussing how it applies in sales. (TRACOM's Social Style model and Wilson's Social Styles model are the same, for informal practical purposes.)

Yale Center for Emotional Intelligence. 2019. *The RULER Model.* [Online] 2019. This describes the RULER model and its application, with a primary focus on using the model in educational settings.

PART III

MORE EFFECTIVE WORK

⌒

This part of the book describes details of how work is performed on Agile projects. It discusses how work is organized and special issues for handling work on large projects. It then discusses specific kinds of work, including quality work, testing, requirements, and delivery.

If you're more interested in top-level leadership issues than detailed work issues, skip ahead to Part IV, "More Effective Organizations." If your organization has struggled with large projects, consider reading Chapter 10, "More Effective Large Agile Projects," before skipping to Part IV.

CHAPTER NINE

More Effective Agile Projects

❧

The preceding chapter discussed how to organize and support the people in Agile development. This chapter discusses how to organize and support Agile development work.

Most software development work is organized into "projects." Organizations use numerous terms to describe their projects, including "product," "program," "release," "release cycle," "feature," "value stream," "work stream," and other similar words and phrases.

Terminology varies significantly. Some organizations believe that "release" is the modern replacement for "project." Others believe that "release" refers to sequential development and have abandoned use of that term. One organization defines a "feature" as a 3–9-person initiative that lasts for 1–2 years. In this chapter, I refer to all those kinds of work as projects—that is, multiple people working on coordinated deliverables over an extended time.

Key Principle: Keep Projects Small

For the past 20 years, the most-publicized Agile successes have come from Agile use on small projects. Agile development for the first 10 years focused strongly on keeping projects small—teams made up of 5–10 people (e.g., 3–9 Development Team members, the Product Owner, and the Scrum Master). This emphasis on small projects has been important because small projects are much easier to complete successfully than large projects, as shown in Figure 9-1.

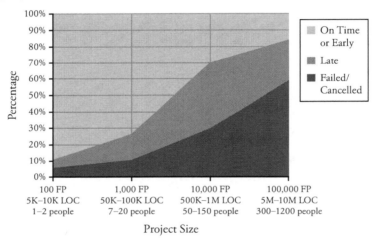

Figure 9-1

The larger the project, the lower the odds of on-time, on-budget delivery and the higher the risk of failure (Jones, 2012). "FP" refers to size in function points. "KLOC" refers to thousands of lines of code. Comparisons of sizes in function points, lines of code, and team sizes are approximate.

Capers Jones has been reporting for more than 20 years that small projects succeed more readily than large projects do (Jones, 1991) (Jones, 2012). I summarized much of the research on the effect of project size in my books *Code Complete,*

2nd Ed. (McConnell, 2004) and *Software Estimation: Demystifying the Black Art* (McConnell, 2006).

Small projects are successful often for many reasons. Larger projects involve more people, and the interconnections among people within the teams and across different teams increase non-linearly. As the complexity of interactions increases, communication mistakes increase. Communication mistakes lead to errors in requirements, errors in design, errors in coding—in general, they lead to errors!

Furthermore, the larger the project becomes, the higher the error *rate* becomes, as shown in Figure 9-2. This is not saying merely that the total number of errors increases—larger projects produce disproportionately more errors.

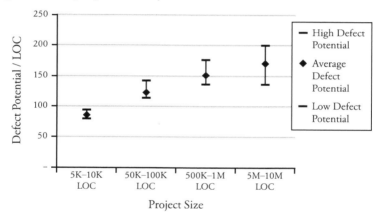

Figure 9-2

The larger the project, the larger the error rate (defect potential). Adapted from (Jones, 2012).

As error rates and total errors go up, the effectiveness of defect detection strategies goes *down*. This means that defects remaining in the software increase disproportionately.

The effort needed to fix the errors also goes up. Consequently, as shown in Figure 9-3, smaller projects have the highest per-person productivity, and productivity declines as project size increases. This is known as a "diseconomy of scale."

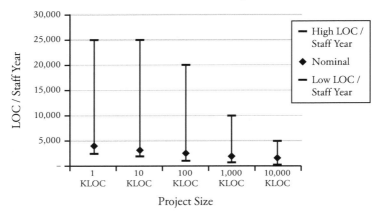

Figure 9-3

The larger the project, the lower the per-person productivity. Adapted from (McConnell, 2006).

The inverse relationship between size and productivity has been extensively researched and verified for more than 40 years. Fred Brooks discussed software's diseconomy of scale in the first edition of *The Mythical Man-Month* (Brooks, 1975). Larry Putnam's work on software estimation validated Brooks's observations (Putnam, 1992). The Constructive Cost Model (Cocomo) estimation-related research confirmed the diseconomy of scale empirically, both in Cocomo's original research in the late 1970s and in the more rigorous, updated research in the late 1990s (Boehm, 1981), (Boehm, 2000).

The bottom line: To maximize the chances of a successful Agile project, *keep the project (and team) as small as possible.*

It isn't feasible, of course, to decree that every project be small. You'll find approaches to large projects, including suggestions for how to make them more like small projects, in Chapter 10, "More Effective Large Agile Projects."

Key Principle: Keep Sprints Short

A corollary to keeping projects small is keeping sprints short. You might think that the small project is good enough on its own. But short sprints of 1–3 weeks support successful projects in numerous ways, as described in the next few sections.

Short Sprints Reduce Midstream Requirements and Increase Responsiveness to New Requirements

In Scrum, new requirements are allowed to be added between sprints. Once a sprint has started, requirements cannot be added until the next sprint. This is reasonable when sprints are only 1–3 weeks long.

If development cycles are longer, pressure to add requirements increases and it becomes less reasonable to ask stakeholders to defer their requirements requests. If a Sequential development cycle is 6 months long, asking a stakeholder to delay implementation of their new requirement until the next cycle means holding it until the beginning of the next cycle, adding it at that point, and then waiting for delivery until the end of the next cycle. That would be an average of 1.5 cycles, or 9 months.

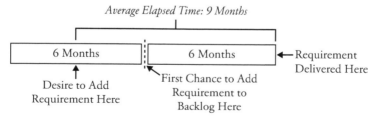

In contrast, Scrum's typical 2-week sprints means the stakeholder who wants a new requirement needs to wait an average of only 3 weeks for the requirement.

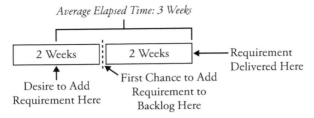

Asking stakeholders to wait 9 months for a new requirement to be delivered is often not reasonable. Asking them to wait 3 weeks is almost always reasonable. This means Scrum teams can work without fear of new requirements being added mid-sprint.

Short Sprints Support More Responsiveness to Customers and Stakeholders

Every sprint provides a new opportunity to demonstrate working software, validate requirements, and incorporate stakeholder feedback. With typical 2-week sprints, teams give themselves 26 opportunities per year to be responsive! With a 3-month development cycle, they give themselves only four opportunities. Fifteen years ago, a 3-month schedule would have been considered a short project. Such a schedule today means you are missing opportunities to be more responsive to your stakeholders, customers, and the market.

Short Sprints Build Stakeholder Trust

As the teams show progress more frequently, with more transparency, stakeholders see steady evidence of progress, which increases trust between stakeholders and the technical team.

Short Sprints Support Rapid Improvement Through Frequent Inspect and Adapt Cycles

The more often a team iterates, the more opportunities it gives itself to reflect on its experiences, learn from them, and incorporate learnings into its work practices. The same reasoning about frequency that applied to customer responsiveness applies in this area: Would you rather give your teams a chance to Inspect and Adapt—and improve—26 times each year or only four times each year? Short sprints help your team improve more quickly.

Short Sprints Help Shorten Experiments

In Cynefin's Complex domain, problems must be probed before the full scope of work can understood. These probes should be defined as, "Doing the smallest amount of work possible to answer a specific question." Unfortunately, Parkinson's Law— "work expands to fill available time"—comes into play. Unless a team has unusually high discipline, if it has scheduled a month to answer a question, it will take the full month. But if it schedules two weeks, it will often take only two weeks.

Short Sprints Expose Cost and Schedule Risks

Short sprints also provide frequent opportunities to check progress. Within just a few sprints on a new initiative, the team will demonstrate its "velocity," or rate of progress. Observed progress makes it easy to forecast how long the overall release will take. If the work is going to take longer than originally planned, that will become evident after just a few weeks—a powerful realization made possible by the sprints' short duration. Chapter 20, "More Effective Agile Predictability," provides more detail.

Short Sprints Increase Team Accountability

When a team is responsible for delivering working functionality every 2 weeks, there's no opportunity for the team to "go dark" for extended periods. They bring their work out in public for the sprint review meetings and demonstrate it to stakeholders every couple of weeks—more often to the Product Owner. Work is accepted by the Product Owner or not, progress is easy to see, and teams become more accountable for their work.

Short Sprints Increase Individual Accountability

For generations, software teams have suffered from *prima donna* developers who go off to work in a dark room for months at a time with no signs of progress. This is no longer an issue with Scrum. The peer pressure of supporting the team's goals for the sprint—combined with the necessity of standing up each day and describing what was accomplished the day before—does not allow that kind of behavior. Either the developer begins to cooperate, which resolves the issue one way, or the developer can't stand the pressure and leaves the team, which resolves the issue another way. In my experience, either outcome is better than having someone work unaccountably for weeks or months, only to discover ultimately that little progress has been made.

Short Sprints Encourage Automation

Because teams are converging frequently, short sprints encourage automating tasks that would otherwise be repetitive and time consuming. Areas commonly automated include building, integrating, testing, and static code analysis.

Short Sprints Offer a Frequent Sense of Accomplishment

A team that delivers working software every 2 weeks experiences a frequent, recurring sense of accomplishment and has many opportunities to celebrate its achievements. This contributes to a sense of Mastery, which increases motivation.

Short Sprints: Summary

The overall value of short sprints can be summarized as, "Speed of delivery beats scope of delivery in all respects." Delivering small amounts of functionality on a frequent cadence provides numerous benefits compared to delivering large amounts of functionality on an infrequent cadence.

Use Velocity-Based Planning

Story points are a means of measuring size and complexity of work items. *Velocity* is a measure of the rate of progress, which is based on the rate at which work is being completed, measured in story points. *Velocity-based planning* is the use of story points and velocity to plan work and track it.

Velocity-based planning and tracking is not part of textbook Scrum, but in my experience it should be. Story points and velocity should be used in the following ways.

Sizing the Product Backlog

Story point estimation is used to size the product backlog. The sizes of items in the product backlog are estimated using story points, and the story points are added to compute a total size for the backlog. This is done early in a release cycle and as work is added to or removed from the backlog. The extent to which this is done is driven by the team's need for predictability, which is discussed in Chapter 20.

Calculating Velocity

The amount of work the team commits to each sprint is counted using story points. The number of story points the team delivers each sprint becomes the team's velocity. Velocity is calculated on a sprint-by-sprint basis, and average velocity is also calculated.

Sprint Planning

The team uses story points as the basis for planning how much work it can commit to in a sprint, based on the team's observed velocity.

If a team has been averaging 20 story points per sprint, and the team's proposed sprint goal would require the team to complete 40 story points, the team should scale back its plans. If one of the team members is going on vacation or if several team members will be attending training, the team should commit to fewer story points for that sprint than it has been averaging. If the average of 20 story points has been accomplished through many late nights and weekends and is not sustainable, the team should plan for a lower number. If the team has been accomplishing its sprint goals comfortably, it might commit to a higher number than its average velocity. In all cases, the team uses its average velocity as a reality check for its sprint planning.

Release Tracking

The average velocity can be used to estimate or forecast how much time is needed to complete the work in the product backlog. If the product backlog consists of 200 story points and the team has a velocity of 20 story points per sprint, it should take the team about 10 sprints to complete the work in the backlog. I cover specifics of how that works in Chapter 20.

Accounting for Effect of Process Changes, Staff Changes, and Other Changes

Velocity can be used to measure the effect of process changes, staff changes, and other kinds of changes. I cover specifics in Chapter 19, "More Effective Agile Process Improvement."

Key Principle: Deliver in Vertical Slices

For short sprints to work, teams need to develop the capability to deliver small chunks of working functionality on a frequent basis. The design approach used to support this is called "vertical slicing," which refers to making changes in each architectural layer to deliver incremental functionality or value.

A vertical slice represents full stack functionality, such as "Add this field to a bank statement" or "Provide confirmation of the transaction to the user one second faster." Each of these examples would typically require work throughout the technology stack, as illustrated in Figure 9-4.

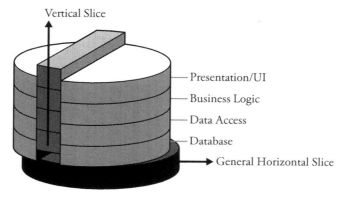

Figure 9-4
Horizontal and vertical slicing. Vertical slicing includes work in all the architectural layers needed to deliver incremental functionality.

Vertical slices are typically easier for nontechnical stakeholders to understand, observe, and assess for business value. They create options for the team to release sooner and realize actual business value and real user feedback.

Teams that focus on horizontal slices can go off into the weeds for several sprints at a time, working on stories that are in some sense "productive" but that don't produce observable business value.

Teams will sometimes object to vertical slicing, typically on the basis of efficiency. They will argue, for example, that it's more efficient to complete a larger chunk of work at the business logic layer before moving to the UX layer. This approach is called "horizontal slicing."

It might be true that in some cases a certain technical efficiency is gained from working in horizontal slices, but that technical efficiency tends to be a localized sub-optimization that's outweighed by larger value-delivery considerations. Contrary to the claims that horizontal slicing leads to increased efficiency, my company has found that many teams experience significant rework arising from delivering in horizontal slices.

Vertical Slices Support Tighter Feedback Loops

Vertical slicing puts functionality in front of business users sooner, which supports earlier feedback on the correctness of the functionality.

Because it requires end-to-end development, vertical slicing forces the team to work through its design and implementation assumptions collaboratively, which provides useful top-to-bottom technical feedback to the team.

And vertical slicing supports end-to-end testing, which tightens the testing feedback loop.

Vertical Slices Support Delivery of Higher Business Value

Vertical slices are easier for nontechnical business stakeholders to understand, which increases the quality of business decision making about the priority and sequencing of new and revised functionality.

Because vertical slices offer complete increments of functionality, they also provide the opportunity to put working functionality into users' hands more often, which increases business value.

Horizontal slicing can lead to a development mentality of architecture as the product rather than the product as the product. This can encourage technical work that is never needed to support delivered functionality and other value-reducing practices.

What Teams Need to Implement Vertical Slicing

Delivering in vertical slices can be challenging. It depends on a team composition that includes business, development, and testing capability, and that includes the skills to work across the full technology stack.

Teams might also need to shift their design and implementation thinking to vertical slices rather than components or horizontal-layer work. Some teams lack the design skill to do this and will need to develop it (and be supported in developing it).

Finally, teams need to be fed work in vertical slices. The Product Owner and the Development Team must approach backlog refinement in a way that produces vertical slices.

Key Principle: Manage Technical Debt

"Technical debt" refers to the accumulation of low-quality work in the past that slows down work in the present. The classic example is a brittle code base in which each attempt to fix a bug exposes one or more additional bugs. Even simple bug fixes become time-consuming, multi-bug-fix exercises.

Technical debt can consist of low-quality code, low-quality design, a brittle test suite, design approaches that are difficult to work with, a clunky build environment, slow manual processes, and other ways in which long-term productivity has been sacrificed for short-term gains.

Consequences of Technical Debt

Debt is typically accumulated as a result of pressure to prioritize near-term releases at the expense of quality. A holistic view of project inputs and outputs includes consideration of the effect of debt accumulation over time:

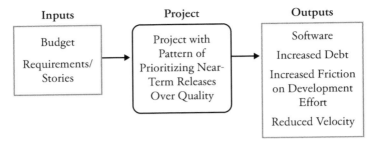

Businesses and technical teams can have good reasons for taking on debt. Some releases are time-sensitive enough that they warrant additional work later in exchange for quicker work now.

However, a pattern of allowing debt to accumulate over time without a plan to manage it will eventually reduce the team's velocity. A team should have a plan for keeping debt at a manageable level so that it can maintain or increase its velocity:

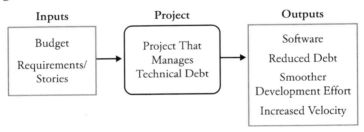

Kruchten, Nord, and Ozkaya have developed an insightful timeline of the way that technical debt is incurred, provides business value (possibly), and eventually becomes more of a liability than an asset. This is shown in Figure 9-5.

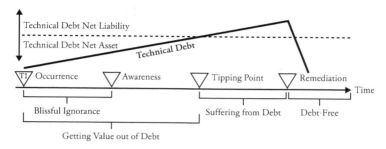

Figure 9-5
A technical debt timeline (Kruchten, 2019).

For greenfield work, teams can avoid accumulating technical in the first place. For legacy work, teams often have no choice but to work with debt that they have inherited. In either kind of work, if the teams manage their debt poorly, their velocity will decrease over time.

Paying Down Technical Debt

Teams vary in their approaches to paying down debt. Some teams allocate a percentage of each development cycle (sprint or release) to paying down debt. Other teams put debt-reduction items into their product backlogs or defect lists and prioritize debt reduction along with the rest of their work. In any case, the key point is that the debt is managed explicitly.

Kinds of Debt and Responses

Not all technical debt is created equal, and various taxonomies for debt have been proposed. I find these categories useful:

* *Intentional debt (short-term).* Debt taken on for tactical or strategic reasons, such as to get a time-sensitive release deployed on time.

- *Intentional debt (long-term).* Debt taken on for strategic reasons, such as a decision to support only one platform at first rather than designing and building multi-platform support from the beginning.
- *Unintentional debt (bad faith).* Debt that arises accidentally due to shoddy software development practices. This kind of debt slows down work in the future and in the present, and it should be avoided.
- *Unintentional debt (good faith).* Debt that arises accidentally due to the error-prone nature of software development ("Our design approach didn't work out as well as we thought it would" or "The new version of the platform invalidated serious aspects of our design").
- *Legacy debt.* Debt that's inherited by a new team on an old code base.

Table 9-1 describes recommended approaches for responding to these kinds of debt.

Table 9-1 Kinds of Technical Debt and Responses

Kind of Debt	Recommended Response
Intentional debt (short-term)	Take on debt if warranted by business concerns; pay off the debt soon.
Intentional debt (long-term)	Take on the debt if necessary; define trigger conditions for paying off the debt.
Unintentional debt (bad faith)	Use high-quality work practices to avoid in the first place.
Unintentional debt (good faith)	By its nature, this debt cannot be avoided. Monitor the debt's effect and pay off when its "interest payment" becomes too high.
Legacy debt	Create a plan for reducing debt over time.

Value of Discussing Technical Debt

I've found technical debt to be a useful metaphor for facilitating discussions between technical and business staff. Business staff tends to be unaware of the cost of carrying technical debt, and technical staff tends to be unaware of the business benefit. In some cases, it's a good business decision to take on technical debt intentionally, and in some cases it isn't. The concept of debt facilitates a meaningful sharing of technical and business considerations, leading to better quality decisions about when and why to take on debt and when and how to pay it down.

Structure Work to Avoid Burnout

The Agile purist view is that sprints should all be the same length (known as "common cadence"). If a team tolerates common cadence well, there's no reason to change it. Common cadence makes calculation of velocity and other aspects of sprint planning more straightforward.

However, a common complaint about Scrum implementations is that an endless succession of sprints leads to sprint fatigue or a feeling of being on the sprint hamster wheel. With Sequential development, there are natural troughs of work, particularly between disciplines, that balance the high-intensity periods. Continuous sprints leave no troughs for rest if every sprint is truly sprinting.

One antidote to sprint fatigue is to vary the lengths of the sprints occasionally. A systematic way to do this is to use a pattern of 6x2x1—6 sprints of 2 weeks plus 1 sprint of 1 week, a total of 13 weeks, which can be performed once per quarter. Alternatively, shorter sprints can be worked in after major releases, around holidays, or at other times when the team's velocity probably wouldn't be stable anyway. During the 1-week sprints, the team can work on infrastructure or tools, attend training or team-building events, have hack days, work on technical debt, concentrate on improvements that are too large to be worked into a regular sprint, or other similar work.

Varying sprint cadence supports the Agile notion of "sustainable pace." Much of the Agile writing today interprets sustainable pace as "no evenings or weekends, ever." I think this is simplistic and ignores differences in individuals' work preferences. A steady 40 hours per week amounts to a sustainable pace for some people, but for others that amounts to a recipe for boredom. I personally have done much of my best work in burst mode—55 hours for a couple weeks, and then 30 hours for a couple weeks after that. The average might work out to about 40 hours per week, but individual weeks aren't very close to 40 hours. The details that make up "sustainable pace" are not the same for everyone.

Other Considerations

Non-Project Software Development Work

Not all software development work occurs in projects, even considering the many definitions described at the beginning of the chapter. Ad hoc, single-person software work is common in handling support tickets, production issues, patches, and so on.

This kind of work certainly qualifies as software development work, and it is also amenable to Agile practices. It can be made more efficient, higher quality, and more methodical through adoption of Agile practices such as Lean and Kanban. However, in my experience, organizations tend to struggle with this kind of work much less than they struggle with project-size software development work, so this book focuses on projects rather than ad hoc work streams.

Suggested Leadership Actions

Inspect

- Review your organization's history of project outcomes. Does your organization's experience match the general pattern that small projects are successful more often than large projects?
- Review your project portfolio. Which of your large projects could be broken into multiple small projects?
- Review your teams' cadences. Are their sprints no more than 3 weeks long?
- Investigate whether your teams are delivering in vertical slices.
- Investigate whether your teams are using velocity-based planning.
- Interview your teams about technical debt. What is their perception about how much debt they're carrying and whether they are allowed to pay it down?

Adapt

- Encourage your teams to consider their velocity when establishing their sprint goals.
- Develop a plan to ensure that your teams have the ability to deliver in vertical slices, including the Development Team's design capability and the Product Owner's approach to backlog refinement.
- Encourage your teams to create plans to manage their technical debt.

Additional Resources

Brooks, Fred. 1975. *The Mythical Man-Month*. Although dated at this point, this book contains the original classic discussion of the challenges of succeeding on large projects.

McConnell, Steve. 2019. Understanding Software Projects Lecture Series. *Construx OnDemand*. [Online] 2019. https://ondemand.construx.com. These lectures extensively discuss software dynamics related to project size.

Rubin, Kenneth, 2012. *Essential Scrum: A Practical Guide to the Most Popular Agile Process*. This comprehensive guide to Scrum describes the use of story points and velocity for sprint planning and release planning.

Kruchten, Philippe, et al. 2019. *Managing Technical Debt*. This is a complete, well-thought-out discussion of all aspects of technical debt.

More Effective Large Agile Projects

☙

The naturalist Stephen Jay Gould tells a story in which two girls are talking on the playground (Gould, 1977). One girl says, "What if a spider was as big as an elephant? Wouldn't that be scary?" The other girl responds, "No. If a spider was as big as an elephant, it would look like an elephant, silly."

Gould goes on to explain that the second girl is right because the sizes of the organisms significantly dictate what the organisms look like. A spider can float through the air without injuring itself because friction from the air is a stronger force than gravity. But an elephant is too heavy to fly. Gravity is a much stronger force than friction at its size. A spider can discard and secrete a new exoskeleton as it grows because it's small, but an elephant is too large to withstand the period between shedding an exoskeleton and regrowing it, so it must have an endoskeleton. Gould concludes that if a spider was as a big as an elephant, it would look more like an elephant, because at that size it really has to.

For us, the analogous question for software projects is, "What if an Agile project was really large? Wouldn't that be scary?" Well, maybe it wouldn't be scary, but a line of reasoning similar to the elephant and spider analysis applies.

What's Really Different About Agile—On Large Projects?

The question of how to be effective on large *Agile* projects is not really the right question. Organizations have struggled with large projects of all kinds since the beginning of software (Brooks, 1975). They have also struggled with small projects. Agile practices and Scrum in particular have allowed small projects to be successful more often, and that has shifted the focus to the large projects that still struggle.

Agile Emphases on Large Projects

Different organizations can have radically different definitions of "large." We've worked with organizations in which any project that requires more than one Scrum team is considered large and others in which a project smaller than 100 people is considered medium or small. "Large" is a sliding scale. The considerations in this chapter come into play any time you have two or more teams involved. Some of the emphases in Agile development support large projects, and some must be modified. Table 10-1 summarizes how Agile emphases play into large projects.

Table 10-1 Agile Emphases on Large Projects

Agile Emphasis	Large Project Implication
Short release cycles	The ideal is to have large-project teams with short release cycles.
End-to-end development work performed in small batches	No change; large-project teams can still complete end-to-end development in small batches, albeit with a higher level of coordination required
High-level up-front planning with just-in-time detailed planning	The proportion of up-front planning will need to increase.
High-level up-front requirements with just-in-time detailed requirements	Larger projects require more requirements coordination, which implies longer lead time from beginning of refinement to completion of implementation.
Emergent design	The cost of error and redesign increases as project size increases; this is the primary Agile factor that must be modified to support a large project.
Continuous testing, integrated into development	This is an excellent emphasis regardless of the size of the project. The type of testing shifts to more emphasis on integration/system test on large projects.
Frequent structured collaboration	This emphasis becomes even more important on large projects; the specific forms of collaboration will change.
Overall approach is empirical, responsive, and improvement-oriented	This emphasis works just as well on large projects as on small projects.

Agile's emphasis on completing end-to-end development work in small batches supports effective work on large projects, as does the focus on continuous testing, frequent structured collaboration, and OODA.

Large projects require more up-front planning, requirements, and design. They don't need all work completed up front as they would in Sequential development, but they need more than regular Agile. This has implications for sprint planning, sprint reviews, product backlog structure, backlog refinement, release planning, and release burndown. Large projects benefit from continuous testing at least as much as small projects do, but test emphasis needs to change—large projects need more integration and system testing.

Here's a visual summary of how Agile emphases change as project size increases:

Agile Emphasis	Number of Teams (of 5–10 People)			
	1	2	7	35+
Short Release Cycles	Emphasis Depends on Project			
Small Batch End-to-end Development	Constant Emphasis			
Just-in-Time Planning				
Just-in-Time Requirements				
Emergent Design				
Continous, Integrated Testing	Constant Emphasis			
Frequent, Structured Collaboration	Constant (Kinds of Collaboration Change)			
Overall Approach Is Empirical, Responsive, and Improvement-Oriented	Constant Emphasis			

☐ Work Performed Just in Time   ◼ Work Performed Up Front

The following sections describe specifics of the adaptations needed to support successful large Agile projects.

Brooks' Law

One perspective on how to infuse more effective Agile practices into a large project was prefigured by Fred Brooks in *The Mythical Man-Month* (Brooks, 1975). In the course of discussing "Brooks' Law"—the idea that adding people to a late project will make it later—Brooks argues that if the work can be *completely partitioned*, Brooks' law doesn't necessarily apply.

This is directly relevant for the large project discussion because the ideal for a large project is to break it up into a set of *completely partitioned* small projects. If you can succeed in doing that, you will benefit in numerous ways. You will increase per-person productivity and reduce error rates, as described in Chapter 9, "More Effective Agile Projects." You will also open the door to emphasizing Agile practices more than Sequential practices.

As Brooks points out, however, the challenge in breaking a large project into multiple small projects is accomplishing the goal of completely partitioning the work. Completely partitioning work is difficult, and if the work is only *mostly partitioned*—meaning it still requires coordination between different project teams—the multiple small projects begin to look and act more like a large project. You will have lost what you were trying to accomplish.

Conway's Law

You can't understand large projects and how to maximize their agility without understanding Conway's Law. As I described in Chapter 7, "More Effective Distributed Agile Teams," Conway's Law states that the technical structure of a system will reflect the structure of the human organization that created it.

If the technical design is based on a large monolithic architecture, the project team is going to struggle tremendously if it tries to be anything other than large and monolithic.

Tying Conway's Law and Fred Brooks's ideas together, the implication for large Agile projects is that the ideal architecture of a large system will support *completely partitioning* the work of the teams that work on it. This ideal will be easier to achieve on some systems than others. Legacy systems, in particular, usually need to adopt some kind of crawl, walk, run approach.

Key Principle: Support Large Agile Projects Through Architecture

For a system's architecture to support completely partitioning the work, some architecture work must be done. Some older systems can evolve toward a loosely coupled architecture, but for new systems the implication is that architecture work must be done up front to partition the work for multiple small teams.

Some Agile teams will balk at the idea of doing "BDUF" (Big Design Up Front), saying that it "isn't Agile." But as Stephen Jay Gould implied, when you take an approach whose core emphases cluster around keeping projects small and try to make it work for projects that are large, *something* has to give. You can't change nothing and expect projects to scale successfully.

If Conway's Law is fully considered, the only factor that really needs to be modified is the emphasis on emergent design and the planning needed to support that. A focus on up-front architecture with a goal of allowing work to be completely partitioned will keep teams small, which means the rest of the Agile emphases can remain. The focus on emergent design can also still remain within the highly partitioned areas in which each small team is working.

It is not coincidence that the focus on small Agile teams has coincided with the emergence of microservices architecture. The goal of microservices architecture is to structure an application as loosely coupled services. Similarly, the goal of structuring a large Agile project is to structure the human organization as loosely coupled small teams.

The organization that succeeds in architecting a large system to support completely partitioned work will not perceive itself as having a large project. It will feel like it has a collection of small teams working independently, with the only thing they have in common being that they all happen to be contributing to a common code base.

A lack of architecture leads to what a colleague refers to as the "snowflake effect"—each development feature is a unique snowflake that is designed differently from every other snowflake. This imposes significant cost on development as team members must learn the details of each snowflake to be able to work effectively in each area of the code. The larger the project becomes, the more significant this issue becomes. If you have enough snowflakes, eventually you have an avalanche!

Specific Architecture Suggestions

An architecture tutorial is outside the scope of this book, but the following sections contain thumbnail descriptions of architectural approaches that support small teams on large projects. The discussion is somewhat technical, so feel free to skip ahead if you are not technically oriented.

The Basics: Loose Coupling, Modularity

Strive for a loosely coupled architecture (modular and layered if possible) with readable and low-complexity code.

The architecture doesn't need to be perfectly factored micro-services code. It just needs to provide enough flexibility to support the business's needs.

The holy grail that is sometimes described is to break your system into, say, 50 microservices. They can be highly modular, running in their own hosted containers with their own databases. They can each have their own versioned and authenticated APIs. They can all be released to production and scaled independently, which approaches the goal of having 50 completely partitioned development teams.

This is all a fantastic vision, and sometimes it actually works! But if some of the processing paths in your system call into numerous other parts of your system, which in turn call into numerous other parts of your system (known as "high fan out"), you can end up with significant processing overhead in the software and significant communication overhead among the teams working on the different microservices. You would probably be better off both in the software and the team structure to aggregate the system into fewer services.

Good solutions depend on applying a combination of technical judgment about design and management judgment about the team's organization.

Avoid Monolithic Databases

Avoiding one big database helps support partitioned teams. Loosely federated databases can support loose coupling and strong modularity within teams. But, depending on the relationships among parts of the system, it's also possible to create complex interactions that lead to significant overhead, latency, and opportunity for errors. A combination of technical judgement and team-management judgment is required to know how much to decompose a system to support loosely coupled teams while maintaining a high-quality technical solution.

Use Queues

Decoupling or time shifting through the use of queues can also support loosely coupled development teams. In abstract terms, this consists of putting tasks into a queue for another part of the system to process later. The "later" could be microseconds later. The key concept in this guideline is that the system is not merely executing most of its code in an immediate, rigid, request-response loop. Using queues supports a high level of decoupling between key parts of system functionality, which allows for decoupling in the architecture and the development team (another instance of Conway's Law).

It can be useful to think about key "seams" in a system architecture. A seam represents a boundary for which, within the boundary, there is a lot of interaction but across the boundary there isn't much interaction. For the sake of loose coupling, it can be useful to use queues for the coupling across the seams. As with the microservices example, it's possible to take this too far—50 processes managing 50 task queues with dependencies can create a different set of coupling issues, which could end up being worse than the problem the queueing is trying to solve.

Use Design by Contract

Design by contract is a design approach in which special attention is paid to interfaces (Meyer, 1992). Each interface is considered to have "pre-conditions" and "post-conditions." The pre-conditions are the promises that the user of a component makes to the component about the conditions that will be true before the component is used. The post-conditions are the promises that the component makes back to the rest of the system about the conditions that will be true by the time the component completes its work.

Bearing Conway's Law in mind, you can use design by contract to eliminate the impact of technical dependencies on workflow.

The "contract" will govern the interface between parts of the software system and will implicitly set expectations for the interfaces among humans too.

Shift in Kinds of Collaboration on Large Projects

Many Agile work practices are based on the efficacy of face-to-face communication. Much information exists only as part of a team's oral tradition. For example, Agile requirements writers explicitly say that a major part of any requirement is the conversation about the requirement. Teams have found this works well on small projects.

Large projects, by their nature, have more people, the people are more spread out geographically (even if in different buildings on the same campus), the projects take longer, new people join the project over time, and long-term team members leave the project over time.

For large Agile projects to be successful, the expectation that all knowledge can be expressed through an oral tradition must be moderated. More work must be done up front, and more of that work must be documented in ways that are understandable by people who weren't part of the original conversations.

Coordination Challenges on Large Projects

Approaches to scaling software development in general, not just on Agile projects, suffer from misdiagnosing the kind of coordination that needs to occur as projects scale. The larger your project becomes, the more you'll need all of the noncoding activities of requirements, architecture, configuration management, QA/Test, project management, and process. The key question is whether any one of these areas needs to scale faster or requires more coordination among teams than the rest.

Experience says that the most common source of challenges is requirements. In my experience, large-project coordination issues occur in this order of frequency:

* Requirements (most frequently)
* Architecture (on design-intensive systems)
* Configuration management/version management
* QA/Test
* Project management
* Process

As you consider how to approach a larger project, you can use this list as a first-order approximation of where challenges will arise. You should also review your organization's large projects, understand those projects' most common sources of challenges, and plan your coordination around those.

A Large Agile Project Scorecard

We have found it useful to score project performance on the main challenge areas that arise on large Agile projects. Figure 10-1 on the next page shows an example of a large-project star diagram. The diagram uses the same key that was used for the Scrum scorecard:

0   Not Used
2   Used infrequently and ineffectively
4   Used occasionally with mixed effectiveness
7   Used consistently and effectively
10 Optimizing

The gray line reflects the average practice that my company has seen. The dashed line shows a healthy large project. To have a good chance of success, a large project should have scores of 7 or higher.

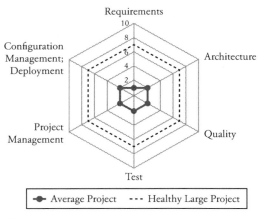

Figure 10-1

A diagnostic tool that shows large-project performance according to key large-project success factors.

Here's more detail on the performance categories:

- *Requirements.* Multi-team requirements practices, including product management, product backlog, backlog refinement, system demos or multi-team sprint reviews.
- *Architecture.* Design practices scaled to suit the size of project; architectural runway or equivalent.
- *Quality.* Multi-team quality practices, including system retrospectives or Inspect and Adapt meetings; product-level and team-level quality metrics; product-level Definition of Done.
- *Test.* Multi-team test automation infrastructure; integration test; end-to-end system test; performance, security, and other specialized testing
- *Project Management.* Dependency management; multi-team planning or PI planning, Scrum of Scrums, Product Owner sync; product-level tracking/release burndown.

- *Configuration Management/Deployment.* Version control of code and infrastructure; DevOps; deployment pipelines; release management.

Consistent with industry experience in general, the average large project we have reviewed performs significantly worse than the average small project.

Start with Scrum

Chapter 4's admonition to "Start with Scrum" is all-the-more relevant in large project environments. If your projects aren't doing well in the small, they'll do even worse in the large. Make sure your small projects are routinely successful, and build up from there. As Barry Boehm and Richard Turner wrote in *Balancing Agility and Discipline*, scaling up a small process tends to work better than scaling down a large one (Boehm, 2004).

Other Considerations

Scrum of Scrums

Scrum of Scrums (SoS) is an approach to scaling Scrum to more than one team. Projects hold an SoS meeting one or more times each week. Each team sends an ambassador to the meetings, which are run similarly to the teams' daily scrum meetings.

Although SoS seems like a logical way to scale up work performed by multiple Scrum teams, we have rarely seen success with the approach. One reason, in my view, is SoS's choice of Scrum Masters being the default ambassadors to the coordination meetings. That choice implies that the most common challenges will arise in the areas of process and general workflow, but experience says that requirements will be the most common source of challenges. In the general case, it is more useful to have Product Owners attend the coordination meetings than Scrum Masters.

Scale Agile Framework (SAFe)

The Scaled Agile Framework (SAFe) is an elaborate framework for scaling Agile across large enterprises. SAFe is by far the most commonly used approach for large Agile projects among the companies we've worked with. SAFe is well thought out, it's been steadily evolving and improving, and it has some truly useful elements. Having said that, only a few of the companies we've worked with have been satisfied with their SAFe implementations, and those have been highly customized.

In my company's work with software organizations, we've found that small companies all think they're unique, and they're not. They have the same problems that can be fixed in the same ways. Large companies all think there must be some other company exactly like them, and there isn't. They've had time grow, develop, and refine distinctive technical practices as well as distinctive business practices and culture.

Scrum makes sense as a template for small projects. SAFe doesn't have the universal applicability to large projects that Scrum has to small projects. It must be highly adapted, often to a point that it is more useful to think of it as a source of useful tools rather than as an integrated framework. If you do choose to use SAFe, we recommend starting with Essential SAFe (the smallest version of SAFe) and building up from there.

Suggested Leadership Actions

Inspect

- Discuss your architecture with your key technical leaders from the perspective of Conway's Law. In what ways do you see the human organization aligning with the technical organization, and vice versa?
- Review the human organization of your largest projects. To what degree is the work truly partitioned vs. monolithic? How complex is the web of communication paths in the human organization, and how do those relate to the software architecture?
- Review the Agile emphases in Table 10-1. Consider whether there is any easier, alternate way for your organization to maintain most of the emphases in the table without doing more design up front.
- Review challenges on your large projects to determine the degree to which coordination issues arise from requirements, architecture, configuration management and version control, QA/test, project management, or process.

Adapt

- Make a plan for evolving your architecture to support a more loosely coupled team structure.
- Revise your approach to large projects to account for the sources of coordination issues you discovered in the Inspect actions above.

Additional Resources

McConnell, Steve. 2004. *Code Complete, 2nd Ed.* Chapter 27 describes some of the dynamics of large vs. small projects, focusing on the way that the proportion of activities change at the project level as project size changes.

McConnell, Steve. 2019. Understanding Software Projects Lecture Series. *Construx OnDemand.* [Online] 2019. https://ondemand.construx.com. Many of the lectures in this series focus on issues related to project size.

Martin, Robert C. 2017. *Clean Architecture: A Craftsman's Guide to Software Structure and Design.* This is a popular guide to software architecture that begins with design principles and builds up to architecture.

Bass, Len, et al. 2012. *Software Architecture in Practice, 3rd Ed.* This is a comprehensive, textbook-style discussion of architecture.

Boehm, Barry and Richard Turner. 2004. *Balancing Agility and Discipline: A Guide for the Perplexed.* This book is a valuable source of insights into specific dynamics of project size and agility—for the expert reader. For the less expert reader the book is too mired in Agile practices circa 2004 to be useful today (main Agile method is XP; doesn't discuss Definition of Done, assumes long, 30-day sprints; no notion of backlog refinement; etc.).

More Effective Agile Quality

⌒

"If you can't find the time to do it right, where will you find the time to do it over?" has been a mantra in quality-focused organizations for generations. The means used to "do it right" have steadily evolved, and modern Agile development has contributed some useful practices.

Key Principle: Minimize the Defect Detection Gap

We don't usually think of it this way, but defect creation is a constant on software projects. For every hour the development team works, some number of defects are created. Thus, graphing the cumulative defect-insertion line on a software project is essentially the same as graphing the cumulative effort line.

In contrast with defect insertion, defect detection and removal are not functions of general effort. They are functions of a specific kind of effort: quality assurance (QA) activities.

As the top part of Figure 11-1 illustrates, defect detection and removal significantly lags defect insertion on many projects. This is problematic because the area between the two lines represents latent defects—defects that have been inserted into the software but haven't been detected and removed. Each of those defects represents extra bug-fixing work that is rarely "on plan." Each of those defects represents work that will unpredictably extend the budget, extend the schedule, and, in general, disrupt the project.

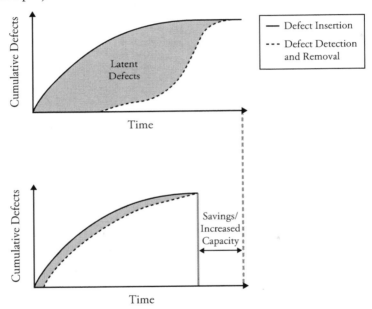

Figure 11-1

The gap between the cumulative defect-insertion line and the defect detection-and-removal line represents latent defects.

Well-run projects minimize the gap between defect insertion and defect detection, as shown in the bottom part of the figure.

Projects in which the defect-correction effort closely follows the defect-creation effort run more efficiently. As the figure shows, these projects end up delivering in less time with less effort. No project is going to detect 100% of defects immediately, but minimizing the number of latent defects present is a useful goal even if the goal can never be achieved completely. If you consider Figure 11-1's two diagrams in terms of release readiness, the project in the lower diagram is more release-ready.

Practices that support the goal of early defect detection include unit testing, pair programming, static analysis, code reviews (if they're performed in a timely way), and continuous integration—these support the goal at a fine-grain level. Agile's focus on routinely bringing the software to a releasable level of quality every 1–3 weeks supports the goal at a large-grain level.

Key Principle: Create and Use a Definition of Done

A clear Definition of Done (DoD) supports minimizing the gap between defect insertion and detection by ensuring that QA work on an item is performed close to all other work.

A good DoD will include completion criteria for design, code, test, documentation, and all other work related to implementation of a requirement. Completion criteria are ideally stated in terms that are unambiguously true or false. Figure 11-2 on the next page shows an example DoD.

☐ Passes code review

☐ Static code analysis passes

☐ Unit tests run without error

☐ 70% statement coverage through unit tests

☐ System and integration testing complete

☐ Automated non-functional tests complete without error

☐ Builds without errors or warnings

☐ Any public APIs documented

Figure 11-2
An example of a Definition of Done, which determines when a backlog item is actually complete.

Teams need to define their own Definition of Done with factors that are relevant to their circumstances. In addition to the factors shown in Figure 11-2, a Definition of Done could include:

- Product Owner accepts the item
- Conforms to UI style guide
- Passes acceptance tests
- Passes performance tests
- Passes selected regression tests
- Code checked in
- Requirements documentation updated
- Automated vulnerability scan passes

Multiple Definitions of Done

Teams will need more than one Definition of Done in the following two general circumstances.

Multiple types of DoD

It is useful or necessary to have different DoDs for different kinds of work. For example, a DoD for code might include full regression testing, whereas a DoD for user documentation would not. Each DoD needs to define the exit criteria to the next activity and embody the principle that no more rework will be needed on an item that has met the Definition of Done.

Multiple levels of DoD

The second circumstance that calls for multiple DoDs is when it is not possible to fully complete work in one sprint. In a combined hardware/software environment, for example, the first-level Definition of Done might include passing all tests in a simulation environment but not necessarily passing on the target hardware if it is not yet available. The second-level DoD would include passing all tests on the actual target hardware.

Similarly, if your software depends on another team's or a contractor's software, you might have a first-level DoD that states that all your tests pass with mock objects if the other team hasn't yet delivered the components you depend on. The second-level DoD would then state that your tests pass with the delivered components.

Although practical reasons exist to allow multiple-level DoDs, doing so creates a risk that "Done" doesn't truly mean "Done" and that poor quality and additional work will accumulate in the cracks between the different definitions. It's best to avoid this if possible.

Evolving Definition of Done

A common issue in legacy environments is that large legacy code bases cannot instantly be transformed to meet a rigorous Definition of Done. Thus, the DoD in a legacy environment might need to initially set a lower bar than it would in a greenfield environment. As the quality level of legacy code improves, you can evolve the DoD to set an increasingly high bar.

Common Issues with Definition of Done

As your teams define and implement Definitions of Done, be aware of these common issues:

- *DoD defines a standard that is too far from releasable.* Details can vary, but the spirit of the DoD should be that when an item is declared "done," it can be released without any further work.

- *DoD is too large.* A DoD checklist that's 50 entries long will be too unwieldy to be followed by your teams, and it won't be followed.

- *DoD is too ambitious for legacy systems.* Avoid creating a DoD that is not possible to follow on legacy systems or that implies an amount of work greater than what has been authorized for the project.

- *DoD describes activities rather than evidence.* A criterion like "Code has been reviewed" describes an activity. A criterion like "Code passes its code review" is evidence.

- *Multiple-level DoDs are too relaxed.* First, beware of using multiple-level DoDs at all. If you do use them, be sure that the criteria for each level accurately capture "done" for that level.

Key Principle: Maintain a Releasable Level of Quality

The Definition of Done applies to individual items. Beyond that, ensuring that the overall code base is kept at a releasable level of quality at all times provides a quality safety net that supports efficiency in many other practices, including coding, debugging, and obtaining meaningful user feedback.

The discipline of frequently driving software to a releasable level of quality provides two important benefits.

The first benefit is that maintaining a releasable level of quality minimizes the gap between defect insertion and detection. If you bring the software to a releasable level of quality every 1–3 weeks, you will never allow that gap to open very wide. This assures a high level of quality. The more often the software is driven to a high level of quality, the easier it is to maintain it at that level and avoid accumulating technical debt.

The second benefit is support for project planning and tracking. If software is driven to a releasable level of quality by the end of each sprint, that implies that there is no more work to do on that functionality later. If software is not driven to a releasable level of quality, that means an undetermined amount of additional quality-improvement work must be done later. Quality-improvement work accumulates across sprints, which undermines the ability to determine the true status of the project. This important dynamic is discussed in more detail in Chapter 11, "More Effective Agile Quality."

For both these reasons, it is important for teams to drive their work to a releasable level of quality by the end of each and every sprint. In many cases, you will put that work into production when it is completed. In some cases, this may not be appropriate—for example, if you work in a regulated environment, your software releases are tied to hardware releases, or the work has not yet crossed the minimal viable product threshold.

Reduce Rework

"Rework" refers to work on items that had previously been declared to be "done." It includes bug fixes, misunderstood requirements, modifications of test cases, and other corrections to work that should have been done correctly in the first place.

Rework is disruptive to projects because the amount of rework is unpredictable, projects don't allow time for it in their plans, and it creates no additional value.

Measuring rework as a means of reducing it is useful, and that is discussed in Chapter 18, "More Effective Agile Measurement."

Other Considerations

Pair Programming

Pair programming is a practice in which two developers sit side by side, one writing code and the other playing a role of real-time reviewer. The roles are sometimes described as pilot and navigator. Pair programming is especially associated with Extreme Programming.

Industry data on pair programming has shown for many years that the output of two people working as a pair is roughly comparable to the total output of two people working individually, the quality is higher, and the work is completed more quickly (Williams, 2002), (Boehm, 2004).

Despite it being strongly associated with Agile development, I have not emphasized pair programming as a more effective Agile practice because in my experience most developers do not prefer to do most of their work in pairs. The result is that pair programming in most organizations has settled into being a selectively used niche practice—mainly for critical or complex parts of the design or code. Beyond that selected usage, if I had a team that wanted to use pair programming extensively, I would support that, but I wouldn't insist on it.

Mob Programming and Swarming

Mob programming is a practice in which the whole team works on the same thing at the same time on the same computer. Swarming has the whole team work on the same story at the same time, but each team member works on their own part of the story at their own computer. (Usage of these terms varies, so you might have heard them used differently than I'm using them here.)

A few teams have experienced success with these practices, but efficacy is still an open question. Even among reviewers of the pre-publication draft of this book, advice ranged from "don't use at all" to "use only with new teams" to "use only with experienced teams." I don't see any clear center of gravity for these practices yet, and so overall I regard both mob programming and swarming as niche practices that should be used selectively or not at all.

Suggested Leadership Actions

Inspect

- Review your QA activities and when and where defects are found. Assess whether Agile practices would allow more defects to be found sooner.
- Review the lists of open bugs for your projects. How many open bugs are there? Does the number imply that your projects are building up a backlog of latent defects as they go, without fixing them?
- Ask your teams to show you their Definition of Done. Do they have a clear, documented definition, and are they using it? Do the details of the definition cumulatively amount to "releasable"?
- Investigate whether your teams measure the percentage of rework on their projects and use it as an input for process improvement work.
- What impediments exist between what your teams are doing today and getting to "releasable"? How can you help your teams address those impediments?

Adapt

- Based on your assessment of when and where defects are found, create a plan to shift your quality practices earlier.
- Make a plan to reduce open bug counts on your projects and then to keep the counts low.
- Work with your teams to measure the percentage of effort that's going into rework on your projects. Monitor this percentage as part of your process improvement efforts.
- Remove the impediments between what your team is doing today and getting to "releasable."

Additional Resources

McConnell, Steve. 2019. Understanding Software Projects Lecture Series. *Construx OnDemand.* [Online] 2019. https://ondemand.construx.com. This series contains an extensive discussion of quality-related issues.

Nygard, Michael T. 2018. *Release It! Design and Deploy Production-Ready Software, 2nd Ed.* This book is a current, entertaining description of how to design and build high-quality systems, addressing non-functional capabilities including security, stability, availability, deployability, and similar attributes.

CHAPTER TWELVE

More Effective Agile Testing

Agile development shifted the traditional test emphasis in four ways. First, it increased the emphasis on testing by developers. Second, it emphasized front-loading testing—testing functionality immediately after it is created. Third, it increased emphasis on test automation. Finally, it emphasized testing as a means of refining requirements and design.

These four emphases provide an important safety net for Agile's other practices, such as just-in-time design and implementation. Without the safety net of a comprehensive automated test suite, the constantly changing design and code environment would give rise to a tidal wave of defects—many of them undetected and going into the latent defect pool described in Chapter 11, "More Effective Agile Quality." With the automated test safety net, most defects are detected immediately after they are created, supporting the goal of minimizing the gap between defect creation and defect detection.

The following sections describe what we have seen as the most effective test practices for Agile projects.

Key Principle: Use Automated Tests, Created by the Development Team

The development team should be writing automated tests, which are incorporated into an automated build/deploy system. The ideal is using multiple levels and types of testing: API tests, unit tests, integration tests, acceptance tests, UI layer tests, support for mocking, random inputs and data, simulations, etc.

Tests are written by the cross-functional *team*, which includes developers, testers, or former testers. The ideal is to have developers write unit tests before writing the corresponding code. Test development and automation are inherent aspects of backlog item implementation that are included in effort estimates.

The team should maintain an on-demand test environment that supports automated testing. A combination of automated unit testing (code-level tests) and automated user-level testing should be a core attribute of any Definition of Done.

Developers should be able to test locally, using unit tests and mocking out the behavior of remote systems. A developer should be able to run unit test suites for a complete component of the product within a few minutes, either on a shared team build server or on the developer's machine.

Local code is promoted to an integration environment, where the developers' unit tests are aggregated, along with the builds. A team should have the capability to run a complete test pass, including all automated unit- and user-level checks, within 1–2 hours. Many environments measure that time in minutes. The complete test pass should be run multiple times per day.

A sophisticated dev org should have the ability to support continuous integration (CI) by running all automated tests every time a check-in is made. For large projects, that requires numerous virtual environments ganging up to run test suites in parallel, which in turn requires a dedicated team (including test specialists) that builds, maintains, and extends the CI server by incorporating test suites from disparate teams.

Large, high-profile companies like Amazon and Netflix are able to support rapid, continuous testing because they have teams that focus solely on this capability, they have invested heavily in computer hardware, and they have developed their capabilities over many years. Companies that are just getting started with CI, or that do not have the needs of an Amazon or Netflix, should scale their expectations appropriately.

Test Automation in Legacy Environments

Inability to develop an ideal test suite should not be taken as a reason not to create automated tests. We've seen teams that inherited poor-quality code bases put basic smoke tests in place, slowly backfill automated tests, and realize significant gains from even a small amount of automation. You can support this with a loose DoD that becomes stricter over time.

It works best to focus legacy test work on areas of the code that are being worked on most actively. There's little benefit in adding coverage for code that's been stable for years.

More Keys to Effective Agile Testing

Aside from including testers on the development teams and using automating tests, keep in mind the following keys to effective Agile testing.

Ensure Developers Take Primary Responsibility for Testing Their Own Code

Integrating testers into development teams can have the unintended consequence of developers not testing their code—the opposite of what is intended! Developers have primary responsibility for quality of their work, including testing. Beware of these warning signs:

- Backlog items are closed only toward the end of each sprint (this implies that testing is occurring after coding, and separately).
- Developers move to other coding tasks before driving previous tasks to the DoD.

Measure Code Coverage

Writing test cases before writing the code ("test-first") can be a useful discipline, but we've found that, for new code bases, code-coverage measurement of unit tests combined with downstream test automation is more critical. A unit test code-coverage percentage of 70% is a useful, practical level to aim for with new code. Code coverage of 100% by unit tests is rare and usually far past the point of diminishing returns. (There are exceptions for safety-critical systems, of course.)

For organizations my company has worked with, best of breed typically approaches approximately a 1:1 ratio of test code to production code, which includes unit test code and higher-level test code. Again, this varies by type of software. Safety-critical software will have different standards than business software or entertainment software.

Beware of Abuse of Test Coverage Measures

We have found that measures like "70% statement coverage" are prone to abuse more frequently than you might expect. We've seen teams deactivate failing test cases to increase their pass ratios or create test cases that always return success.

In cases like these, it's more effective to fix the system than the person. This behavior suggests that the teams believe that development work is a higher priority than test work. Leadership needs to communicate that test and QA are as important as coding. Help your teams understand the purpose and value of the tests and emphasize that a number like 70% is simply an indicator—it is not the goal itself.

Monitor Static Code Metrics

Code coverage and other test metrics are useful but don't tell the entire quality story. Static code-quality metrics are also important: security vulnerabilities, cyclomatic complexity, depth of decision nesting, number of routine parameters, file size, folder size, routine length, use of magic numbers, embedded SQL, duplicate or copied code, quality of comments, adherence to coding standards, and so on. The metrics provide hints about which areas of code might need more work to maintain quality.

Write Test Code with Care

Test code should follow the same code-quality standards as production code. It should use good naming, avoid magic numbers, be well-factored, avoid duplication, have consistent formatting, be checked into revision control, and so on.

Prioritize Maintaining the Test Suites

Test suites tend to degrade over time, and it isn't uncommon to find test suites in which a high percentage of the tests have been turned off. The team should include review and maintenance of the test suite as an integral cost of its ongoing development work and include test work as part of its DoD. This is essential for supporting the goal of keeping the software close to a releasable level of quality at all times—that is, for keeping defects from getting out of control.

Have the Separate Test Organization Create and Maintain Acceptance Tests

If your company still maintains a separate test organization, it's useful to have that organization assume primary responsibility for creating and maintaining acceptance tests. The development team will still create and run acceptance tests—continuing to do that provides important support for minimizing the gap between defect insertion and defect detection. But it will have secondary responsibility for that kind of work.

We often see acceptance tests performed in a separate QA environment. This is useful when the content of the integration environment is constantly in flux; the QA environment can be more stable.

Keep Unit Tests in Perspective

A risk with Agile testing is overemphasizing code-level (unit) tests and underemphasizing tests of emergent properties such as scalability, performance, and so on—which become apparent when running integration tests of the larger software system. Be sure to include sufficient system-wide testing before a team declares itself done with a sprint.

Other Considerations

Manual/Exploratory Testing

Manual tests continue to have a role in the form of exploratory testing, usability testing, and other kinds of manual tests.

Not Your Father's Testing

The software world is in the middle of a sea change of testing approaches made possible by cloud computing, the ease with which changes can be promoted and rolled back, and, in some cases, new error modes arising from cloud computing. If your understanding of test practices is based on premised software and hasn't been updated, spend some time learning about modern test practices such as Canary Releases (A/B testing), Chaos Monkey/Simian Army, and other cloud-specific test practices.

Suggested Leadership Actions

Inspect

* Review whether your teams' approaches to automated testing include defining standards for test coverage and minimum acceptable test coverage.
* Determine tests your teams are performing manually. Does your team need a plan for which of these manual tests can be automated?

Adapt

* Define a goal level for test automation on each of your projects. Create plans to achieve those levels over the next 3–12 months.

Additional Resources

Crispin, Lisa and Janet Gregory. 2009. *Agile Testing: A Practical Guide for Testers and Agile Teams.* This is a popular reference about how testing is different for Agile teams and projects.

Forsgren, Nicole, et al. 2018. *Accelerate: The Science of Lean Software and DevOps: Building and Scaling High Performing Technology Organizations.* This book summarizes current data on the most effective Agile testing practices.

Stuart, Jenny and Melvin Perez. 2018. *Retrofitting Legacy Systems with Unit Tests.* [Online] July 2018. This white paper addresses specific issues involved in testing legacy systems.

Feathers, Michael. 2004. *Working Effectively with Legacy Code.* This book goes into more detail on working with legacy systems, including testing.

More Effective Agile Requirements Creation

For the first 25 years I worked in software development, every study I saw that examined causes of project challenge and failure found that the leading cause of problems was poor requirements—requirements that were incomplete, incorrect, contradictory, and so on. For the past 10 years, the most common cause of challenges my company has found on Agile projects has been difficulty in filling the Product Owner role, which is really about—you guessed it—requirements.

Because requirements have been such a widespread and persistent source of software project challenges, I'm going to use the next two chapters to dive deeper into requirements specifics than I have into other topics.

Agile Requirements Lifecycle

Compared to 25 years ago, today we have some very effective requirements practices that can be used on Agile projects. These practices help with each of the main requirements development activities:

- *Elicitation*—initial discovery of requirements.
- *Analysis*—development of a richer and more refined understanding of requirements, including priorities among them.
- *Specification*—expression of the requirements in a persistent form.
- *Validation*—assurance that the requirements are the correct requirements (will satisfy customer needs) and that they are captured correctly.

For most of the techniques, there isn't much difference in how a team would use them for an Agile or a Sequential project. What is different is *when* the team performs the activities.

This chapter describes the elicitation and specification activities and begins the discussion of analysis. The next chapter focuses on the prioritization aspect of analysis. The main techniques for validation of requirements on Agile projects include ongoing conversations about the requirements and the end-of-sprint review (that is, demonstrating the working software).

What's Different About Agile Requirements?

Requirements work occurs at different times on Agile projects than it does on Sequential projects. Figure 13-1 illustrates this difference.

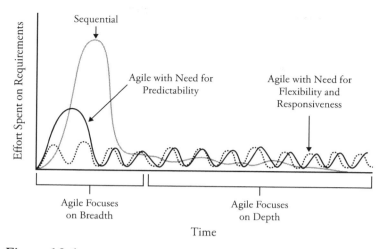

Figure 13-1

Differences in front-loading of requirements work for Agile projects that need predictability, Agile projects that need flexibility, and Sequential projects. Adapted from (Wiegers, 2013).

On Sequential projects, a significant percentage of requirements work is performed in a large batch at the beginning of the project. Up-front work on Agile projects is much smaller and is focused mostly on understanding the scope of requirements. Agile projects that need predictability work more on up-front requirements than other Agile projects do. Detailed refinement of individual requirements (elaboration) is deferred in both cases until shortly before development work on those requirements begins.

Agile projects aim to define just the essence of each requirement at the beginning of the project, leaving most of the detailed elaboration work to be performed just in time, and in some cases leaving all of the work to be performed just in time. Requirements are not elaborated less on Agile projects, but they are elaborated later. Some Agile projects make the mistake of not doing the elaboration, but that is more characteristic of code-and-fix development than Agile. More effective Agile projects elaborate their requirements by using the practices described later in this chapter.

Here's a pictorial view of how Agile projects approach requirements:

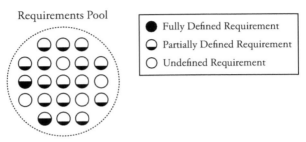

On Sequential projects, the details of each requirement are elaborated up front, with little requirements work left until later in the project. The whole requirement is developed early, not just the essence, as shown here:

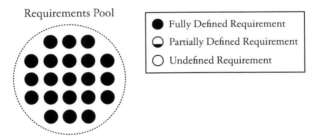

Detailed requirements work is performed in both Agile and Sequential approaches, but it is performed at different times. Over the course of a project, this leads to having different kinds of work completed at different times, as shown in Figure 13-2.

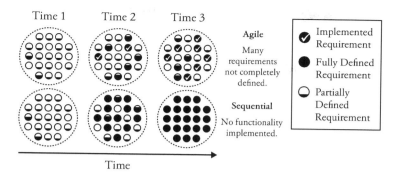

Figure 13-2

Differences in degree of requirements completion vs. functionality completion at different points in time in Agile and Sequential projects.

By performing the bulk of the requirements work up front, the Sequential project is essentially saying, "I'm betting that having detailed requirements up front will add value to the rest of the project, that working on detailed requirements up front will reduce uncertainty, and that the spoilage rate of this up-front work will be acceptable." ("Spoilage" is requirements work that becomes out of date before implementation work begins.)

The Agile project is essentially saying, "I'm betting that doing end-to-end implementation work (not just requirements work) and gaining feedback will reduce uncertainty. I'm betting that doing a lot of detailed requirements work up front will specify a lot of details that spoil by the time we get to implementation. The waste arising from requirements spoilage will be higher than whatever value-add there might have been from fully defining the requirements up front."

There's some truth in both arguments, and which approach works better is a function of whether the team is working in Cynefin's Complicated or Complex domain, the skill of the people doing the requirements work, and how confident the team is that the work it's doing is really Complicated rather than Complex.

Cynefin and Requirements Work

For Cynefin's Complicated problems, it is possible to model a complete system up front, if the team is adequately skilled at requirements development work.

For Cynefin's Complex problems, it isn't possible to know what the system needs to do up front. Requirements development work is a learning process for both the development team and the business. In this domain, even smart people can't know all the details of what they need to do until they try to do it.

The attempt to define requirements up front for Complex problems includes these challenges:

- *Requirements change,* and they have to be re-elaborated between the time they're initially elaborated and the time that implementation work begins. The initial elaboration work was waste.
- *Requirements are eliminated* after significant elaboration work has already been done. The elaboration work was waste.
- *Requirements are implemented that aren't really needed,* which is discovered only after users see the working software.
- *Some requirements are overlooked or emerge during the project,* which causes problems for design and implementation approaches that assumed that requirements were defined completely or nearly completely up front. The misguided design and implementation work was waste.

Figure 13-3 illustrates the waste that occurs when requirements change after the point in the project at which requirements would be fully defined on a Sequential project, using "Time 3" from Figure 13-2.

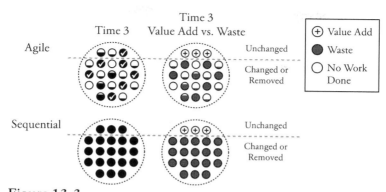

Figure 13-3

Differences in waste when requirements change mid-project in Agile and Sequential projects.

In the upper part of the figure, referring to the Agile project, there is, of course, no waste in unchanged requirements. Waste for changed and removed requirements varies, depending on the degree of completion of the work. Partially defined requirements result in less waste—note the dots in the partially filled-in circles—and fully defined requirements result in more waste.

In the lower part of the figure, referring to the Sequential project, there is a higher degree of waste in changed and removed requirements, due to the higher level of investment in those requirements prior to them being changed or removed.

False starts and dead ends still occur with Agile requirements, but less up-front investment in those false starts and dead ends means less waste overall.

Agile Requirements: Stories

Agile requirements are most commonly expressed in the form of stories, which take the form of:

As a <type of user>, I want <goal/desire> so that <benefit>

A story is a limited, defined set of functionality. Not all stories are requirements. Some examples are shown in Table 13-1.

Agile projects usually rely on stories as the primary means of expressing requirements. Stories can be captured in Agile tools, in a document or spreadsheet, on index cards, or on sticky notes on a wall. As you can see from the examples in the table, stories are not detailed enough to support development work on their own. The story is the documented and trackable placeholder for a conversation between the business and the technical staff. Stories are refined through conversations that include business, development, and testing perspectives—plus other perspectives if appropriate to the story.

Table 13-1 Examples of User Stories

	Type of User		Goal/ Desire		Benefit
As a	software leader	I want to	know my project status quantitatively	so that	I can keep the rest of my organization informed
As a	business leader	I want to	see status of all projects in one place	so that	I can understand which projects need my attention
As a	technical staff member	I want to	report status with low effort	so that	I can spend most of my time on hands-on technical work

The Agile Requirements Container: The Product Backlog

Agile requirements are typically contained in a product backlog, which contains stories, epics, themes, initiatives, features, functions, requirements, enhancements, and fixes—all the work needed to define the remainder of a project's scope. The "back-log" term is standard in Scrum. Kanban teams might call it an "input queue," but the concepts are similar. Teams working in formal contexts such as regulated industries might need more formal requirements containers (documents).

Most teams find that having about two sprints' worth of refined backlog items beyond the current sprint provides enough detail to support workflow planning and technical implementation. For teams doing work that's mostly in Cynefin's Complex domain, a shorter planning horizon can be more practical.

Figure 13-4 illustrates the way that the product backlog items become more refined as implementation of those backlog items approaches. I've shown the backlog as a funnel with near-term work at the bottom. (Agile teams typically refer to the backlog as a queue, with near-term work at the top.)

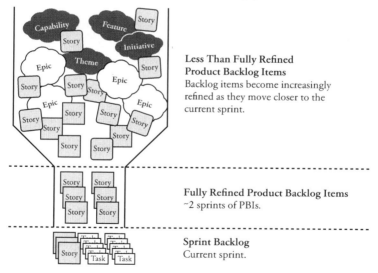

Figure 13-4
The Agile product backlog emphasizes just-in-time refinement.

What Goes into the Product Backlog?

In general, the product backlog contains requirements, but the definition of "requirement" is loose. The most common product backlog items (PBI's) look like this:

Requirement—an umbrella term that includes features, epics, stories, fixes, enhancements, and so on. "Requirement" doesn't necessarily mean "fully formed, rigorous requirement." Indeed, as discussed earlier in this chapter and as illustrated in Figure 13-2, most requirements in Agile work are kept in a partially defined state until just before they are implemented.

Feature—an increment of functionality that delivers capability or value to a business. The connotation of "feature" is that it requires more than one sprint to deliver. It is often described as a collection of user stories.

Epic—a story that requires more than one sprint to deliver. There is not widespread agreement on the specific details of epics and features, except that both are too large to complete within a single sprint.

Theme, investment theme, capability, initiative, enhancement, and similar terms—because there is an expectation that the backlog will be refined, relatively amorphous items can be added to it, especially at the far end of the backlog, with the understanding that those items will be refined in due course.

User story or *story*—a description of a function or capability described from the perspective of the person using the system. Some people make a distinction between story and user story, but usage of the two terms is not standardized—in most cases the two terms are synonyms. Stories are commonly defined as fitting within a single sprint. If a story is discovered through the refinement process to require more than one sprint, it is reclassified as an epic.

Fixes, technical debt reduction, spikes—development-oriented work that doesn't implement user requirements. This kind of work is generally called "enablers."

The terminology associated with contents of the product backlog is extensive and sometimes ambiguous. For this reason, some Agile practitioners simply refer to all product backlog items as "PBIs," which is a handy way of sidestepping a raft of terminology issues.

How Requirements Get into the Product Backlog

The backlog plays a key role on Agile projects, and many Agile texts are completely silent about how the Product Owner and the rest of the Agile team are supposed to populate it.

Requirements can get into the product backlog through a variety of techniques. The overall approaches can be described as top-down or bottom-up.

Top-Down Requirements Elicitation

In the top-down approach, the requirements process begins with the big picture. The team identifies actors, features, epics, initiatives—top-level business goals, functions and capabilities. These are then decomposed into stories. Good techniques for starting the top-down approach include the following:

- Create a story map
- Define a product vision
- Craft an elevator pitch
- Write the press release and FAQ
- Create a lean canvas
- Design an impact map
- Identify personas

Each of these techniques is intended to define a general direction for the release, and each is intended to help generate the more detailed stories that will guide implementation.

Bottom-Up Requirements Elicitation

In the bottom-up approach, the requirements process begins with specific details, typically stories. Good techniques for the bottom-up approach include these:

- Hold a user story–writing workshop
- Conduct focus groups with typical users
- Hold requirements elicitation interviews
- Observe users performing their jobs
- Review problem reports from the current system
- Review existing requirements (if replicating functionality of an existing system)
- Review existing enhancement requests

After specific stories are generated, they are aggregated into themes, features, and epics.

Top-Down vs. Bottom-Up

New development work will typically take a top-down approach. Legacy systems and evolutionary development are well-suited to bottom up. On a greenfield project that's using iterative development, the team might transition from top-down to bottom-up after enough functionality has been developed to generate user feedback.

When using the top-down approach, challenges arise from not diving deep enough into the details to expose the full scope of work, leaving too many details to be discovered during later backlog refinement.

With bottom-up requirements elicitation, the challenge is obtaining a meaningful view of the overall system—that is, "not being able to see the forest for the trees." You might overlook top-level constraints that override detailed work. Additional work is needed to ensure that the team's work adds up to a coherent overall direction.

The bottom-up and top-down approaches end up meeting in the middle to some degree. A workshop for writing user stories can draw in many of the top-down techniques, a press release draft can be used as a prompt in a requirements elicitation interview, and so on.

Details of specific Agile requirements elicitation practices are beyond the scope of this book. "Additional Resources" at the end of this chapter contains suggestions for where to find more information.

Key Principle: Refine the Product Backlog

After the product backlog is initially populated, it needs to be "refined" on an ongoing basis so that each PBI contains enough detail to support effective sprint planning and development work. I typically want to see about two sprints' worth of fully refined PBIs in the backlog at all times, not including the work in the current sprint.

Insufficient backlog refinement can cause a number of significant problems for the Agile team:

* The backlog items are not defined in sufficient detail to guide the work, so the team goes in the wrong direction.
* The team spends too much time refining during the sprint and encounters too many surprises as it goes.
* The backlog items have not been updated, so the team implements out-of-date concepts of the work.

- The backlog is not prioritized properly, so the team works on lower value items and delays work on more valuable items.

- Backlog items are misestimated and are too large, so the team cannot complete its sprint commitment because items were larger than expected.

- The team might be outright starved for work because there aren't enough refined items in the backlog.

Backlog Refinement Sessions

Backlog refinement is done in a session that includes the Product Owner, Scrum Master, and the Development Team. The whole team attends so that shared understanding can be developed of the upcoming work.

Work includes discussing stories and epics, splitting epics into stories, splitting stories into smaller stories (and splitting epics into smaller epics), clarifying details of stories, defining acceptance criteria for stories, and estimating stories.

Backlog refinement meetings are typically held mid-sprint. If questions need to be answered, the work to answer those questions should be done prior to the next sprint planning meeting so that open questions don't undermine sprint planning.

The Product Owner brings a prioritized (ordered) list of PBIs to the backlog refinement session and should have already completed most of the requirements-related elaboration work.

Key Principle: Create and Use a Definition of Ready

Just as the Definition of Done helps a team avoid moving work to the next stage before it is really done, a clear, documented Definition of Ready (DoR) helps a team avoid moving requirements into development before they are ready. A PBI is considered to be ready when it is:

- Understood by the Development Team well enough to decide whether it's doable in the sprint
- Estimated, and it fits comfortably into a single sprint
- Free from dependencies that would block it from being implemented during the sprint
- Defined with acceptance criteria (testable)

Teams can create their own DoR, which will be a variation on these points. The goal is to have the targeted PBIs fully refined before the next sprint planning meeting so that the team will have all the information it needs to plan effectively and not be sidetracked by open issues.

Other Considerations

Requirements Fundamentals

Requirements have been a thorny issue for decades. Agile has contributed useful practices to the requirements canon, but it has not changed the importance of high-quality requirements.

In Sequential development, requirements issues were conspicuous because the aggregate inefficiency was experienced all at once, cumulatively, at the end of the project. On a year-long project, if poor requirements contributed 10% inefficiency to a project, the project would be more than a month late. That pain is difficult to ignore.

In Agile development, the pain of poorly defined requirements is metabolized in smaller increments, more frequently, over the course of a project. A team experiencing 10% inefficiency from poorly defined requirements might re-do a story every few sprints. That doesn't seem as painful because the pain isn't borne all at once, but the cumulative inefficiency can be just as significant.

When performing reviews and retrospectives, Agile teams should be especially attentive to requirements issues. A team that finds that it's misunderstanding user stories should consider a focused effort to improve its requirements skills.

A discussion of detailed requirements practices is outside this book's scope, but you can check your knowledge with the self-assessment below. If most of the terms are unfamiliar to you, recognize that software requirements is now a well-developed discipline and many good techniques are available.

Requirements Self-Assessment

- ☐ Acceptance Test Driven Development (ATDD)
- ☐ Behavior Driven Development
- ☐ Checklists
- ☐ Context diagram
- ☐ Elevator pitch
- ☐ Event lists
- ☐ Extreme characters
- ☐ Five whys
- ☐ Hassle map
- ☐ Impact mapping
- ☐ Interviews
- ☐ Laddering questions
- ☐ Lean canvas
- ☐ Minimum Viable Product (MVP)
- ☐ Personas
- ☐ Planguage
- ☐ Press release
- ☐ Product vision
- ☐ Prototypes
- ☐ Scenarios
- ☐ Story mapping
- ☐ User stories

Suggested Leadership Actions

Inspect

* Review your teams' approaches to requirements through the lens of up front vs. just in time. What would you estimate is your "requirements spoilage rate" (percentage of requirements that are out of date or need to be redefined between the time you define them and the time you implement them)?

* Are your teams using top-down or bottom-up approaches to elicit requirements? To what degree are you seeing the typical challenges described in this chapter for each of these approaches? Do the teams have plans in place to account for them?

* Attend a backlog refinement session with the goal of understanding the status of the team's backlog. Do they have enough requirements defined to support efficient sprint planning and efficient development work during their sprints?

* Investigate whether your teams have a documented Definition of Ready and are using it.

* Review the past sprint reviews and retrospectives and identify backlog items that could not be completed because of insufficient backlog refinement. Has the team taken actions to prevent that from happening in the future?

Adapt

* Take steps to create a Definition of Ready.
* Take steps to ensure product backlog refinement is occurring in a timely way.

Additional Resources

Wiegers, Karl and Joy Beatty. 2013. *Software Requirements, 3rd Ed.* This is a highly readable, comprehensive description of requirements practices for both Sequential and Agile work.

Robertson, Robertson Suzanne and James. 2013. *Mastering the Requirements Process: Getting Requirements Right, 3rd Ed.* This is a good complement to the book by Wiegers and Beatty.

Cohn, Mike. 2004. *User Stories Applied: For Agile Software Development.* This book focuses on the ins and outs of user stories.

Adzic, Gojko and David Evans. 2014. *Fifty Quick Ideas to Improve Your User Stories.* As its title suggests, this short book provides numerous suggestions to improve user stories.

More Effective Agile Requirements Prioritization

⌒

One of the key emphases of Agile development is to sequence delivery of functionality from highest business priority to lowest. Highest-priority stories move toward the top of the backlog for additional refinement and implementation in the near-term sprints. Prioritization is also used decide which stories to implement and which stories not to.

Prioritizing requirements has always been useful, but for Agile projects requirements prioritization becomes a more prominent focus. A few really effective techniques have been developed to support this. But first let's take a look at the role most responsible for prioritizing requirements in Agile projects.

Product Owner

As I described in Chapter 4, "More Effective Agile Beginnings: Scrum," one of the most common failure modes in Scrum is an ineffective Product Owner (PO). In my company's experience, an effective PO has the following attributes:

Domain area expertise. An effective PO is an expert in the application, industry, and customers their application serves. Their understanding of the industry provides a foundation for prioritizing their team's deliverables, including understanding what is really required in a minimum viable product (MVP). They have the skill needed to communicate business context to the technical team.

Software requirements skill. An effective PO understands the level of detail and type of detail needed to define requirements appropriate to their specific environment. (The level of detail needed for business system requirements and medical devices are different.) The PO understands the difference between requirements and design—the PO stays focused on "the what" and leaves "the how" to the Development Team.

Facilitation skills. A strong PO can bring people together toward a common goal. Software requirements work is all about reconciling competing interests: tradeoffs between business goals and technical goals; tradeoffs between the team's local technical concerns and larger, organizational architectural concerns; conflict between different product stakeholders; and other tensions. An effective PO will help stakeholders work through different perspectives for the sake of a strong product.

Courage. An effective PO needs to be able to make decisions from time to time. An effective PO is not autocratic but knows when to employ the paradigm of "decision leader decides" vs. "group decides."

General personal-effectiveness attributes. An effective PO also has the general personal-effectiveness attributes of high energy level, proactive behavior for backlog refinement, leading meetings efficiently, and consistent follow-through.

This list of desirable attributes implies some aspects of an effective PO's background. The ideal PO has an engineering background, experience in the field, and business experience, though as I mentioned earlier, with appropriate training, business analysts, customer support staff, and testers can all make excellent POs.

T-Shirt Sizing

As I discussed in my book *Software Estimation: Demystifying the Black Art* (McConnell, 2006), T-shirt sizing is a useful way to prioritize partially refined functionality based on approximate return on investment.

In this approach, technical staff classifies each story's size (development cost) relative to other stories as Small, Medium, Large, or Extra Large. ("Stories" can also be features, requirements, epics, and so on.) In parallel, the customer, marketing, sales, or other nontechnical stakeholders classify the stories' business value on the same scale. These two sets of entries are then combined, as shown in Table 14-1 on the next page.

Creating this relationship between business value and development cost allows the nontechnical stakeholder to say things like, "If the development cost of Story B is Large, I don't want it because the value is only Small." This is a tremendously useful decision to be able to make early in the elaboration of that story. If you were instead to carry that story through some amount of refinement, architecture, design, and so on, you would be expending effort on a story that ultimately isn't cost-justifiable. The value of a quick "No" in software is high. T-shirt sizing allows for early-in-the-project decisions to rule out stories, without needing to carry those stories further.

Table 14-1 Using T-shirt Sizing to Classify Stories by Business Value and Development Cost

Story	Business Value	Development Cost
Story A	Large	Small
Story B	Small	Large
Story C	Large	Large
Story D	Medium	Medium
Story E	Medium	Large
Story F	Large	Medium
…		
Story ZZ	Small	Small

The discussion about what to carry forward and what to cut is easier if stories can be sorted into a rough cost/benefit order. Typically, this is done by assigning a "net business value" number based on the combination of development cost and business value.

Table 14-2 shows one possible scheme for assigning a net business value to each combination. You can use this scheme or come up with one of your own that more accurately reflects the value arising from combinations of development cost and business value in your environment.

Table 14-2 Approximate Net Business Value Based on Relationship of Development Cost and Business Value

Business Value	Development Cost			
	Extra Large	*Large*	*Medium*	*Small*
Extra Large	1	5	6	7
Large	-4	1	3	4
Medium	-6	-2	1	2
Small	-7	-3	-1	1

This lookup table allows you to add a third column to the original cost/benefit table and to sort that table by approximate net business value, as shown in Table 14-3.

Table 14-3 Sorting T-shirt Sizing Estimates by Approximate Net Business Value

Story	Business Value	Development Cost	Approximate Net Business Value
Story A	L	S	4
Story F	L	M	3
Story C	L	L	1
Story D	M	M	1
Story ZZ	S	S	1
Story E	M	L	-2
...			
Story B	S	L	-3

The "Approximate Net Business Value" column is what it says—an *approximation*. I don't suggest just counting down the list and drawing a line. The value of sorting by approximate business value is that it supports getting quick "definitely yes" responses for the stories at the top of the list and quick "definitely no" decisions for the stories at the bottom. You'll still need to discuss the items in the middle. Because the net business values are approximate, you'll occasionally see cases in which a story that has a value of 1 is a better idea than a story that has a value of 2 when you look at the details.

T-Shirt Sizing and Story Points

This discussion of T-shirt sizing has used the same T-shirt scale for development cost and business value. If stories have been refined enough to assign story points, the technique works equally well if story points are used for the development costs and the business values are still expressed in T-shirt sizes. You can still calculate the approximate net business value so that the highest-ROI ideas rise to the top. This can be done regardless of what scale is used for development cost.

Story Mapping

Because product backlogs often consist of dozens or hundreds of stories, it's easy for priorities to get confused and the collection of items delivered at the end of each sprint to be incoherent even if, individually, they represent the highest-priority backlog items.

Story mapping is a powerful technique for prioritizing the sequence in which stories are delivered while simultaneously shaping the collections of stories into coherent packages (Patton, 2014). It also helps with elicitation, analysis, and specification of requirements, and it becomes an aid to status tracking during development.

Story mapping is conducted with the whole team and consists of three steps:

1. Capture major chunks of functionality on sticky notes, and arrange them in a prioritized line from left to right, highest priority to lowest. Major chunks of functionality will consist of features, epics/big stories, themes, initiatives, and other large-grain requirements. I'll refer to these generically as epics in the rest of this discussion.

2. Decompose top-level epics into steps or themes. This elaboration does not change the prioritization of the epics.

3. Decompose each of the steps or themes into stories captured on sticky notes. Arrange these below each step or theme in priority order.

This process results in a story map that lists requirements in priority order both from left to right and top to bottom.

The following sections describe these steps in more detail.

Step 1: Prioritize Epics and Other Top-Level Functionality

Top-level functionality is prioritized using sticky notes from left to right, as shown in Figure 14-1.

The epics can be prioritized using T-shirt sizing or other techniques, including Weighted Shortest Job First, discussed in Chapter 22, "More Effective Agile Portfolio Management."

Top-Level Priority (High to Low)

Figure 14-1
Story mapping begins with listing epics (and other top-level items) in priority order from left to right.

Lower-priority epics on the right side of the story map might not be important enough to be included in the release. If they are, they still might not be important enough to be included in a minimum viable product (MVP).

Step 2: Decompose Top-Level Epics into Steps or Themes

Most epics will be intuitively describable as sequential steps. Some will not consist of sequential steps and can be decomposed into themes, as shown in Figure 14-2.

Top-Level Priority (High to Low)

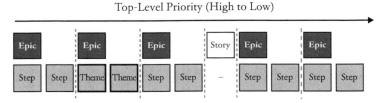

Figure 14-2
Story mapping enumerates steps or themes below epics, which doesn't change the prioritization order of the epics.

This second-level decomposition into steps and themes is called "the backbone" in story mapping. Walking through a description of the backbone should provide a coherent description of the overall functionality being built.

Step 3: Decompose Each Step or Theme into Prioritized Stories

Below the backbone, each step or theme is further decomposed into one or more stories. These are arranged in priority order from top to bottom, as shown in Figure 14-3, using T-shirt sizing or more informal judgment by the team.

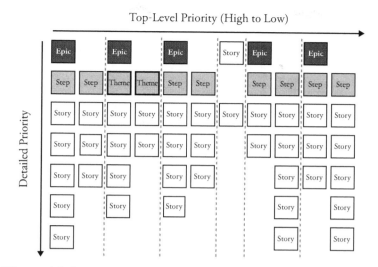

Figure 14-3

The team decomposes each step or theme into stories and sorts them in priority order left to right and top to bottom.

The vertical stacks of stories under each step or theme are called "ribs" in story mapping. The minimum set of stories immediately below the backbone that make up a coherent implementation is called the "walking skeleton." The walking skeleton is coherent but is not normally sufficient to be an MVP, which includes additional stories beyond the walking skeleton.

The ways these terms apply to the story map are shown in Figure 14-4 on the next page.

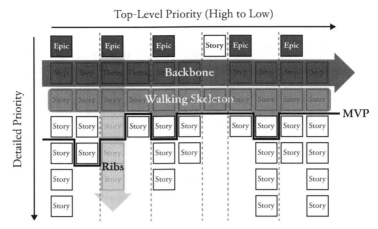

Figure 14-4

The horizontal slice of functionality immediately below the backbone makes up the minimal coherent implementation of the release, called the "walking skeleton." MVP usually includes functionality beyond the walking skeleton.

Teams can define long lists of fine-grain functionality that don't add up to a coherent release. By defining a backbone, walking skeleton, and MVP, the Development Team obtains clear direction for delivering prioritized *and* coherent functionality.

Story Mapping and User Roles

A useful variation can be to start with user roles at the top instead of epics, prioritize those from left to right, and then decompose epics below those.

Story Mapping as an Example of an Information Radiator

Effective Agile practices emphasize *making work visible*—not just accessible on a web page but a visible part of the work environment. A story map on the wall is a constant reminder of team priorities, current assignments, and future work flow. Agile teams refer to this kind of display as an "information radiator."

Research has found that visual displays of this kind are necessary for improved delivery performance (Forsgren, 2018).

Story Mapping as an Example of the Agile Pendulum Swing

Story mapping is a fascinating example of how the software development pendulum has swung from pure Sequential development to early Agile, and it has now swung back to a *better Agile*. Early Agile development avoided doing up-front requirements work at all costs, leaving requirements to be done just in time—and only just in time. Story mapping, strongly associated with Agile development, is an approach for organizing and prioritizing requirements *up front*. But it is not an old, Sequential, fully elaborated requirements-up-front practice. It is a practice that helps define the broad scope of a release up front and then continues to provide prioritization and guidance for incremental requirements refinement throughout the release.

Story mapping is a terrific example of the way that Sequential development and Agile development can be synthesized to provide the best of both worlds. Story mapping provides support for identifying requirements up front and refining them only shortly before they are implemented. It helps avoid the common Agile failure mode of delivering functionality in priority order but missing the big-picture view. And the act of walking through the stories from left to right and top to bottom often exposes missing steps in epics, misunderstandings of priorities, and other mistakes.

Other Considerations

As with requirements elicitation, requirements prioritization has been a thorny issue for decades. In addition to T-shirt sizing and story mapping, consider the following useful techniques.

Dot Voting

In dot voting, each stakeholder is given a fixed number of dots—for example, 10 dots. Stakeholders allocate their dots among requirements any way they see fit. All 10 dots on 1 requirement, 1 dot each on 10 different requirements, 5 on 1 and 1 each on the rest—anything is possible. The technique provides a quick way to discover the priorities of a group.

MoSCoW

"MoSCoW" is a mnemonic for Must have, Should have, Could have, Won't have. It is a useful method of partitioning proposed requirements into categories.

MVE

MVE is an acronym for Minimum Viable Experiment, which refers to the smallest release that can be used to provide valuable feedback to the team. MVE is supportive of work in Cynefin's Complex domain; it amounts to a probe that's used to explore a possible product direction.

Alternatives to MVP

Some teams find that keeping the minimum viable product to a minimum can be a challenge. If you encounter that problem with your teams, consider alternative formulations of "minimum," including earliest testable product, earliest usable product, and earliest lovable product.

Weighted Shortest Job First (WSJF)

Weighted Shortest Job First is a technique for maximizing value based on the sequence in which work is performed. WSJF is discussed in Chapter 22.

Suggested Leadership Actions

Inspect

* Review staffing for the Product Owner role on your teams. How effective are the people you have in this critical role? Are they adding to the teams' effectiveness, or are they weak links in the chain?
* Investigate the techniques that your teams are using for requirements prioritization. Do the techniques support implementing based on ROI order?
* Investigate whether your teams are implementing functionality purely on a fine-grain, descending business value basis without any consideration of the big picture.

Adapt

* If your Product Owners are not effective, develop them or replace them.
* Work with your teams to adopt a technique for prioritizing product backlog items—such as T-shirt sizing or story mapping.
* Work with your teams to implement story mapping for the purpose of supporting coherent packages of functionality.

Additional Resources

Patton, Jeff. 2014. *User Story Mapping: Discover the Whole Story, Build the Right Product.* Jeff Patton is the recognized authority on user story mapping.

McConnell, Steve. 2006. *Software Estimation: Demystifying the Black Art.* Section 12.4 of this book contains a more detailed discussion of T-shirt sizing.

More Effective Agile Delivery

⌒

Delivery is the activity in which the rest of the development process comes together. As such, delivery provides a useful lens through which to discuss several aspects of more effective Agile development.

In this chapter, I refer to both *delivery* and *deployment*. "Delivery" refers to preparing the software in every way needed to make it ready for deployment but not actually deploying it. "Deployment" refers to taking that last step to put the software into production.

The last step required to get to delivery is integration. In Agile development, the goal is to have both continuous integration (CI) and continuous delivery or deployment (CD). CI and CD are cornerstone practices of DevOps.

Continuous integration is not literally "continuous." The term is used to mean that developers are checking code into a shared repository often—typically multiple times per day. Likewise, continuous delivery does not literally mean "continuous." In practice, it means delivery that is frequent and automated.

Key Principle: Automate Repetitive Activities

Software development activities tend to flow from more open-ended, creative, nondeterministic activities, such as requirements and design, to more closed-ended, deterministic activities, such as automated testing, commit to trunk, user acceptance testing, staging, and production. People are good at the more open-ended upstream activities that require thinking, and computers are good at the more deterministic downstream activities that need to be done repetitively.

The closer you get to delivery and deployment, the more sense it makes to automate the activities so that they are performed by computers.

For some companies the ideal is fully automated deployment, which requires a fully automated deployment pipeline, including automating repetitive tasks. Figure 15-1 shows which tasks can potentially be automated.

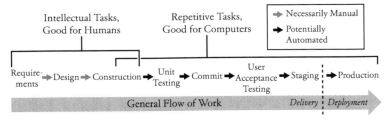

Figure 15-1
The closer software work gets to deployment, the better suited it is for automation.

The potential for frequency of deployment is essentially unlimited. For several years Amazon has been deploying every few seconds, with as many as 1,000 deployments per hour (Jenkins, 2011). Most organizations do not have any business reason to deploy anywhere near this often, but Amazon's performance shows that virtually any frequency of deployment is possible.

As Figure 15-1 suggests, the key idea in achieving automated deployment is to separate requirements, design, and construction, which can't be automated, from delivery and deployment, which can be.

Automating the later stages of the pipeline provides the benefits of increased efficiency and faster deployment. There is also a human benefit. If you consider the effect of automation through the lens of Autonomy, Mastery, and Purpose, automation also increases motivation. It eliminates a repetitive task that offers no opportunity for growth, and it frees up time that can be applied to upstream activities that do offer opportunity for growth.

Work Practices That Support CI/CD

Several work practices are required to support CI/CD, some of which have been discussed in earlier chapters.

Automate Almost Everything

To fully achieve CI/CD, the entire development environment needs to be automated. This includes versioning artifacts that might not otherwise be versioned: code, system configurations, application configurations, build, and configuration scripts.

Increase Emphasis on Automated Testing

The automated test environment should support each proposed change passing automated tests of several different types, including unit tests, API tests, integration tests, UI layer tests, tests for random inputs, tests for random data, load testing, and so on.

A major benefit of CI/CD is automatic detection and rejection of changes that are unacceptable due to error introduction or unacceptable performance degradation.

Increase Priority of Deployability

Maintaining the automated deployment pipeline requires effort, and for CI/CD to work, the team must prioritize keeping the system in a deployable state over doing new work (Humble, 2015). Prioritizing new work over maintaining the automated deployment pipeline is a choice to incur long-term pain and reduced velocity.

Broaden Your Definition of Done

While the Definition of Done is an important concept on any project, the specifics become more important in a CI/CD environment.

In a CI/CD environment, DoD needs to include standards for unit tests, acceptance tests, regression tests, staging, and revision control. Figure 15-2 shows a DoD that's appropriate for such an environment.

- ☐ All the PBIs in the product increment satisfy the acceptance criteria*
- ☐ Static code analysis passes
- ☐ Unit tests run without error
- ☐ 70% statement coverage through unit tests
- ☐ System and integration testing complete
- ☐ All regression tests passed*
- ☐ ...
- ☐ Demonstrated in production-like environment (staging)*
- ☐ Code is in the version control trunk and is releasable or released*

Figure 15-2

Example Definition of Done for a CI/CD environment. Items marked with asterisks are different from the single-project DoD.

Emphasize Incremental Work Practices

Several steps need to be taken to support the goal of minimizing the gap between defect insertion and defect detection:

- Commit/push code frequently (at least daily, preferably more often).
- Don't commit/push broken code.
- Fix breaks in the deployment pipeline immediately, including broken builds.
- Write automated tests with the code.
- All tests must pass.

These practices are useful in assuring that your team's software is in a releasable state every time a new feature is added or a correction is made.

Use Continuous Deployment as a Yardstick for Overall Development Effectiveness

Humans repetitively doing tasks that could be performed by computers is a form of waste. The lead time for getting code changes to production is a useful measurement proxy for how much manual effort is occurring throughout that pipeline.

Measuring deployment lead time can lead to increases in test automation; simplification and automation of the build, release, and deployment process; and an increased emphasis on designing applications with testability and deployability in mind. It can also lead to developing and deploying functionality in smaller batches.

Humble, Molesky, and O'Reilly recommend, "If it hurts, do it more often and bring the pain forward" (Humble, 2015). In other words, if it hurts, automate it so that it will stop hurting. For downstream activities that are amenable to automation, this is excellent advice.

Benefits of CI/CD

CI/CD produces both obvious and not-so-obvious benefits. The obvious benefits include getting new functionality into the hands of users faster and more often. The not-so-obvious benefits of CI/CD might be more significant.

Teams learn faster, because they go through the develop-test-release-deploy cycle more often, which provides more frequent learning opportunities.

Defects are detected closer to when they are introduced, so they cost less to fix, as discussed in Chapter 11, "More Effective Agile Quality."

Teams experience lower stress because push-button releases become easy, without any fear of human error causing the release to fail.

As deployment becomes more reliable and routine, releases can be performed during normal business hours. If mistakes are found, the whole team can be involved, not just (tired) on-call individuals.

An emphasis on releasing multiple times per day can be beneficial even if you're working on mission-critical software that is released to the public infrequently. Releasing frequently, even if only internally, makes quality a constant consideration. It accelerates team learning because each time a release cannot be completed, the team has an opportunity to understand why it didn't release and improve in that area.

Finally, as described earlier in this chapter, CI/CD can increase motivation by allowing teams to spend more time on work that provides higher opportunity for growth.

Other Considerations

Continuous Delivery

The phrase "CI/CD" has become common in the software industry, which implies that organizations are routinely doing *both* continuous integration and continuous delivery. However, we do not see most organizations practicing the "CD" part of CI/CD. DZone Research reports that while 50% of organizations believe they have implemented CD, only 18% actually meet the textbook definition (DZone Research, 2015).

CI is a prerequisite for CD, so we have found that it makes sense to get CI right first. Despite much recent attention on environments like Netflix and Amazon, which deploy hundreds of times per day, environments that deploy weekly, monthly, quarterly, or less often are common and will be for the foreseeable future. You might be working on embedded systems, on combined hardware/software products, on regulated systems, in an enterprise space, or on legacy systems that can't accept frequent releases. However, you can still benefit from automating the repetitive parts of CI. You can also benefit from the discipline associated with continuous delivery even if continuous deployment will never be desirable.

This is an area where the concept of the Agile boundary is useful—you might have good reasons to draw your Agile boundary so that it includes CI but doesn't include CD.

The Agile boundary applies to external customers as much as it does to internal development organizations. We've worked with organizations that have developed the ability to release software externally much more frequently than they actually do—they release less often because their customers have requested that. Their customers are on the other side of the Agile boundary. They still deliver frequent internal releases for the sake of obtaining the benefits described in this chapter.

Suggested Leadership Actions

Inspect

* Familiarize yourself with the extent of automation in your delivery/deployment pipeline.
* Interview your teams to determine how much of their effort is going into repetitive delivery/deployment activities that could be automated.
* Inventory the activities in your delivery/deployment process that are still being done manually. Which activities are preventing your teams from having push-button deliveries?
* Investigate to determine whether your teams' work is planned to a level that supports frequent integration.
* Consider measuring the lead time from code change to software deployment.

Adapt

* Encourage your staff to integrate their work frequently, at least daily.
* Create a Definition of Done that supports automated delivery and deployment.
* Create a plan for your teams to automate as much of their build and deployment environments as they can.
* Communicate to your staff that their work to keep the delivery/deployment pipeline working is higher priority than creating new functionality.
* Set a quantitative goal to reduce the lead time from code change to deployment.

Additional Resources

Forsgren, Nicole, et al. 2018. *Accelerate: The Science of Lean Software and DevOps: Building and Scaling High Performing Technology Organizations.* This book lays out a compelling case for the deployment pipeline being the central focus of an effective and healthy delivery organization.

Nygard, Michael T. 2018. *Release It!: Design and Deploy Production-Ready Software, 2nd Ed.* This book covers architecture and design issues as well as deployment issues related to faster and more reliable deployment.

PART IV

MORE EFFECTIVE
ORGANIZATIONS

⌒

This part of the book deals with Agile development concerns that are best addressed at the top level of an organization—and in some cases that can be addressed *only* at the top level.

More Effective Agile Leadership

❧

Agile enthusiasts often refer to Agile implementations as depending on "servant leadership." I believe this to be true, but I also believe it is too vague to be specifically useful for Agile adoptions. More direct guidance is required. Whether you've decided to go full-blown Agile or adopt Agile less extensively, leadership is a make-or-break aspect of Agile implementations, so this chapter is full of key principles.

Key Principle: Manage to Outcomes, Not Details

Organizations live and die based on the commitments they make and the commitments they keep. Effective Agile implementations consist of commitments both to and from the teams and both to and from leadership.

Agile teams (specifically Scrum teams) commit to leadership that they will deliver their sprint goal at the end of each sprint. In a high-fidelity Scrum implementation, the commitment is seen as absolute—the team will work mightily to live up to its sprint goals.

In return, leadership commits to the Scrum team that the sprint is sacrosanct. Leadership will not change requirements or otherwise disrupt the team while it's in the middle of a sprint. In traditional Sequential projects, this was not a reasonable expectation because the project cycles were so long and circumstances were bound to change. In Scrum projects, it's entirely reasonable because sprints are typically only 1–3 weeks long. If the organization can't maintain its focus without changing its mind during this time, the organization has larger problems than whether its Scrum implementation is going to work.

The idea of treating teams and sprints as black boxes and managing only the inputs and outputs from the sprints has the desirable side effect of helping business leaders avoid micromanagement and encouraging more of a leadership posture. Business leaders need to give direction to the teams, explain the purpose of the work, elaborate the priorities among different objectives, and then set the teams free to amaze them with the outcomes.

Key Principle: Express Clear Purpose with Commander's Intent

Autonomy and Purpose are connected because a team cannot have meaningful, healthy Autonomy unless it understands the Purpose of its work. A self-managed team needs to make the vast majority of decisions internally. It has the cross-functional skills and the authority to do so. However, if it does not have a clear understanding of the purpose of its work, its decisions will be misguided (literally). Figure 16-1 describes possible outcomes for the team, depending on its Autonomy and the clarity of its objectives (Purpose).

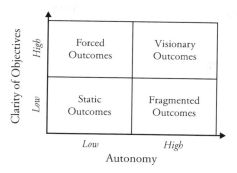

Figure 16-1
Autonomy vs. clarity of objectives.

The US military uses a notion of "Commander's Intent," which refers to a public statement of the desired end state, the purpose of the operation, and the key tasks to be accomplished. Commander's Intent is specifically useful in cases where events are not unfolding as originally planned, communication is disrupted, and a team needs to make a decision without the ability to confer higher up in the chain of command.

Your goal in a software context is similar. Communication with company leadership will probably not be forcibly disrupted, but often company leadership is not readily accessible for extended periods of time,[3] events are not unfolding as originally planned, and the team still needs to make decisions. In those circumstances, teams benefit from having a "guiding light" or "north star" or "Commander's Intent" from which they can obtain direction.

A good description of Commander's Intent will include the following:

---

[3] I once worked with a software executive who met with his boss only 30 minutes every six months.

- A statement of the reasons and motivation for the project or initiative; the purpose.
- A vivid visualization of the desired end state. It should allow team members to understand what success looks like and their part in achieving it.

An organization that wants to become Agile needs to develop the ability to describe purpose clearly. Its managers should focus on leading through objectives rather than managing by focusing on details.

> *"Don't tell people how to do things. Tell them what to do and let them surprise you with their results."*
> —George S. Patton

Prioritize, and Communicate Priorities

Effective Agile leaders support their teams by communicating unambiguous priorities. We've seen many organizations that prioritize everything as highest priority and leave it to the teams to figure it out. Or they reprioritize too frequently. Or they prioritize at too fine a level of detail. Or they refuse to prioritize at all. These mistakes are both exceedingly common and exceedingly ineffective.

Refusal to prioritize is a sign of weak leadership. It amounts to abdicating responsibility for making decisions. If you care about what gets done, you have to make decisions about priorities and communicate those decisions to your teams unambiguously.

Frequent reprioritization can be just as damaging. Frequent changes in priorities undermine both the team's sense of Autonomy and its sense of Purpose. Leaders should ask themselves, "Will this reprioritization matter six months from now?" If it won't, it isn't important enough to randomize the team.

Commander's Intent is a good lens through which to view the appropriate level of prioritization. The leader should define what success looks like—objectives, outcomes, impacts, and benefits—but stop short of defining details.

Prioritization is an area in which an effective Agile implementation can highlight an organization's weaknesses in ways that are threatening to its leaders. We have occasionally seen leaders shut down Agile implementations because frequent delivery (or lack thereof) highlights the leader's inability to provide clear priorities to their teams.

It's impossible to overstate how important this point is. If you are not effectively prioritizing your teams' work, you are not leading. Your projects will achieve results far short of the results they could achieve—and far short of the results that your teams deserve. The organization that wants to be effective will not avoid the discomfort that can arise from shining a bright light on prioritization weaknesses—it will instead use the discomfort as motivation to improve.

Key Principle: Focus on Throughput, Not Activity

Ineffective leaders tend to focus more on the perception of progress than the reality of progress. But not all motion is progress, and busyness is often a poor proxy for results.

The goal of an effective organization should be to maximize *throughput*—the rate at which work is completed—not the rate at which work is started or the level of activity. Leaders must accept that some amount of slack is necessary to maximize throughput (DeMarco, 2002).

One reason Scrum keeps accountability at the team level, rather than at the individual level, is that it allows the team to decide how the team will be most productive. If the team can be most productive by having one of its members sit out for a day, the team is free to make that decision.

Allowing individuals to have slack time is a counterintuitive way to maximize throughput, but at the end of the day, what matters to the organization is the total output from each team, not the output from each individual. If the team is effectively optimizing for team productivity, the organization shouldn't care about what's happening at the individual level.

Key Principle: Model Key Agile Behaviors

Effective leaders embody the behaviors they want to see from the people they lead. Those behaviors should include:

- *Develop a Growth Mindset*—commit to continuous improvement at both the personal and organizational levels.
- *Inspect and Adapt*—constantly reflect, learn from experience, and apply the learnings.
- *Decriminalize mistakes*—model the approach of accepting each mistake as an opportunity to learn.
- *Fix the system, not the individual*—when problems occur, treat them as opportunities to look for flaws in the system rather than blame individuals.
- *Commit to high quality*—use your actions to communicate a clear commitment to high quality.
- *Develop business focus*—show how business considerations are included along with technical considerations in your decision making.
- *Tighten feedback loops*—be responsive to your teams (even if they shouldn't need it, because you've expressed your Commander's Intent so clearly).

Suggested Leadership Actions

Inspect

Review your own performance as a leader:

* Are you treating your Agile teams as black boxes, managing to their performance in meeting their commitments rather than managing details?

* Have you expressed your "Commander's Intent" clearly? Can your teams express a vivid, current definition of success for their work? Can they work for a few weeks without your involvement, if necessary?

* Have you set clear and realistic priorities for your teams and communicated them?

* Do you stay focused on your team's throughput rather than their apparent level of activity?

Adapt

* Ask your teams to conduct a 360-degree review of your leadership performance according to the "Inspect" criteria above. Welcome your teams' feedback in a way that models learning from mistakes.

* Based on the results of your self-evaluation and your team's input, develop a prioritized list of personal leadership self-improvement actions.

Additional Resources

U.S. Marine Corps Staff. 1989. *Warfighting: The U.S. Marine Corp Book of Strategy.* This short book decribes the U.S. Marine Corp approach to planning and operations. I find many parallels to software projects in the description.

Reinertsen, Donald G. 2009. *The Principles of Product Development Flow: Second Generation Lean Product Development.* This book contains an extended discussion of throughput or "flow." Reinertsen makes a compelling argument that not focusing on flow for product development is, as he puts it, "wrong to its very core."

DeMarco, Tom. 2002. *Slack: Getting Past Burnout, Busywork, and the Myth of Total Efficiency.* DeMarco argues the case for not fully loading staff.

Storlie, Chad, 2010. "Manage Uncertainty with Commander's Intent," *Harvard Business Review*, November 3, 2010. This article provides a slightly more detailed description of Commander's Intent than the one I've given in this chapter.

Maxwell, John C. 2007. *The 21 Irrefutable Laws of Leadership.* Maxwell's book is a good counterpoint to the sometimes overly analytical approach to leadership that I see from software leaders. He includes key advice, such as, "The heart comes before the head" and "People don't care how much you know until they know how much you care."

More Effective Agile Organizational Culture

⌐

The majority of Agile practices are team-based practices that provide support for team performance, learning, and improvement. Leaders also have an opportunity to expand team-level principles to organization-level work. This chapter describes how to support more effective Agile practices at the organizational level.

Key Principle: Decriminalize Mistakes

As I've mentioned, Agile development depends on the use of Inspect and Adapt, a learning cycle that depends on making calculated mistakes, learning from them, and improving. By "calculated mistake" I mean making a decision when you know you are not confident in the result and being attentive to learn from the result, regardless of how well it turns out.

In Cynefin terms, Complicated projects depend on making small numbers of calculated mistakes; Complex projects depend on making large numbers of calculated mistakes. It is thus essential that an organization decriminalize errors so that they are visible, examined, and ultimately beneficial to the organization, rather than hidden, shameful, and ultimately harmful to the organization.

As Jez Humble says, "In a complex adaptive system, failure is inevitable. When accidents happen, human error is the starting point of a blameless post-mortem" (Humble, 2018). Some organizations such as as Etsy publicize and *celebrate* mistakes—the focus of the celebration is based on the idea that, "We're happy we made this mistake, because otherwise we never would have learned about *X*."

Make Necessary Mistakes Quickly

Complex projects depend not just on learning from mistakes but on making the mistakes in the first place. It's important to create an organizational culture that does not hesitate to make mistakes when necessary. As Figure 17-1 suggests, this is not a license to make careless mistakes. But it's healthy to establish a culture of jumping in and learning from experience in cases where a decision's outcome cannot be determined in advance.

	Unintentional	Calculated (Intentional)
Slow	Improve skill at making mistakes in calculated ways and learning from them.	Speed up mistakes to accelerate learning.
Fast	Careless—avoid!	Aim for most mistakes in this category; necessary for success on Complex problems.

Figure 17-1

Types of mistakes—a taxonomy of decriminalized mistakes.

Correct Mistakes within their Recovery Windows

Issues have recovery windows within which they can be corrected with low pain. Once an issue is beyond its recovery window, the pain increases. Correcting a mistake in an internal release is inexpensive. Correcting the mistake after it's been rolled out to customers is expensive. The earlier an issue is surfaced, the greater the chance that it can be corrected while it's still in its recovery window. Good news travels fast. Bad news needs to travel faster.

Decriminalize Escalation

An organization that is serious about decriminalizing errors needs to decriminalize escalation of errors. Information about errors should propagate freely to the level needed to correct the error. Microsoft did an excellent job of this when I was there in the early 1990s. By boss came into my office one afternoon and said, "I need to vent. I was just in a BillG review meeting, and I got my ass chewed. I'd been sitting on an issue for two weeks, and Bill pointed out he could have solved the issue with a 5-minute phone call. He chewed me out for not delegating upwards to him. I feel bad because I deserved to get chewed out. I knew I should have delegated the issue to him, and I didn't."

Psychological Safety

Decriminalizing mistakes is important, among other reasons, because it contributes to teams' feelings of psychological safety. A two-year research project conducted by Google's People Operations (HR) found that five factors contributed to team effectiveness at Google, described in Figure 17-2 on the next page.

229

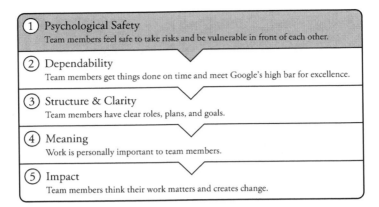

Figure 17-2

The most important contributor to successful teams at Google is psychological safety.

Google's research found that, by far, the most important influence on team effectiveness was psychological safety, which they defined as, "Can we take risks on this team without feeling insecure or embarrassed?" Google described psychological safety as the underpinning of the other four factors. They found that:

> *"Individuals on teams with higher psychological safety are less likely to leave Google, they're more likely to harness the power of diverse ideas from their teammates, they bring in more revenue, and they're rated as effective twice as often by executives."*
> *(Rozovsky, 2015)*

Google's research is consistent with prior research by Ron Westrum (Westrum, 2005; Schuh, 2001). Westrum developed a "Three Cultures Model" of organizational cultures: pathological, bureaucratic, and generative. The attributes of these cultures are shown in Table 17-1.

Table 17-1 Attributes of Different Cultures in Westrum's Three Cultures Model

Pathological	Bureaucratic	Generative
Power-oriented	Rule-oriented	Performance-oriented
Low cooperation	Modest cooperation	High cooperation
Messengers shot	Messengers neglected	Messengers trained
Responsibilities shirked	Narrow responsibilities	Risks are shared
Interdepartmental bridging discouraged	Interdepartmental bridging tolerated	Interdepartmental bridging encouraged
Failure → scapegoating	Failure → justice	Failure → inquiry
Novelty crushed	Novelty causes problems	Novelty implemented

Westrum found that generative cultures are more effective than pathological and bureaucratic cultures—they perform beyond expectations, demonstrate higher flexibility (agility), and show better safety records.

Pathological organizations are characterized by suppression of bad news. Generative organizations publish bad news internally. Through subsequent inquiry, they leverage the bad news into improvements. Westrum's work reinforces the importance of decriminalizing mistakes.

Key Principle: Plan Based on Measured Team Capacity

An effective organization views each team and the organization overall as having a particular amount of capacity for software development work. This capacity is a function of individual productivity, team productivity, staff additions and losses, and gradual, measured productivity improvements over time.

An effective organization measures its capacity and makes plans based on its measured, empirical performance history—typically based on each team's velocity. This approach contrasts with a more visceral approach in which an organization bases its plans on the expectation that its teams will demonstrate abrupt increases in capacity (that is, "insert miracle here").

The difference in approaches to self-assessed capacity for technical work comes into play in project-portfolio planning and in setting project deadlines. If the organization views its own capacity clearly, it will distribute work and assign deadlines that can be met by the teams. If the organization bases its plans on the assumption of abrupt increases in capacity or on unknown capacity, it will overload its teams and set up the teams and the overall organization for failure.

Aggressive views of organizational capacity—and the project pressure that ensues—give rise to several unintended, ultimately destructive consequences:

- Teams aren't able to meet their commitments (sprint goals), which in turn means the organization isn't able to meet its commitments.
- Because teams aren't able to meet their commitments, team members do not feel a sense of Mastery over their work and their motivation suffers.

- Excessive loading on teams competes with the Growth Mindset, which undermines the ability of the team and organization to improve over time.
- Excessive loading also results in burnt-out teams, higher turnover, and reduced capacity.

As I wrote in *Rapid Development* more than 20 years ago, leaders apply pressure to their teams in the belief that the pressure will create a sense of business urgency and force useful prioritization. In practice, the attempt to instill business urgency most often has the effect of sending teams into full-scale, counterproductive panic—even when the leaders perceive themselves as applying only a tiny amount of pressure (McConnell, 1996).

Agile development today offers useful tools for prioritizing work at both the team level and organization level. Use those tools instead of applying pressure.

Establish Communities of Practice

Organizations we've worked with have found that establishing communities of practice to support the Agile roles accelerates effective performance of the roles. Composed of people who share an interest in what they do and want to get better at it, each community defines the kind of interaction that works best for its members. For example, meetings can be in-person in real-time, or they can be online.

The focus of community-of-practice discussions can be any or all of the following:

- Share knowledge generally; coach junior members
- Discuss common problem scenarios and solutions
- Share experiences with tools
- Share lessons learned from retrospectives (and invite feedback)

- Identify areas of weak performance in the organization
- Network
- Identify best practices within the organization
- Share frustrations, vent, and support one another

You can set up communities of practice for Scrum Masters, Product Owners, Architects, QA staff, SAFe Program Consultants (SPCs), Agile Coaches, DevOps staff, and other specialties. Participation is usually voluntary and self-selected so that only people who are interested participate.

The Role of the Organization in Supporting More Effective Agile

Some attributes that support successful teams are under the teams' control; many are controlled at the organizational level.

Agile teams cannot be successful if their organizations undermine their efforts. Organizations do this by blaming teams for mistakes, not supporting the teams' Autonomy, not adequately communicating the teams' Purpose, and not allowing for growth of the teams over time. Of course, this is not unique to Agile teams; it's true of teams in general.

Teams can be most successful if their organizations support them by establishing a blame-free culture organization-wide, staffing the teams with the full skill set needed, loading the teams with appropriate workloads, regularly communicating the teams' purposes, and supporting the teams' growth over time.

Depending on where you are in your Agile journey, other leaders in your organization might need to take this journey with you. If you refer back to the Agile boundary you drew in Chapter 2 ("What's Really Different About Agile?"), you can identify those other leaders and make plans for how to work with them.

Suggested Leadership Actions

Inspect

* Reflect on your reactions to your teams' mistakes over the past few weeks or months. Would your teams interpret your reaction as decriminalizing mistakes and emphasizing the opportunity to learn from them? Do you model learning from mistakes in your behavior?

* Interview your team members to assess their level of psychological safety. Can they take risks without feeling insecure or embarrassed?

* Perform a gap analysis between your organization and the generative culture in Westrum's model.

* Review your organization's approach to assigning workloads to teams. Are you setting expectations based on observed empirical capacity for work?

Adapt

* Make a personal resolution to decriminalize mistakes in your interactions with your teams.

* Communicate to your teams that you expect them to work at a sustainable pace that allows for learning and growth. Ask them to let you know if schedule expectations are preventing that.

* Make a plan to close the gaps identified in your gap analysis of Westrum's Three Cultures Model.

* Make a plan for how to bring other leaders in your organization along with you on your Agile journey.

Additional Resources

Rozovsky, Julia. 2015. *The five keys to a successful Google team.* [Online] November 17, 2015. [Cited: November 25, 2018.] https://rework.withgoogle.com/blog/five-keys-to-a-successful-google-team/. This article describes the work on organizational culture at Google.

Westrum, Ron, 2005. "A Typology of Organisational Cultures." Quality and Safety in Health Care, January 2005, pp. 22-27. This is Westrum's definitive paper on his Three Cultures Model.

Forsgren, Nicole, et al. 2018. *Accelerate: The Science of Lean Software and DevOps: Building and Scaling High Performing Technology Organizations.* This book contains a discussion of Westrum's organizational culture model applied to IT organizations.

Curtis, Bill, et al, 2009. *People Capability Maturity Model (P-CMM), Version 2.0, 2nd Ed.* This document describes an approach to maturing Human Resources practices in technical organizations. The approach is logical, and the value seems apparent. The document can be difficult to read. I suggest starting with Figure 3.1 for context.

More Effective Agile Measurement

⌐

Less effective Agile implementations sometimes treat measurement as the enemy. More effective Agile implementations use measurement to include quantitative data in their process-change decisions, rather than basing decisions on subjective opinion alone.

This is the first of three chapters that discuss quantitative approaches to Agile development. This chapter describes how to establish a meaningful measurement baseline. Chapter 19, "More Effective Agile Process Improvement," discusses how to use the measures for process and productivity improvement. Chapter 20, "More Effective Agile Predictability," discusses estimation.

Measuring Quantity of Work

Measurement begins by measuring how much work is being done. On Agile projects, that means measuring work-item sizes in *story points*. A story point is a measure of a work item's size

and complexity. Agile teams use story points primarily for estimating, planning, and tracking their work. Story points are
useful for measuring process improvements and productivity
improvements, too.

Agile teams most often use story point scales based on the Fibonacci numbers from 1–13 (1, 2, 3, 5, 8, and 13). Each work
item is assigned a size in story points, and the sizes of the individual work items are added to arrive at the work's total size in
story points.

Non-Fibonacci values, such as 4 and 6, are not used. This helps
to avoid the false precision of debating whether a story is a 5 or
a 6 when the team doesn't really even know whether the story is
a 3, 5, or 8.

In an ideal world, there would be a universal standard for how
each story point is measured and assigned. But in the real world,
each team defines its own scale for how large a story point is on
that particular team. After working with its scale a while, the
team gets synched up on how big a 1 is, how big a 5 is, and so
on. Most teams need experience actually assigning story points
before their story point scale stabilizes.

Once story points have been assigned, the team does not change
story point assignments based on actual performance. If a story
was assigned 5 story points initially but feels more like an 8 by
the time it's completed, it remains a 5.

Velocity

Once the size of the work has been established through story
points, the next step is to calculate the rate at which work is
completed.

On Agile teams, "story points per sprint" make up the team's
velocity. A team that completes 42 story points in a sprint has a
velocity of 42 for that sprint. A team that completes 42 story

points in one sprint, 54 in the next sprint, 51 in the next, and 53 in the sprint after that has an average velocity of 50.

Velocities of individual sprints fluctuate and are not usually meaningful. Trends in average velocity over time are more revealing. Once the team has established a baseline velocity that it believes accurately represents its work-completion rate, the team can begin experimenting with process changes and observe how those changes affect its velocity. How to do that is discussed more in Chapter 19.

Some teams also track *scope velocity*, which is the rate at which work is added to an ongoing project.

Small Stories

For general use (not in support of measurement), some teams will use additional story point values—such as 21, 40 and 100 (round numbers) or 21, 34, 55, 89 (Fibonacci numbers)—to represent themes, epics, and larger backlog items.

For the sake of supporting meaningful measurement, stories should be decomposed so that they fit onto the scale of 1–13, and teams should take care to apply the story points proportionately. A story that's assigned 5 story points should be about 5/3 as large as a story that's assigned 3 story points. This allows a team to perform meaningful numeric operations, such as adding up total story points.

Numbers like 21, 40 and 100 are not meant to be used in the same way. They are more metaphorical than numeric, and for measurement purposes they should be avoided.

Short Iterations

Velocity is computed on a per-sprint basis, so the shorter you make your sprints, the more often you can update your team's velocity. When compared to Sequential software development, in which whole-lifecycle iterations can take quarters or years, and therefore require quarters or years to fully calibrate a team's productivity, short iterations allow a team's velocity to be calibrated within only a couple of months.

Comparing Teams' Velocities

Each team creates its own story point scale, based on the specific kind of work it's doing. Leaders naturally want to compare team performance, but there are too many differences in teams' work to allow for meaningful cross-team comparisons. Teams vary based on:

- Different kinds of work (greenfield vs. legacy, front end vs. back end, scientific vs. business systems, and so on)
- Different technical stacks, or different parts of the same stack
- Different stakeholders who provide different levels of support
- Different numbers of team members, including team members being added and subtracted at different times
- Different responsibility for production support
- Different exceptions to their usual velocities because of training, vacation schedules, release schedules, holiday schedules at different geos, and other factors

Even though all teams are using story points, it is not meaningful to compare one team's velocity to another. It's as though one team is playing baseball, another team is playing soccer, and another is playing basketball. Or one is playing NBA basketball and another is playing summer league basketball. Comparing runs, goals, and points across teams is not meaningful.

Leaders who have tried to compare team performance by using velocity say that the effort is toxic. It pits teams against one another. Teams are aware that the comparisons are based on unreliable data, so they regard the comparisons as unfair. The result is a reduction in morale and productivity—the opposite of the purpose of comparing the teams in the first place.

Measuring Quality of Work

In addition to quantity of work, quality of work can be measured—and should be measured—so that the team doesn't focus solely on quantity and neglect quality.

Rework percentage (R%) is the percentage of effort focused on rework vs. new development. As I mentioned in Chapter 11, "More Effective Agile Quality," rework is a useful proxy for inefficiency or waste on software projects. A high R% can indicate that the team is not spending enough time refining stories before implementing them, does not have a strict enough Definition of Done, is not adhering to its Definition of Done, is not testing adequately, is allowing technical debt to accumulate, or other problems.

On Sequential projects, rework tends to accumulate at the end of the project—unplanned—and is therefore quite visible. On Agile teams, rework tends to be worked off more incrementally, and it is therefore less noticeable. But it's still there, and it's useful to monitor R% on Agile teams.

The use of story points provides a foundation for measuring rework. Stories can be classified as new work or rework. R% is calculated as the amount of rework in story points divided by total work in story points. The team can then monitor whether its R% increases or decreases over time.

Teams often need to align on what counts as rework. For teams working on legacy systems, reworking issues created by earlier teams should count as new work. For a team that is fixing issues that it created earlier itself, that work should count as rework.

An alternative to measuring R% is to set a policy that rework is simply not assigned story points. You won't be able to calculate a rework ratio, but if the team spends much time on rework, you'll see its velocity decrease because the time spent on rework does not add to the team's story point count.

In either approach, the purpose is to balance the quantity-oriented measure of velocity with a quality-oriented measure.

General Measurement Considerations

While using Agile-specific measures, leaders of Agile teams should keep in mind a few general keys to successful software measurement.

Set Expectations About Measurement

Be transparent about why you're measuring and how you intend to use the measures. Software teams are concerned that measures might be used unfairly or incorrectly, and many organizations' track records make that a valid concern. Be clear that the measures are intended to support each team's self-improvement—this will help adoption of the measures.

What Gets Measured, Gets Done

If you measure only one thing, people naturally optimize for that one thing, and you can experience unintended consequences. If you measure only velocity, teams can cut retrospectives, skip daily scrums, relax their Definitions of Done, and increase technical debt in the attempt to improve velocity.

Be sure to include a balanced set of measures for teams to optimize against, including quality and customer satisfaction, so that teams don't optimize for velocity at the expense of other objectives that count as much or more.

Similarly, it's important to measure what's most important, not just what's easiest to measure. If you could have a team deliver half as many story points but twice as much business value, that would be an easy choice, wouldn't it? So be sure that measuring story points doesn't inadvertently undermine your team's focus on delivering business value.

Other Considerations

Use Data From Tools With Caution

Organizations invest in tools, and technical staff enters defect data, time-accounting data, and story point data. The organization naturally believes the data collected by the tool is valid. This is often not the case.

We worked with one company that was certain it had accurate time-accounting data because it had been requiring staff to enter their time for years. When we reviewed the data, we found numerous anomalies. Two projects that should have had similar amounts of effort varied by a factor of 100 in the hours entered for them. We found that staff didn't understand why the data was being collected and viewed it as bureaucratic. One staff member had written a script to enter time-accounting data, and that script was being widely used—unaltered—so everyone was entering the same data! Other staff members were entering no time-accounting data at all. The data was meaningless.

Suggested Leadership Actions

Inspect

- Review your team's attitudes toward measurement. Do your teams understand that measurement supports them in making changes that will ultimately improve the quality of their work lives?
- Review your teams' story sizes and iteration length. Are the story sizes small and the iterations short, to support more accurate productivity measurement?
- What measure or measures are you using for quality? Do they adequately balance any quantity-oriented measures you are using? In other words, does your set of measures account for everything that's important to your business?
- Review any data your organization is using that is being collected from tools. Investigate whether the data means what you think it does.

Adapt

- Communicate to your teams that the purpose of measurement is to support their work.
- Encourage your teams to begin using story points and velocity if they are not already using them.
- Encourage your teams to begin using a quality-oriented measure such as R% if they are not already using one.
- Discontinue the use of measures that are meaningless or misleading, including invalid data from tools and invalid cross-team comparisons.
- Educate your organization about the hazards of comparing different teams' velocities, if needed.

Additional Resources

Belbute, John. 2019. *Continuous Improvement in the Age of Agile Development.* This practical book contains a detailed discussion of software team measurement and process improvement issues, mostly focusing on quality.

More Effective Agile Process Improvement

☙

How do you summarize effective Agile's approach to process in four words? My answer is, *"Fix systems, not individuals."* I talked previously about decriminalizing mistakes, which is important. But decriminalizing mistakes does not mean ignoring them—it means coming together in an open, respectful, collaborative way to understand the factors that led to the mistake and changing them so that the mistake cannot happen again.

A common misimplementation of Agile is, "Work as fast as possible"—but this prevents ever really getting better. More effective Agile implementations concentrate on going faster by getting better.

Scrum as a Process Improvement Baseline

If we go back to the days of Software Capability Maturity Model (SW-CMM), Level 2 was a "repeatable" process. That established a baseline that supported measured improvements at higher levels in the SW-CMM. A high-fidelity Scrum implementation accomplishes the same purpose. The Scrum team has a baseline process that it follows consistently, and the team can improve from there.

Improving Productivity

The desire to improve productivity is pervasive, but how do you know whether your team is improving? How do you measure productivity?

Although software productivity is next-to-impossible to measure on an absolute scale, story points and velocity provide a way to measure productivity improvement on a *relative* scale, and that sets the stage for dramatic improvements in productivity.

Comparing a team to itself over time is the primary, valid use of story points for productivity measurement. If a team had been averaging 50 story points its first 5 sprints, and it averaged 55 story points its second 5 sprints, that suggests that the team's productivity has increased.

Team Productivity Improvement

The first step in improving productivity is to establish a measured, believable productivity baseline using velocity, as described in Chapter 18, "More Effective Agile Measurement."

Once you have established a velocity baseline, you make a change and compare the team's velocity for the next few sprints to the baseline velocity. After a few sprints, you'll gain insight into whether the change increased or decreased productivity.

Here are some examples of changes whose effects you can measure by using velocity over time:

- You introduce a new collaboration tool
- You change part of the technology stack
- You move the Product Owner from onshore to offshore on a geographically distributed team
- You tighten up your Definition of Ready and spend more time refining stories before implementation work begins
- You change your sprint cadence from 3 weeks to 2
- You move your team from cubes to an open work bay
- You add a team member partway through a release

A change in the numbers will not always be definitive, of course. In general, with productivity measurement, it's good to adopt the attitude that, "Measurements give you questions to ask and suggest places to look, but they don't necessarily give you the answers."

What's Possible With Team Productivity Improvement

Short sprints provide frequent opportunities to experiment with process changes, track the results of changes, and build on the successful changes. Improvements accumulate rapidly with this approach. We have seen teams double their productivity or better.

Some implications of this can be unexpected. We've seen multiple instances in which teams wanted to "vote a problem team member off the island" because of poor performance. In each case, the story was similar. The manager asked, "If we remove that person, will you commit to keeping your velocity the same?" The team responded, "No, we will commit to *increasing our velocity*, because that person is dragging us down."

In another instance, we worked with a digital content firm that had teams at two sites. The first site had a team of 15 staff members, and the second site had a team of 45. Through rigorously tracking its velocity, monitoring work in progress, and analyzing its wait states, the team at the first site concluded that it was spending more time and effort coordinating with the second site than the second site's work was worth. The second site was retasked to a different project, and the original project's *overall output increased* with just the 15-person team at the first site. They effectively quadrupled their productivity through a disciplined use of Agile productivity measures.

Organizational Influences on Productivity

Scrum experts repeat this mantra: "Scrum doesn't solve your problems, but it shines a bright light on them so that you can see what they are." Sometimes Scrum exposes issues the team can work on by itself, and sometimes it exposes issues that need to be addressed by the organization. Organizational issues we have seen include these:

- Difficulty hiring qualified staff

- High staff turnover

- Too little professional development

- Too little manager training

- Unwillingness to remove problem team members

- Unwillingness to follow Scrum rules, such as "No changes mid-sprint"

- Inability to staff special roles (Scrum Master, Product Owner)

- Frequent changes in business direction

- Dependencies on other teams; unresponsive other teams

- Excessive multi-tasking across projects, including required product support

- Lack of support from business staff; slow decisions

- Slow decisions from executives

- Bureaucratic company work practices

- Team scattered across numerous development sites

- Inadequate support for travel across sites

Comparing Productivities Across Teams

While most cross-team velocity comparisons cannot be made meaningfully, one type of comparison is valid—the rate of productivity increase across teams. If most of your teams are increasing their productivities 5–10% per quarter and one team is increasing 30% per quarter, you can review that team's performance and investigate whether it is doing something the other teams can learn from. You'll still need to account for changes in team composition or other non-productivity factors that might have influenced the change.

Bottom Line on Productivity Improvement

Software productivity measurement is a minefield, but saying that measures are imperfect and infallible is not the same as saying they can't be used. Used with care, productivity measurement supports rapid increases in team performance.

Disciplined Mapping and Monitoring of Work in Progress

As organizations move beyond basic Scrum, it becomes useful to mix in Lean as a way to support improvements in quality and productivity. Kanban is the Lean technique most often used to implement Lean's requirement to visualize and map work flow across a value stream.

Kanban emphasizes examining "work in progress" (WIP), defining how much WIP exists in a system at present, and then gradually imposing limits on WIP to expose delays that are limiting throughput.

Kanban systems typically use a physical Kanban board like the one shown on the next page:

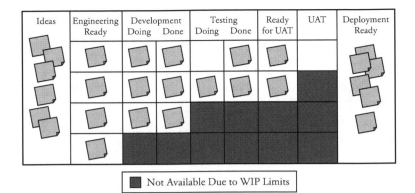

■ Not Available Due to WIP Limits

"Kanban" means signboard or billboard in Japanese. Work items on a Kanban board ("Kanban cards") are captured on sticky notes. Work items move left to right, but work is pulled from the right rather than pushed from the left, as open spaces on the Kanban board allow. In the board shown above, a work item could be pulled into UAT or Testing, but there is no open capacity for work to be pulled into any other state.

In Lean terms, work is always in one of three categories:

- *Value*—work that immediately adds concrete value and that the customer is willing to pay for.
- *Necessary waste*—work that doesn't add value on its own but that is the supporting work necessary for adding value, such as testing, procuring software licenses, and so on.
- *Unnecessary waste*—work that doesn't add value, that hurts throughput, and that can be eliminated.

The function of WIP limits is to expose waiting time, which is a large source of waste on software projects. Examples of waiting time include:

- Waiting for completion of manual acceptance testing after code has been unit tested, integration tested, and checked in before the functionality can be deployed.

- Waiting for bugs detected by an independent testing organization to be fixed by development before the software can be deployed.
- Waiting for a code review before a story can be completed in a sprint.
- Waiting for a team at one location to check in code that needs to be completed before a team at another location can proceed with its work.
- Waiting for a Product Owner to refine a story before the Development Team can begin implementing the story.
- Waiting for an executive decision maker to make a decision that determines which path a team will take.

One way or another, waiting time on software projects delays functionality from being released and, therefore, is always a form of waste.

When teams first map their work flows, they usually find that they have too much WIP—usually, far too much WIP!

A disciplined focus on WIP will highlight that improvements to throughput are rarely related to maximizing utilization of individual staff members. The desire to keep every staff member busy at all times more often creates WIP, which creates bottlenecks, which reduces throughput. Attention to WIP can be incredibly useful in helping an organization shift from maximizing busyness to maximizing throughput.

A detailed discussion of Kanban and Lean is beyond the scope of this book. Further reading is suggested at the end of this chapter.

The Agile Retrospective

The retrospective meeting is the primary time at which new improvements are considered and prior improvements are assessed. On Scrum projects, the sprint retrospective is held at the end of the sprint, after the sprint review and prior to sprint planning for the next sprint.

The purpose of the retrospective is to inspect how the sprint went, generate improvement ideas, evaluate improvement ideas that have been implemented from prior retrospectives, and create a plan for implementing improvements in the next sprint. The Scrum Master facilitates the meeting, and the whole Scrum team participates.

The general flow of the meeting follows this sequence:

1. Set the stage. Suggest an improvement mindset; remind everyone to focus on fixing the system. One organization begins each retrospective with a joke, which sets a tone of decriminalizing errors and psychological safety.
2. Gather input; create a shared pool of information.
3. Generate insights; look for patterns; look for root causes; review the big picture.
4. Decide what to do; identify experiments to be conducted by the team; create an action plan.
5. Close the retrospective, including reviewing how the retrospective itself could be improved.

The focus of the retrospective can be on any areas that could improve performing during the next sprint, including

* Processes and practices
* Communication
* Environment
* Work products
* Tools

The retrospective is time-boxed. A typical length for a 2-week sprint is 75 minutes.

Teams vary in their perspective on whether outside participants should be allowed to observe or participate in retrospectives. Management can always review the improvement plans that emerge from the retrospective, but I believe that maximizing candor within the retrospective itself is more valuable than allowing outside observers.

Allow Time for Changes to Take Effect

Current Scrum practice is to ensure that each retrospective results in at least one change being made in the next sprint. The effect of that change is reviewed at a future retrospective, and it is either retained or discontinued. Changes can go into the product backlog and be scheduled as future sprint deliverables.

The desire to keep a team from becoming complacent is sensible; however, I think the practice goes too far. It should be balanced against the need to measure the effects of each change. Too many changes introduced too quickly will obscure the effect on velocity.

Allow time for the environment to stabilize around any changes so that you can understand the effect of each change. Changes sometimes introduce an initial productivity drop before improving productivity, so allow for that.

Review of Story Point Assignments in Retrospectives

Story point assignments are not changed after they have been assigned, but they can be reviewed during retrospectives. If the team agrees that a story's as-built size was within one Fibonacci number of its assignment (e.g., it was assigned a 3 but turned out to be more like a 5), the assignment is considered to be good enough. If the assignment was off by more than one, count it as a miss, and track how many stories missed.

The number of misses can be used as an indicator of whether the team is doing sufficient backlog refinement prior to assigning story points, whether it is decomposing stories sufficiently, whether it is discussing stories thoroughly enough during sprint planning, and so on.

Beware of Gaming of Measures

As you work on process improvement, be sure that improvements are genuine, not just changes in what work is being measured or team composition.

Different teams take different approaches to what kinds of work are assigned story points (which is one of many reasons that cross-team comparisons are such a challenge, and cross-organization comparisons are pointless). Some teams assign story points to defect correction work, and some don't. Some assign story points to spikes, some don't. Some of these variations work better than others, in my experience, but what never works is changing the kind of work that counts as story points instead of making genuine process improvements.

If you find a team that's gaming its measures, treat that as an opportunity to decriminalize the mistake. Take a systems view of the behavior, and fix the system that's causing the problem. According to the "Mastery" part of Autonomy, Mastery, and Purpose, teams generally want to improve. If you find a team that is gaming the system rather than using measurement to improve, investigate what is undermining the team's natural desire to improve. Is it excessive schedule pressure? Insufficient time for reflection and adaptation? Lack of permission to make process changes that would lead to improvement? This is an opportunity to reflect on your performance as a leader and assess the effect that's having on your teams.

Inspect and Adapt

In addition to the formal retrospective, the Inspect and Adapt mentality should apply end to end on Agile projects. Scrum provides several structural opportunities for Inspect and Adapt to occur:

* Sprint planning
* Sprint review
* Sprint retrospective
* Any time a defect is discovered to have escaped beyond its sprint

Effective use of Inspect and Adapt depends on having some *impatience*. Teams that are patient with their problems end up living with them for a long time and not improving. Teams that insist on doing something about their problems can improve incredibly rapidly.

Effective use of Inspect and Adapt can also benefit from some structure and transparency. We've had success with teams putting proposed process changes into their product backlogs and prioritizing and planning process improvement work along with their other work. This helps avoid the failure mode of retrospective findings becoming "write-only" documents and avoids the issue of too many changes being made at one time.

Other Considerations

Measuring Individuals

Numerous fields have attempted to measure productivity of individuals, including medicine, education, and software. In all cases, there is no valid way to measure individual productivity. The best doctors might take on the most challenging patients; they can have lower cure rates than other doctors, even though they are the best. The best teachers might work in the most difficult schools; their students might have lower test scores, even if the teachers are better. The best software developers might get assigned the most complex work, in which case their apparent productivity will be lower than average developers.

Differences in technical task assignments, multi-tasking across multiple projects, interpersonal dynamics with other team members, level of stakeholder support for their projects, time spent mentoring other staff members, and countless other factors affect each individual's output. Outside of research settings, software projects contain too many confounding variables to allow for meaningful productivity measurements of individuals.

Agile's focus is on the team, rather than on individuals. Team-level measures are more culturally consistent with Agile, and they're also much more valid.

Suggested Leadership Actions

Inspect

- Investigate whether your teams' Scrum practice is consistent enough to form a baseline against which you can measure.
- Review your team's performance in their sprint reviews, retrospectives, and sprint planning. Are they taking advantage of these opportunities to Inspect and Adapt?
- How well are you as a leader supporting your teams in improving, especially when balancing short-term delivery needs against longer-term improvement objectives?
- Map your work flow and look for delays. Assess how much waste you have in your delivery process due to unnecessary delays.

Adapt

- Begin measuring the effect of process changes by using story points.
- Encourage your teams to make consistent use of Inspect and Adapt during the relevant Scrum events.
- Proactively communicate to your teams that retrospectives are important and that you support your teams making changes immediately, in the next sprint, based on findings in their retrospectives.
- Visualize your teams' work by using Kanban, and look for delays.

Additional Resources

Derby, Esther and Diana Larsen. 2006. *Agile Retrospectives: Making Good Teams Great.* This is a resource on conducting Agile retrospectives.

Hammarberg, Marcus and Joakim Sundén. 2014. *Kanban in Action.* A good introduction to Kanban in a software context.

Poppendieck, Mary and Tom. 2006. *Implementing Lean Software Development.* This is another software-focused introduction to Lean/Kanban.

Oosterwal, Dantar P. 2010. *The Lean Machine: How Harley-Davidson Drove Top-Line Growth and Profitability with Revolutionary Lean Product Development.* This book describes a case study of turning around Harley-Davidson's product development efforts through an application of Lean.

McConnell, Steve. 2011. What does 10x mean? "Measuring Variations in Programmer Productivity." This chapter in *Making Software: What Really Works, and Why We Believe It* describes the variations in individual developer productivity and provides more detail about the challenges of measuring it in a commercial setting.

McConnell, Steve. 2016. "Measuring Software Development Productivity" [online webinar]. This webinar provides more detail on measuring team productivity.

CHAPTER TWENTY

More Effective Agile Predictability

⌇

Decades ago, Tom Gilb asked the question, "Do you want predictability, or do you want control?" (Gilb, 1988). With little fanfare, Agile has caused a shift in many organizations' answer to that question. Sequential development tended to define a fixed feature set and then estimate the schedule—the focus was on *predicting* the schedule. Agile development tends to define a fixed schedule and then define the most valuable functionality that can be delivered in that time frame—the focus is on *controlling* the feature set.

Much of the Agile literature has focused on software development for markets that prioritize timeliness above predictability: consumer-oriented mobile applications, games, SaaS applications, Spotify, Netflix, Etsy, and so on. But what do you do if your customers still want predictability? What if your organization needs to deliver a specific feature set *and* it still needs to know how long it will take to deliver that feature set? Or what if you just want to get an idea of approximately how much functionality can be delivered in approximately how much time as an aid to optimizing the combination of functionality and schedule?

Agile has most often emphasized feature set control, but Agile practices also provide excellent support for predictability, if appropriate practices are selected.

Predictability at Different Points in the Release Cycle

Agile-specific estimation practices are not available in the very early days of a project. Prior to populating the product backlog, the practices used for early-in-the-project estimates will be the same regardless of whether the project will later be conducted as Sequential or Agile (McConnell, 2006). It is not until the team begins working in sprints that the distinction between Agile and Sequential becomes relevant.

Figure 20-1 shows the point in the project at which Agile-specific estimation practices become relevant, expressed in terms of software's Cone of Uncertainty.

There is an exception to this pattern, which is that if you want a combination of predictability and control, rather than pure predictability, Agile practices come into play slightly earlier.

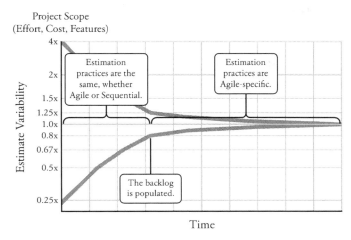

Figure 20-1

Estimation practices in terms of the Cone of Uncertainty. Agile-specific practices come into play after the backlog has been populated. Adapted from (McConnell, 2006).

Kinds of Predictability

Approaches to predictability are introduced and described briefly below and then are discussed in more detail in the sections that follow.

Strict predictability of cost and schedule. Sometimes you need to predict the cost and schedule for an exact feature set. Maybe you're replicating an exact set of functionality on a new platform. Maybe you're developing a specific set of functionality for a hardware device that has already been built. Maybe you're developing software under a non-Agile contract. All of these scenarios are about prediction and downplay feature-set control. They are not the most common cases, but they do come up from time to time.

Strict predictability of features. Sometimes you need to predict the exact features that will be available at a fixed date with a fixed budget. This is a variation of the first scenario, and the practices used to support it will be similar.

Loose predictability. Sometimes you need to predict the feasibility of an approximate combination of functionality, cost, and schedule. None of the parameters is strictly fixed; each has at least a little flexibility. This kind of predictability is often needed during budgeting when you're trying to assess whether a business case for developing loosely defined functionality exists. Loose predictability is also often needed while a project is underway to track progress. Loose predictability can be accomplished through an iterative process that involves prediction combined with control.

The next two sections describe what's required to achieve strict predictability. Even if you don't need strict predictability, the considerations involved in achieving it are relevant to achieving the loose predictability I describe in the last section.

Strict Predictability of Cost and Schedule

If you need predictability about cost and schedule with an exact, fixed feature set, predictability comes into play after the exact feature set has been defined—which is usually 10–30% of the way into a release cycle.

These key Agile practices support strict predictability:

- Story point assignment
- Velocity computation
- Small stories
- Up-front population, estimation, and refinement of the product backlog
- Short iterations
- Release burndown

- Accounting for variability in velocity

If you don't need strict predictability of cost and schedule, you might skip ahead to the next section, "Strict Predictability of Feature Set." However, some of the concepts in this section are referenced in later sections, so you might at least skim the headings before moving on.

Predictability Support: Story Point Assignment

Direct estimation of effort is subject to issues of both bias and subjectivity (McConnell 2006). Bias is the intentional adjustment of the estimation in the desired direction. Subjectivity is the unintentional adjustment of the estimate due to wishful thinking or insufficient skill in estimation. The history of software development is that estimation is nearly always on the optimistic side, leading to a systemic tendency for individuals and teams to underestimate.

Story points are useful in part because they are not subject to bias. Instead of estimating effort directly, teams use story points to assign relative sizes to work items. People will often have a conversion factor in mind from hours to story points when they assign story points, but errors in those conversion factors don't undermine the estimate because of the way that story points are used. Story points are used to compute velocity, which is calculated empirically, based on actual performance. A team might be optimistic in thinking, "We can complete 100 story points this sprint." At the end of the sprint when they've completed 50 story points rather than 100, their velocity is 50, not 100, and that's the number that is used for future planning.

Predictability Support: Velocity Computation

The most common use of velocity is for sprint planning, one sprint at a time. An equally valuable use of velocity is to support predictability. If a team has been working at a sustainable pace and completing 50 story points per sprint for the past 3 sprints (an average velocity of 50), the team can use its average velocity to predict when it will deliver the total amount of functionality.

Suppose your company is planning a release that's 12 months out and consists of 1,200 story points. A 12-month schedule allows 26 biweekly sprints. The team works for 8 weeks (4 sprints) and sees an average velocity of 50 story points per sprint. At that time it's valid to predict that the team will require 1,200/50 = 24 sprints to complete the planned work. The team can likely deliver that feature set in its one-year timeframe.

There are a few ifs, ands, or buts on this statement. The stories that are used to calibrate the team's velocity need to be 100% complete—they must fully meet a rigorous Definition of Done. Also, the team can't be accumulating technical debt that it will need to pay off later in the release cycle, because that will drag down its velocity in later sprints. The projection of velocity needs to account for vacation and holiday schedules. Plans need to account for any work still needed after Definition of Done, such as User Acceptance Test, System Test, and so on. The velocity must also account for the sprint-to-sprint variability shown by the team (more on that later). But compared to traditional Sequential project estimation, the ability of a team to produce an empirically based calibration of its productivity early into a release cycle—and to use that to predict a completion date—is a powerful capability.

Predictability Support: Small Stories

As discussed in Chapter 18, "More Effective Agile Productivity Measurement," keeping stories small supports measurement of progress on Agile projects.

Predictability Support: Up-front Population, Refinement, and Estimation of the Product Backlog

The team that needs strict predictability will need to populate the product backlog with their release's full set of stories up front—that is, adopt a more Sequential approach to populating the backlog.

They don't need to refine the stories in as much detail as they would in a full Sequential approach. They need to refine them enough to be able to assign story points to each backlog item, which is more than they would refine them up front in a typical Agile approach. Then they actually assign story points to each backlog item, which is known as "story pointing the backlog."

It's difficult to elaborate every single story into enough detail to support meaningful story point assignments on the 1–13 scale early in a project. I'll provide suggestions about how to address that issue later in this chapter.

Predictability Support: Short Iterations

As discussed in Chapter 18, the shorter your iterations are, the more quickly you develop productivity data that can be used to forecast a team's progress.

Predictability Support: Release Burndown

Monitoring ongoing progress against the team's initial prediction is handled organically, in the normal flow of work. The team uses a release burndown to track the number of story points completed each sprint. If the team's velocity begins to change from its initial average of 50, it can inform stakeholders and adjust plans accordingly.

Predictability Support: Accounting for Variability in Velocity

Any team's velocity will show variability from sprint to sprint. A team that averages 50 story points per sprint might actually have completed sprints of 42, 51, 53, and 54 story points. This suggests that using the team's velocity to predict a long-range outcome includes some variability or risk.

The team with those four sprints showed a sample standard deviation of 5.5 story points vs. its average of 50. You can calculate a confidence interval based on the number of sprints completed to estimate risk to the team's ultimate, whole-project velocity. And you can update that as the team completes more sprints and gains more experience.

Figure 20-2 shows an example of using initial velocity and a confidence interval to illustrate potential low and high velocity.

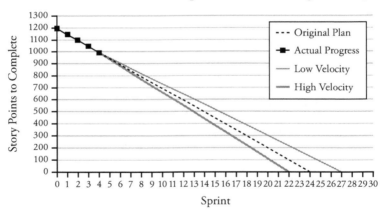

Figure 20-2

The team's average velocity, variability in velocity, and a mathematical computation of a confidence interval can be used to compute variations in project outcomes.

As shown in the figure, based on a 90% confidence interval,[4] the team is showing that it will require a total of 22–27 sprints to complete the work of 1,200 story points, with a nominal of 24 sprints. The team has demonstrated low variability in its velocity, which produces a narrow range of possible outcomes. There's a risk of a one-week overrun, but it's most likely that the team will complete within its one-year timeline.

Because of how confidence intervals are calculated, the more sprints the team completes, the more the range will tighten up and the better the predictability will be. If the team's next four sprints showed the same variability as the first four, the 90% confidence interval would shrink the range to 23–26 total sprints to complete the work.

Working with a team's velocity is never an exercise in pure predictability because one of the goals is to help teams achieve stability in their velocities. As teams work to improve their practices, their variability should come down and predictability should improve.

---

[4] A "confidence interval" is a specific (and complicated) statistical calculation of how confident you can be that the observed mean (average) is close to the actual mean. In this example, a 90% confidence interval says you can be 90% confident that the actual mean of the velocity will be between 44 and 56, implying a number of sprints between 22 and 27 (taking into account the 4 sprints that have already been completed). Some teams use standard deviation to compute possible outcomes, but that is not mathematically correct. Standard deviation provides a prediction of the individual sprint velocities that will fall within a range. A confidence interval is the appropriate technique for calculating the range of likely average velocities for the complete set of sprints.

Strict Predictability of Feature Set

If you have a fixed cost and schedule and need to predict exactly what features can be delivered for that fixed cost and schedule, the approach is similar to what was just described. Here's how the strict-feature-set approach plays out across the key Agile practices involved.

Creation of the Product Backlog

The backlog must be fully populated just as it was in the approach used to achieve strict predictability of cost and schedule.

If the team defines and refines stories that add up to more story points than the team has time for, some of that definition and refinement work will be wasted. The more the team can perform its backlog population work from high priority to low priority, the less waste there will be.

Computation of Velocity, used to Predict Functionality

Velocity is used similarly to how it is used in the strict predictability of cost and schedule scenario. However, instead of using velocity to predict an end date, velocity is used to predict the amount of functionality that can be delivered (that is, a number of story points). The variability transfers onto the feature set rather than into the schedule.

Using the same example as above—with a one year schedule—you can apply the confidence interval to predict the story points that can be completed within a fixed number of sprints, rather than predicting the number of sprints required to deliver a fixed number of story points.

Based on a 90% confidence interval after the first 4 sprints, the team should deliver a total of 1,158–1,442 story points after a total of 26 sprints, and chances are good that the team will be able to meet its goal of 1,200 total points.

Looser Approaches to Predictability

The discussion so far has been based on a pure predictability approach. At some point in the project, the organization wants to be able to predict the exact combination of cost, schedule, and functionality that will ultimately be delivered—without changing any of them very much. The need for this level of predictability is common in some industries and comes up only occasionally in others.

The more common need I see is for a looser level of predictability that allows for ongoing management control of cost, schedule, functionality, or all three. As I've written previously, many times the role of estimation is not to make a pin-point prediction but to gain a general sense of whether this general type of work can be completed in that general time frame (McConnell, 2000). This is not really "prediction," because the entity you're predicting keeps changing. It's really a combination of prediction and control. Regardless of how it's characterized, it can meet the organizational need for "predictability" and it can be an effective way to conduct a software project. Agile practices provide good support for this loose predictability.

Loose Predictability During Top-Level Budget Planning

Some Agile coaches recommend using the larger story point values of 21, 40, 100—or the larger Fibonacci numbers such as 21, 34, 55, and 89—for top-level budget planning even if they are not used for detailed estimation. For reasons already described, using those numbers in that way is not valid from a strict prediction point of view. From a looser pragmatic point of view, using numbers in that way can serve a useful purpose. The organization just needs to be aligned on what those larger numbers mean.

Use Large Numbers as Proxies for Risk

You can assign numeric values to epics (or other large items such as themes, features, and so on), recognizing that each use of a larger number adds a little bit more risk to your predictability. Review the ratio of points from detailed stories vs. points from epics. If 5% of your points are from epics, there's not much risk to your overall predictability. But if 50% of the points are from epics, risk to predictability is higher. Depending on how important predictability is to you, that might matter or it might not.

Use Epics as Budgets, When Predictability is Needed

Another approach to estimating epics and other large items is to use numeric estimates and treat those numbers as budgets for detailed work in each area. For example, if you're using a Fibonacci scale and the team estimates an epic as 55 story points, from that point forward you treat the 55 story points as the allowable budget for that epic.

With the epic-as-detailed-budget approach, when your team refines the epic into detailed stories, it is not allowed to exceed the 55-point budget for that epic. Your team will need to prioritize its more detailed stories and choose those that provide the highest business value within the 55-point budget.

This kind of approach is common in other kinds of work. If you do a kitchen remodel, you'll have a total budget for the remodel, and you'll have a detailed budget for cabinets, appliances, countertops, hardware, and so on. The detailed budget approach works equally well for software teams. It provides the organization with a feeling of predictability, one that is achieved through the combination of predictability and control.

From time to time the team will blow its budget—in the example, it won't be able to deliver the essence of the intended functionality within the 55-point budget. That will force a conversation with the business about the priority of the work and whether it's worth extending the budget. This kind of dialog is healthy, and story point assignments facilitate it. It might not provide the same level of predictability that strict-predictability approaches do, but it might be acceptable or even preferable if you value incremental course corrections more than you value pure predictability.

Predicting Delivery Dates for a Combination of Core Feature Set and Additional Features

Some organizations don't need predictability of 100% of a feature set. They need assurance that they can deliver a core feature set within a particular time frame, and they can be opportunistic about the features they deliver beyond that.

If the team we've been using as an example needs to deliver a core feature set of 1,000 story points, it can predict that it will complete that core feature set after about 20 sprints (40 weeks). That leaves a capacity of about 6 sprints or 300 story points for the remainder of the year. The organization can make long-range commitments to its customers about the core features, while still leaving some capacity available to deliver just-in-time functionality.

Predictability and the Agile Boundary

Most organizations can use the looser approaches described in this chapter most of the time and meet their business purposes. Some organizations have higher needs for predictability and need the stricter approaches.

Some Agile purists will complain that elaborating the product backlog to the degree needed to support fine-grain story-pointing up front is "not Agile." But the goal isn't simply to be

Agile (at least not if you care about the topic of this chapter). The goal is to use Agile practices and other practices to support the objectives and strategies of your business, including predictability, if that's what your business needs.

As shown in Figure 20-3, the "Agile boundary" concept described in Chapter 2 ("What's Really Different About Agile?") is useful here.

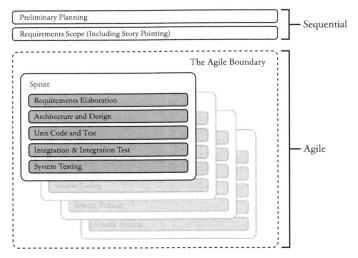

Figure 20-3
The concept of the Agile boundary helps to support long-range predictability—for organizations that need that.

For the sake of strict predictability, some of the early activities will need to be approached more Sequentially, and after that the rest of the project can be conducted in a fully Agile way.

Predictability and Flexibility

The discussion in this chapter has been focused on organizations that have a business need for long-range predictability. Agile practices provide excellent support for that objective.

The fact that an organization needs long-range predictability does not mean it will never change its plans. The business that maps out 1,200 story points of functionality early in the year will sometimes decide to change course halfway through the year. *There is nothing wrong with that.* If the team is using Agile practices, it will be able to respond to the course change in an organized and efficient way. Yes, some of the work on early requirements elaboration will be discarded, amounting to waste, but less work will be discarded than if the team had been using a Sequential approach that fully elaborated each requirement up front. Plus, the team will be able to change direction more easily because of the short-iteration structure of its work.

Other Considerations

Predictability and Cynefin

Fully defining the product backlog early in a release cycle depends on most of the work being in the Cynefin framework's Complicated domain. If the work is mostly Complex, it won't be possible to elaborate the work fully and reliably until it's done. Recall that a major focus of a project operating primarily in the Complex domain is conducting probes to determine the very nature of the problem that needs to be solved.

Strategies such as Barry Boehm's spiral model (Boehm, 1988) have been suggested to investigate projects that have significant Complex aspects and convert them to Complicated before diving into full-scale work. That can be a useful approach for an organization that values predictability. However, not every Complex problem can be converted to Complicated, and work on problems that are mostly Complex will never be very predictable. If you see a project that has mostly Complex elements, ask whether predictability is even theoretically possible for that project.

Predictability and Agile Culture

Predictability can be a touchy subject for Agile teams. One failure mode we've seen with Agile adoptions is teams that refuse to provide estimates, even after their businesses describe sensible reasons for needing them. We've seen more than one Agile adoption shut down for this reason.

We've also seen instances of Agile purists advising teams to avoid providing estimates and instead to coach their whole organization into becoming more Agile so that estimates aren't needed. Aside from being instances of the tail trying to wag the dog, these examples amount to attempts by the development teams to dictate business strategy to the business.

One of the original values described in the Agile Manifesto is *customer collaboration*. If you are the customer and, rather than providing what you're asking for, your Agile teams are insisting that your business needs to redefine itself, you might suggest a renewed focus on that particular Agile value.

Suggested Leadership Actions

Inspect

- What is your particular business's need for flexibility vs. predictability?

- Does your business need strict predictability, or will looser predictability suffice?

- Do your teams understand that the goal of Agile development is to support the needs of the business and that sometimes the business needs predictability?

- Consider the practice of treating epics as budgets. How would that approach work on your teams?

- Assess each of the projects in your portfolio according to the Cynefin framework. Are your teams being asked to estimate work that is inherently Complex?

Adapt

- Talk with your teams about your business's need for predictability. Explain why it's important to your business (if it is important).

- For each Complex project, assess whether the project can be converted to Complicated. For those that remain Complex, shift your focus from prediction to exploration.

- Ask your teams to refine their use of Agile practices to better support your business's need for predictability, including treating epics as budgets.

Additional Resources

McConnell, Steve. 2006. *Software Estimation: Demystifying the Black Art.* This book contains a detailed discussion of software estimation on Sequential and Agile projects. It includes numerous techniques that can be used for early-in-the-project estimation (before the Agile vs. Sequential distinction comes into play). In the time since the book was published in 2006, some of its discussion of requirements' role in estimation has been superceded by the progressive approach to requirements elaboration that's described here in *More Effective Agile.*

More Effective Agile in Regulated Industries

⁓

The early Agile focus on flexibility at all costs created the impression that Agile practices were not well-suited for regulated industries such as life sciences, finance, and government. The focus on "go full Agile or go home" reinforced the impression that Agile practices were not applicable for companies that could not see how to make their customers or their overall product development cycles fully Agile.

This was unfortunate, because so much software is developed under overt regulations, including FDA, IEC 62304, ASPICE, ISO 26262, FedRAMP, FMCSA, SOX, and GDPR. And other software that might not seem regulated can still be subject to rules for privacy, accessibility, and security.

As Agile has matured, it turns out that Agile practices can be as useful and appropriate in many regulated industries as they are anywhere else. It is certainly possible to practice Agile development in a way that will not meet the standards of regulated industries, but it's equally possible to practice Agile development in a way that does.

In 2012, the FDA adopted AAMI TIR45:2012 ("Guidance on the use of AGILE practices in the development of medical device software") as a recognized standard. My company has been working for more than 10 years with numerous companies in FDA-regulated environments and other regulated environments to adopt Scrum and other Agile practices successfully. The discussion in this chapter applies to all but the most heavily regulated industries. FAA/DO-178 regulations, in particular, are more extensive than described in this chapter, and when I refer to "regulated environments" in this chapter, I am not including FAA/DO-178.

How Agile in General Supports Work in Regulated Environments

In general terms, the software-related requirements for regulated environments boil down to this: "Document what you plan to do; do what you said you were going to do; and prove, with documentation, that you did it." Some environments add an additional requirement: "Provide extensive traceability to prove you did all that at a fine level of detail."

Agile practices don't make work on regulated products more or less difficult. The documentation around Agile practices is the greater concern. The efficiency with which documentation can be produced is probably the most important consideration in adapting Agile practices for use in regulated environments.

Sequential practices support efficient creation of documentation on regulated products. Agile's emphasis on incremental and just-in-time practices increases the number of times that documentation must be created or updated. This is not necessarily a problem. Many leaders have told me that Agile development makes documentation easier, because documentation is created more incrementally, just as the software is. However, some aspects of Agile culture need to be modified, such as the focus on the oral tradition and tribal knowledge.

On the next page, Table 21-1 summarizes how the Agile emphases affect compliance in regulated environments.

At a conceptual level, several Agile practices provide support for the intent of regulations, which is to guarantee high-quality software:

* Definition of Done (which is created in a way that meets or exceeds regulatory requirements, including documentation-related requirements)
* Definition of Ready
* Software quality maintained at a releasable level at all times
* Test development either preceding development of code or following immediately behind it
* Automated regression test use
* Regular Inspect and Adapt activities to improve product and process quality

Table 21-1 How the Agile Emphases Come into Play in Regulated Environments

Agile Emphasis	Regulated Environment Implication
Short release cycles	No effect on compliance per se, but the cost of each release can be significant and might affect how often the organization chooses to release.
End-to-end development work performed in small batches	No effect on compliance per se but affects when documentation can be created.
High-level up-front planning with just-in-time detailed planning	Plans must be documented, even just-in-time plans, and traceability can be required, depending on the type of regulation.
High-level up-front requirements with just-in-time detailed requirements	Requirements must be documented, even just-in-time requirements; affects time that documentation is created.
Emergent design	Design must be documented, even just-in-time design; affects time that documentation is created.
Continuous, automated testing, integrated into development	Supports compliance.
Frequent structured collaboration	Some collaboration must shift from oral tradition to documentation.
Overall approach is empirical, responsive, and improvement-oriented	No effect on compliance.

How Scrum in Particular Supports Work in Regulated Environments

Regulations can be slow to be updated. The regulated environment requirements I described above were initially created decades ago, at a time when software development amounted to the Wild West. An organization could have been using practically any approach to develop software, and most of the approaches didn't work very well. Regulations are intended, in part, to avoid chaotic, ad hoc practices with unknown levels of efficacy.

U.S. federal regulations do not generally require a specific software development approach or lifecycle. They require that organizations choose an approach, define it, and document it, as described above. In addition, sometimes they require obtaining approval from the regulator.

Agile practices, especially Scrum, have been formalized and extensively documented (including in this book), which supports this requirement. If a team agrees to use Scrum and documents that it's using Scrum, as defined in a specific document, that contributes to creation of a defined process, which supports regulatory compliance.

Mapping Scrum onto Required Process Documentation

Regulations vary, and this section uses IEC 62304 ("Medical device software—Software life cycle processes") for the sake of illustration.

IEC 62304 requires activities and documentation in the following categories:

* Software development planning
* Requirements analysis
* Software architectural design
* Software detailed design

- Software unit implementation and verification
- Software integration and integration testing
- Software system testing
- Software release

As suggested by AAMI TIR45, these activities can be mapped onto an Agile lifecycle model, as shown in Figure 21-1. This approach effectively divides the regulated Agile project into four layers:

- *The project layer*—the entire set of activities for a project. A project consists of one or more releases.
- *The release layer*—the activities needed to create a usable product. A release consists of one or more increments. (Certain regulatory environments impose significant requirements on releases—for example, the requirement to be able to recreate an exact bit-wise image of any software that has ever been released for the life of the device— which makes releases rare.)
- *The increment layer*—the activities needed to create useful functionality but not necessarily a usable product. An increment consists of one or more stories.
- *The story layer*—the activities needed to create a small, possibly incomplete, piece of functionality.

In a Sequential approach, each activity would be performed mostly in a single phase. With an Agile approach, most activities are spread across layers.

In a nonregulated Agile approach, most activities would be documented informally. With a regulated Agile approach, the activities will be documented more formally.

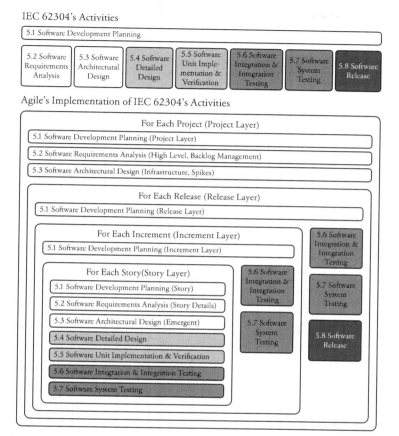

Figure 21-1

Mapping of example regulatory process documentation categories onto Scrum activities. Adapted from (AAMI, 2012).

Partly in support of generating documentation efficiently, the allocation of work across sprints will be adapted to meet regulatory requirements. This approach has been used successfully:

- Use the first sprint (or sprints) to define the general scope of the project, plan for release, and lay out architectural foundations.

- Conduct normal Scrum sprints, by the book. The Definition of Done includes as-built documentation for the sprint, including mapping each user story to code and test cases.
- In preparation for release, perform a documentation sprint that focuses on buttoning up documentation to meet regulatory requirements, including synchronizing requirements and design documentation with code and test outputs and running tests in a formal way that creates verification records.

There are variations on this approach that I'll discuss next.

The Agile Boundary for Regulated Systems

The cost of documentation is a considerable concern in development of regulated software, and it can be useful to apply the "Agile boundary" concept to software development activities. Consider the generic set of software activities.

With no documentation requirements, you might find great value in applying a high degree of iteration from planning, into requirements, all the way through acceptance test. You might find value leaving requirements to be defined just in time, right before unit implementation begins.

With documentation requirements, however, you might decide that it's too costly to provide a high degree of iteration in requirements and it's more cost-effective to use a more Sequential approach. With that in mind, you might draw your Agile boundary after architecture and before software system test, as shown in Figure 21-2.

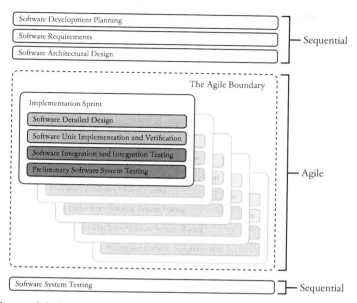

Figure 21-2

An example of where a development initiative in a regulated industry might draw their Agile boundary.

In this scenario, you'll use a mostly Sequential approach for planning, requirements, and architecture; shift to a more incremental approach for detailed implementation work; and shift back to a Sequential approach for software system testing.

Some Agile purists would complain that this approach is "Not really Agile," but, again, the goal is not to be Agile. The goal is to use available software development practices to best support the business. When you factor in the cost of producing documentation, a combination of Sequential and Agile approaches sometimes works best in regulated environments.

Overall, an Agile implementation in a regulated industry will be more formal and structured and require more documentation than a nonregulated Agile implementation. Software teams working in regulated industries will nonetheless benefit from

Agile's shorter end-to-end unit development cycles, continuous testing, tighter feedback loops, frequent structured collaboration, and reduced waste due to a higher proportion of just-in-time planning—and possibly just-in-time requirements and design. They might benefit from building documentation incrementally, too.

Other Considerations

In our work with companies in regulated industries, we have found that "regulatory requirements" do not always come from regulations. Sometimes they come from calcified organizational policies that have lagged behind regulations.

We worked with one life sciences company that enforced design traceability—tracing features through to the specific software modules affected. We analyzed which of the development process requirements were mandated by the FDA and which were required by the company's regulatory group. We were able to eliminate about one-third of the design documentation, which was not mandated by the FDA and was essentially useless.

We have found requirements being treated as regulatory requirements that come from a company's experience with client audits rather than from any regulatory agency. We've also seen that sometimes documentation requirements come from software capitalization rules rather than regulatory requirements.

Overall, I suggest that you be sure to understand the sources of your regulatory requirements. Have a discussion with your regulatory groups to understand which are real regulatory requirements and which are the regulatory group's opinion about what is needed for clients or for financial practices. You can then make decisions about the necessity of carrying forward your company's historic documentation requirements into your current development efforts.

Suggested Leadership Actions

Inspect

- Investigate the sources of the regulatory requirements in your company. Which requirements actually arise from current regulations, and which arise from other sources?
- Review the way in which documentation is being created in your environment. Could Agile practices be used to reduce the cost of documentation?
- Determine where you are currently drawing the Agile boundary for software development activities in your organization. Is it drawn in the best location?

Adapt

- If indicated by your documentation review, create a plan to reduce documentation costs by creating documentation more incrementally.
- Create a plan to redraw the Agile boundary for activities in your organization to better support your organization's goals, including the goal of cost-effective documentation.

Additional Resources

AAMI. 2012. *Guidance on the use of AGILE practices in the development of medical device software.* 2012. AAMI TIR45 2012. This is the definitive reference for Agile in regulated industries at this time.

Collyer, Keith and Jordi Manzano. 2013. Being agile while still being compliant: A practical approach for medical device manufacturers. [Online] March 5, 2013. This readable case study describes how one team met regulatory requirements using an Agile approach.

Scaled Agile, Inc. 2017. "Achieving Regulatory and Industry Standards Compliance with the Scaled Agile Framework® (SAFe®)" Scale Agile, Inc. White Paper, August 2017. This white paper describes how to achieve compliance using SAFe as the specific approach to Agile. It is short and a good complement to this chapter.

More Effective Agile Portfolio Management

Many organizations sequence their project portfolios quite informally. They use intuitive practices to decide which projects to start first and which to finish first.

These organizations do not realize just how much their informal approach to project portfolio management is costing them. If they did, they would choose to burn stacks of $100 bills before they would choose to manage their project portfolios by using seat-of-the-pants methods.

The gap in value between intuitive approaches to portfolio management and mathematically based approaches is wide, and Agile projects' shorter cycle times create even more opportunities to increase the value delivered through a well-managed portfolio.

Weighted Shortest Job First

The primary tool for managing an Agile project portfolio is Weighted Shortest Job First (WSJF).

The concept of Weighted Shortest Job First comes from Don Reinertsen's work on lean product development (Reinertsen, 2009). In Agile development, it's primarily associated with SAFe, but the concept is broadly applicable regardless of whether an organization is using SAFe.

WSJF starts with an identification of the "cost of delay" (CoD) associated with each feature or story. CoD is a not-very-intuitive term that refers to the opportunity cost of *not* having a feature available. If a feature will save your business $50,000 per week once it goes online, the cost of delay is $50,000 per week. If the feature will generate $200,000 per week in revenue once it goes online, the cost of delay is $200,000 per week.

WSJF is a heuristic for minimizing the cost of delay for a set of features. Suppose you have the features in Table 22-1.

Table 22-1 Example Set of Features with Information Needed to Calculate WSJF

Feature	Cost of Delay (CoD)	Development Duration	WSJF: CoD / Duration
Feature A	$50k/week	4 weeks	12.5
Feature B	$75k/week	2 weeks	37.5
Feature C	$125k/week	8 weeks	15.6
Feature D	$25k/week	1 week	25

According to the table, the initial total CoD is $275,000 per week—the sum of all the CoDs for the features. Once you start delivering functionality, you stop incurring CoD for the functionality you've delivered.

The rule in WSJF is that you deliver the feature with the highest WSJF first. If multiple items have the same WSJF, you do the shortest one first.

Suppose that we implemented the features in order from largest CoD to smallest CoD. A diagram of total CoD would look like Figure 22-1.

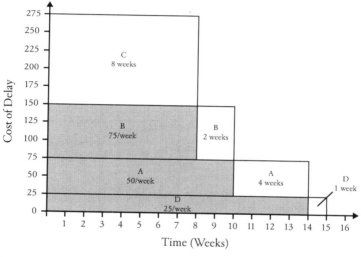

Figure 22-1
Total CoD for example features delivered in descending-CoD order.

The white rectangles represent the feature that is currently in progress—work begins initially on Feature C (highest CoD), then on Feature B, then on A, and finally on D (lowest CoD).

CoD accumulates for each feature until it is completed. Total CoD is calculated as the total area occupied by the rectangles, shaded and unshaded. In this example, the total CoD is $2.825 million: 8 weeks times $125,000/week for Feature C, plus 10 weeks times $75,000/week for Feature B, and so on.

Figure 22-2, on the other hand, shows the features sequenced by descending WSJF—CoD divided by duration—rather than by CoD. The dashed line shows the curve from delivering in simple CoD order.

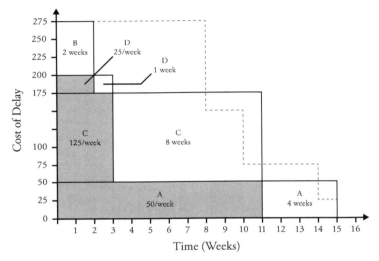

Figure 22-2
Total CoD for example features delivered in descending-WSJF order.

Visually, you can see that the total area in the rectangles when the features are delivered in this order is smaller than the area for the descending-CoD ordering. Mathematically, the total CoD with this sequencing works out to $2.35 million, a decrease in CoD (or increase in business value) of $0.475 million. This is an incredible increase in business value achieved simply by resequencing the order in which you deliver features!

A Common Alternative to WSJF Sequencing That's Much Worse

Sub-optimal sequencing based on cost of delay is common, even though WSJF is a demonstrably better way to sequence delivery. An even worse delivery order—and a common one—

is to level-load all four features on a budgeting cycle, beginning all four features at the beginning of the cycle and not delivering any of them until the end of the cycle.

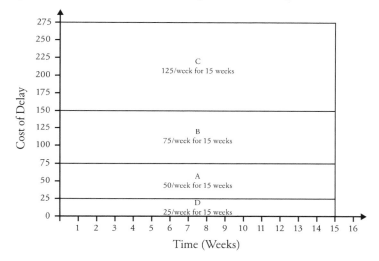

Figure 22-3
Total CoD for features delivered on a budget-cycle basis.

Total CoD for this approach is $4.125 million, which is far worse than either of the other approaches.

A mantra in Lean is "Stop starting, start finishing." The lost opportunity represented in this example would not be very visible in an organization using Sequential development on a quarterly or annual cadence. It becomes much more visible when an organization moves to a weekly or biweekly cadence.

Alternatives to Using Money for Cost of Delay

The examples so far have shown cost of delay in dollars. There are two circumstances in which you might choose to express CoD in different terms.

The cost is a non-monetary cost. In safety-critical environments, the CoD might be that a medical device is not available to save lives or a 911 system is not available to take emergency calls. In these circumstances, you can express CoD in lives, injuries, or other appropriate units. Aside from that, the WSJF calculations are the same.

You don't have good information on cost. A more common scenario is that the cost is a monetary cost, but you don't have accurate or reliable information about the cost of delay. In that case, you can assign a relative cost. Agile teams typically use Fibonacci numbers for this (1, 2, 3, 5, 8, 13, 21). After assigning relative costs, the WSJF calculations are the same.

Other Considerations

T-Shirt Sizing

Described in Chapter 14, "More Effective Agile Requirements Prioritization," the T-shirt sizing approach can be used to plan at the portfolio level, and we have worked with companies that have done that successfully. However, if a company is able to calculate cost of delay for its initiatives, especially if it can calculate it in monetary terms, the significant business value available from using WSJF makes WSJF preferable.

Suggested Leadership Actions

Inspect

- Reflect on what size feature, requirement, or project would be large enough to support calculation of cost of delay in your organization. Would using CoD and WSJF improve your teams' feature-level planning or just project portfolio–level planning?

- Examine your current project portfolio using CoD and WSJF. Obtain CoD information from your business and development duration from your teams. Calculate the total CoD of your current prioritization. Calculate the WSJF order for your portfolio, and then calculate what your overall CoD would be if you resequenced your portfolio in WSJF order.

Adapt

- Sequence your project portfolio using WSJF.
- Consider applying the WSJF approach to smaller-grain items such as epics.

Additional Resources

Reinertsen, Donald G. 2009. *The Principles of Product Development Flow: Second Generation Lean Product Development.* This book contains the description of CoD and WSJF and goes into deep discussions of queueing theory, batch sizes, and increasing flow.

Humble, Jez, et al. 2015. *Lean Enterprise: How High Performance Organizations Innovate at Scale.* This book also discusses WSJF and is more software-specific. It renames WSJF "CD3" (Cost of Delay Divided by Duration).

Tockey, Steve. 2005. *Return on Software: Maximizing the Return on Your Software Investment.* This book contains a detailed discussion of economic decision making in an engineering context, including interesting discussions of decision making under risk and uncertainty.

CHAPTER TWENTY-THREE

More Effective Agile Adoptions

☞

Other parts of this book describe the specific Agile practices that make up the details of an Agile adoption. This chapter discusses adoption itself, a form of organizational change. Whether you're partway through an Agile adoption that's struggling or you're just beginning a new adoption, this chapter describes how to make your adoption successful.

General Change Approach

At the 40,000-foot view, the intuitive approach to Agile adoption seems straightforward:

Phase 1: Begin with a pilot team. Charter an initial team to trial an approach to Agile development in your organization. Work out the stumbling blocks at the single-team level.

Phase 2: Propagate Agile practices to one or more additional teams. Roll out Agile practices to additional teams, making use of lessons learned from the pilot team. Establish communities of practice to share lessons learned. Work out additional kinks, including inter-team issues.

Phase 3: Roll out Agile practices to the entire organization. Making use of lessons learned in Phase 1 and 2, roll out Agile practices to the remainder of the organization. Use the team members from Phase 1 and 2 as coaches for the remaining teams.

This is all logical and intuitive, and it even kind of works. But it omits important elements needed to support a successful rollout, and it overlooks a pivotal relationship between pilot teams and larger scale rollouts.

The Domino Change Model

Organizational change is a big topic, and researchers have been studying it and writing about it for a long time. Harvard professor John Kotter talks about an eight-step process for successful change that follows three phases (Kotter, 2012):

- Creating the climate for change
- Engaging and enabling the organization
- Implementing and sustaining for change

The early 20th-century psychologist Kurt Lewin presented a similar idea:

- Unfreeze
- Change
- Refreeze

These models can be thought-provoking. For anticipating the kinds of support needed for a successful Agile adoption, I like a change model that is inspired by the work of Tim Knoster, which I will refer to as the "Domino Change Model."

In the Domino Change Model (DCM), a successful organization change requires these elements:

- Vision
- Consensus
- Skills
- Resources
- Incentives
- Action plan

If all elements are present, a successful change occurs. If any of the elements is missing, however, the change will not occur. You can think of it as dominoes that must be in place. If any of the dominoes is missing, change will not occur. Figure 23-1 shows what happens when each of the dominoes is missing.

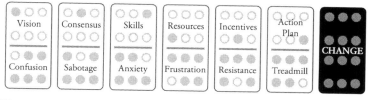

Figure 23-1

The Domino Change Model describes required elements for change and the effects of each missing element.

The remainder of this section walks through these elements.

Vision

According to the DCM, a lack of vision leads to confusion. And this starts with the definition of Agile itself. As I described in Chapter 2 ("What's Really Different About Agile?"), different people can have vastly different understandings of what "Agile" means. Without clear vision, one person will believe that "Agile adoption" refers to the whole business being redesigned to be more nimble. Another will believe it simply means implementing Scrum company-wide. Leadership needs to communicate a clear definition of "Agile."

Beyond that definition, the vision should include a *detailed articulation of the desired end state.* That articulation should include why the Agile adoption needs to occur, what the expected benefits are, how deep and widespread the adoption will be, and how will it affect each person individually—ideally not generically or by category, but one by one.

Pushing a change without clear vision will lead to the perception that "Leadership doesn't know what it's doing."

Consensus

In the DCM, lack of consensus leads to sabotage, and my company has witnessed numerous examples of that. Variations of sabotage include "scrummerfall" (doing waterfall but renaming the practices using Scrum terms), "Scrum-but" (omitting necessary elements of Scrum), little or no energy exerted to overcome minor obstacles, and grumbling and passive resistance.

Leadership pushing a change without building consensus leads to the perception that "Leadership doesn't care about us."

Articulating a clear vision goes a long way toward building consensus, and communicating that actively—far more than you think you need to—is necessary. A clear articulation of benefits is one of the easiest ways to lead an Agile adoption—the teams decide that's what they need to be successful in their jobs.

True consensus building involves two-way communication: leaders describing the vision and being receptive to feedback about the vision. In a true consensus process, the vision might be affected. A leader needs to be open to the possibility of adjusting the vision—which is really just another instance of Inspect and Adapt.

Skills

You can't compel someone to do something they aren't capable of doing, and so trying to perform an Agile adoption without developing the necessary skills leads to anxiety. When leadership tries to push a change without building necessary skills, it creates the perception that "Leadership is unreasonable."

Building skills requires basic nuts-and-bolts professional development, including formal training in the classroom or online, discussion groups, reading clubs, lunch and learns, time to practice new techniques, internal coaching, external coaching, and mentoring.

Resources

One common dynamic we've seen in our work is management wanting to make a change and wondering why it's taking so long while their staff also want to make the change but believe that management won't let them make the change. We refer to this as management and staff being in *violent agreement*—they just don't know it.

One cause of this dynamic is staff being asked to make a change without necessary resources—they necessarily will feel they are being prevented from making the change.

Bearing in mind that software development is intellectual, skills-based work, the kinds of resources needed for software change include access to training, access to coaching, and licenses to tools. Although it might not seem necessary, staff also need explicit permission to work on the adoption and time explicitly approved for this work. Without that, day-to-day task focus will take precedence. Larger organizations usually need full-time staff driving the adoption.

Without adequate resources, staff perception will be that "Leadership doesn't really mean it."

Incentives

Without incentives, you can expect resistance. This is natural, because people don't want to make changes that are not in their self-interest. Most people feel that the comfort of the status quo is in their self-interest—any change requires justification.

This is another area in which a vividly articulated vision helps. The incentives don't have to be monetary, and they don't have to be tangible. Each individual needs to understand why the change matters to them, why it is in their personal self-interest. This is a lot of work and requires a lot of sustained communication. But without it, the perception will be that "Leadership is taking advantage of us."

Remember to consider Autonomy, Mastery, and Purpose. A high-fidelity Agile implementation will increase individuals' and teams' Autonomy. The focus on empirically based planning and a Growth Mindset will support learning and Mastery. The leadership style most appropriate to support Agile teams will regularly communicate Purpose.

Action Plan

Without an action plan, the adoption will stall. Specific tasks need to be assigned to specific people, and timelines need to be established. The plan needs to be communicated to everyone involved, which, in an Agile adoption, is everyone. It's basic but often overlooked: If people don't know what to do to support the adoption, they aren't going to do it!

Pushing an adoption without an action plan leads to the perception that "Leadership is not committed to the change."

A common pattern in large organizations is to initiate numerous change cycles, most of which never reach fruition. After experiencing a few of these cycles, staff adopt the approach of keeping their heads down and hoping the change blows over before it affects them. Their organization's track record says there's a lot of merit to that approach.

Remember to incorporate Inspect and Adapt into the action plan. The change should be incremental and should involve improvements throughout the rollout based on regular retrospection and the application of lessons learned.

Table 23-1 summarizes the general effect and effect on the perception of leadership for each element that might be missing in the DCM.

Table 23-1 Effects of Missing Elements in the DCM

Lack of	Leads to	Which Creates Perception That
Vision	Confusion	Leadership doesn't know what it's doing.
Consensus	Sabotage	Leadership doesn't care about us.
Skills	Anxiety	Leadership is unreasonable.
Resources	Frustration	Leadership doesn't really mean it.
Incentives	Resistance	Leadership is taking advantage of us.
Action plan	Treadmill	Leadership is not committed to the change.

Propagating Change Through the Organization

The Domino Change Model is useful for both planning an Agile adoption and diagnosing the causes of a stalled adoption.

There's another aspect to adoption that's not contained in that model, however, one related to problems in how organizations pilot Agile practices and how they then proceed to roll out the practices on a larger scale.

In contrast to the idealized rollout described at the beginning of this chapter, many organizations' rollouts look more like this:

- The organization commits to an Agile adoption.
- The initial pilot team succeeds.
- The second or third teams to adopt the changes stumble or fail—the teams fail outright, the team abandons the new practices and reverts to old practices, or no teams can be found that will follow the pilot team.

Why does this happen? You're probably familiar with Geoffrey Moore's "Crossing the Chasm" model as it applies to market adoption of innovative products (Moore, 1991). I've found that the same dynamic applies to adoption of innovations *within* organizations.

Moore's model was based on seminal work by Everett Rogers in *Diffusion of Innovation* (Rogers, 1995). Because this discussion doesn't depend on Moore's notion of the "Chasm," I'm going to concentrate on Rogers' description.

In Rogers' model, innovations are adopted from left to right across the categories of adopters shown in Figure 23-2.

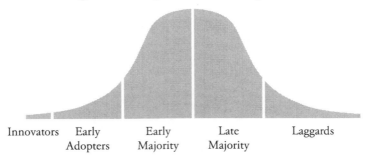

Figure 23-2
The innovation adoption sequence.

Each category of adopters displays certain attributes. The *Innovators* (the earliest adopters) are adventurous and eager to try new technologies or practices. They are attracted to novelty for its own sake. They can cope with a high degree of uncertainty—they're highly risk-tolerant. They fail often, and they aren't bothered by that because they're so motivated by the prospect of being the first person to get something new to work. Because they fail often, they might not be respected by adopters in the other categories.

Early Adopters share some attributes with the Innovators but toned down somewhat. They are also attracted to new technologies and practices, primarily because they are trying to get a big "win" before anyone else does. Early adopters don't fail as often as innovators, so they are respected opinion leaders in their organizations. They are role models for other adopters.

Innovators and Early Adopters have a few attributes in common. They are both attracted to innovation for its own sake. They are looking for revolutionary, game-changing gains. They are highly risk-tolerant and highly motivated to see the change work. They are willing to exert substantial personal energy and initiative to make the change work. They will read, seek out colleagues, experiment, and so on. They see challenges with the new thing as opportunities to make the new thing work before others do. Bottom line is that these people can succeed with little external support.

Now, the big question: Who typically works on pilot teams?

Innovators and Early Adopters! This is problematic because they are not representative of the majority of adopters in the organization, and they represent a fairly small percentage of adopters in the organization.

As Figure 23-3 on the following page shows, the innovation adoption sequence is a standard normal distribution (bell curve). Innovators are the third standard deviation from the mean, and Early Adopters are the second. Together, they represent only 15% of the total adopters.

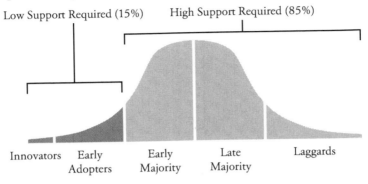

Figure 23-3
Different levels of support are required for different parts of the innovation adoption sequence. Later adopters require a higher level of support than earlier adopters.

In contrast with the earlier adopters (Innovators and Early Adopters), the later adopters (the 85%) also have some characteristics in common. They are attracted to novelty for the sake of improved quality or productivity but not for the sake of innovation or for its own sake. They are looking for low-risk, safe, incremental gains. They are not very risk-tolerant—many are risk-averse. Far from being willing to exert personal energy to overcome obstacles, they view obstacles as evidence that the change is a bad idea and should be abandoned. They aren't highly motivated to see the change succeed; their motivation ranges from half-heartedly wanting the change to work to wanting the change to fail.

What this means is that pilot teams don't tend to tell you most of what you need to know to lead a successful rollout. Later adopters will need more support, and most adopters will be later adopters.

Some leaders in tech organizations will argue that their staff consist of higher percentages of Innovators and Early Adopters and lower percentages of Early Majority, Late Majority, and Laggards. Indeed, percentages can vary for different populations, and that view might be true. But within their staff the same relative breakdown will be true. Their earlier adopters will perform the evaluations, and their later adopters will need relatively more support.

40,000-Foot Rollout View, Take 2

Here's the 40,000-foot view of a more reality-based Agile adoption approach:

Phase 1: Begin with a pilot team. Charter an initial team to trial an approach to Agile development in your organization. Work out the stumbling blocks at the single-team level.

Phase 2: Propagate Agile practices to one or more additional teams. Communicate a detailed vision of how Agile will benefit your organization and the people in it. Describe the benefits realized by the pilot team in detail. Communicate a detailed vision of how the Agile adoption will benefit the specific people on the next teams. Provide explicit training during work hours, coaching, and time to work on the rollout to the new teams. Establish communities of practice and support them. Check in regularly with the new teams, and offer to provide additional support. Work out additional kinks, including inter-team issues. Develop a plan for the level of training and support needed for the wider rollout.

Phase 3: Roll out Agile practices to the entire organization. Communicate a revised vision of how Agile will benefit your organization based on the first few teams' experience. Describe the benefits realized by those teams in detail, and explain what lessons have been learned that will help guarantee that additional teams will be successful. Listen to people's feedback, and revise the vision as needed. Communicate the revised vision, and acknowledge that it includes people's feedback.

Schedule meetings with each person who will be affected by the Agile adoption, and communicate a detailed vision of how the Agile adoption will benefit that person specifically. Prepare for each of these meetings by understanding the individual's specific case; do not treat the individual as just a generic member of a group.

Describe the specific plan for making Agile successful in your organization. Describe who is leading the adoption effort, what tasks will be needed to make the adoption successful, and the timeline for adoption.

Provide training and coaching during work hours. Emphasize that each team has permission to do the work needed to make the rollout successful. Check in regularly with the teams, and provide additional support. Make staff available to help work out issues within teams and across teams. Explain that challenges are expected and that support will be available when challenges occur.

Overall, apply the idea of Commander's Intent to the adoption. Set the vision (collaboratively), and then turn people loose to work out the details.

Inspect and Adapt

As the rollout continues, refer back to the Domino Change Model periodically, looking for signs of problems in each area. Each adoption is unique in some respects. Be open to feedback and changing direction if needed. This is an opportunity to model Inspect and Adapt behavior at the leadership level.

Suggested Leadership Actions

Inspect

* Review the Domino Change Model and how it applies to your past or current change initiatives. In what parts of the model has your organization typically been successful, and where is there room for improvement?
* Reflect on the innovation diffusion model and how it applies to your organization's track record with pilot teams. Do you agree that your pilot teams have consisted of Innovators and Early Adopters? How representative have they been of the rest of your organization?

Adapt

* Based on a gap analysis between your current Agile adoption and the Domino Change Model's categories, create a plan to improve performance in the gaps.
* Based on the gap analysis between your current support for later adopters and the innovation diffusion model, create a plan to provide a level of support appropriate for your later adopters.

Additional Resources

Rogers, Everett M. 1995. *Diffusion of Innovation, 4th Ed.* This is the definitive work on innovation diffusion.

Moore, Geoffrey. 1991. *Crossing the Chasm, Revised Ed.* This book popularized Rogers' work on innovation diffusion. It's highly readable and much shorter than Rogers' book.

Heifetz, Ronald A. and Marty Linsky. 2017. *Leadership on the Line: Staying Alive Through the Dangers of Change, Revised Ed.* This is a somewhat dry book that nonetheless provides a really useful way to think about the leader's role in leading change ("view from the balcony") and some important and seldom-discussed obstacles to change.

Kotter, John P. 2012. *Leading Change.* This is Kotter's definitive work on leading change.

Kotter, John and Holger Rathgeber. 2017. *Our Iceberg Is Melting, 10th Anniversary Edition.* This is an entertaining version of Kotter's change theory told in the form of a parable about penguins. If you like books like *Who Moved My Cheese* and *Fish! A Proven Way to Boost Morale and Improve Results*, you'll like this book.

Madsten, Corey. 2016. *How to Play Dominoes.* Every author gets a little bit punchy toward the end of writing a book. This citation is here just to see who's still reading.

PART V

CLOSING

~

This part of the book provides a vision of a high-functioning Agile organization, and it summarizes the Key Principles described throughout the book.

Enjoy the Fruits of Your Labor

⌒

From the beginning, "Agile" has served both as a rallying cry for better software development and as an umbrella term for a large collection of practices, principles, and philosophies that have been developed in support of that rallying cry.

Agile itself continues to Inspect and Adapt and to improve, which is why today's Agile is better than the Agile of 20 years ago. Modern Agile understands that the goal of Agile isn't simply to be agile. The goal is to use Agile practices and other practices to support the objectives and strategies of your business.

Effective Agile begins with leadership—you set the tone for your Agile teams. Clearly communicate your expectations through Commander's Intent, empower your teams, develop their ability to self manage, and then let them iterate and improve. Concentrate on fixing systems and processes rather than individuals. Help your organization decriminalize mistakes and develop a Growth Mindset. Use mistakes as learning opportunities, Inspect and Adapt, and gradually become better.

When this is done well, your organization will create teams that stay focused on the goals of your organization. The teams will be responsive to your organization's needs, even when they change. This will improve your organization's ability to respond to the changing needs of your customers.

Your teams will monitor the effectiveness of the practices they are using and replace ineffective practices with better ones. Their throughput will increase over time.

Your teams will continuously monitor their workflows. They will know where the work is and whether it's progressing as it should. They will provide extensive visibility to others. They will deliver what they say they are going to deliver, when they say they are going to deliver it, with high quality.

Your teams will work well together, with other teams, with other project stakeholders, and with the world beyond your organization.

Discoveries will be constant, but disruptive surprises will be few and far between. In the event of such surprises, the teams will provide early notification, which will allow both the teams and the rest of your organization to respond quickly and effectively.

The teams will maintain high quality at all times and identify opportunities for improvement regularly. Motivation will be high, and attrition will be low.

✎

As your organization progresses toward this vision of effective software development, it will move through a few maturation phases.

Initially, the focus will be on the team's internal performance. Teams will require several sprints to learn Scrum and other supporting Agile practices. They will work on their ability to plan in small increments, design in ways that support short iterations, prioritize, commit, maintain high quality, make decisions on behalf of your organization, work together as a team, and deliver. Depending on how well they are supported and on how much friction they encounter from the rest of the organization, they might require numerous sprints to reach this level of capability.

Over time, the focus will shift to the organization's interaction with your teams. Because your teams' capacity has increased, your organization will need to support them with clear product leadership on requirements priorities and other priorities and with timely decision making that matches pace with the team's increased capacity.

Eventually, iterative changes will transform your teams. They will deliver quickly and change direction quickly. This will open up strategic opportunities for your organization to plan and execute differently and better, using your enhanced development capability.

The focus on a Growth Mindset and on Inspect and Adapt means that, over time, all of this just gets better and better.

Enjoy!

Summary of Key Principles

Inspect and Adapt. Agile is an empirical approach that depends on learning from experience. This requires creating opportunities to reflect periodically and make adjustments based on experience. (Page 30)

Start with Scrum. Scrum is not necessarily the final destination on an Agile journey, but it is the most-structured, best-supported place to start. (Page 38)

Build Cross-Functional Teams. Work on Agile projects occurs within self-managed teams. To be self-managed, teams must include the full set of skills needed to make well-informed decisions that are binding on the organization. (Page 63)

Integrate Testers into the Development Teams. Tighten the feedback loop between development and test by having the people doing the work work more closely together. (Page 68)

Motivate Teams Through Autonomy, Mastery, and Purpose. Agile practices inherently support the factors that contribute to motivation. Teams are intended to work with Autonomy and to become better over time (Mastery). In order to do so, they need to understand their Purpose. The concepts of "healthy Agile team" and "motivated Agile team" are strongly intertwined. (Page 77)

Develop a Growth Mindset. Whether you look at it from the point of view of the "Mastery" part of Autonomy, Mastery, and Purpose or from the point of view of Inspect and Adapt, effective Agile teams maintain a steady focus on getting better. (Page 81)

Develop Business Focus. Developers frequently need to fill in gaps in requirements and in direction from their Product Owner. Understanding their business helps them fill those gaps in ways that are beneficial to the business. (Page 84)

Tighten Feedback Loops. Don't take any longer to learn lessons than you need to; keep the feedback loops as tight as possible. This supports more rapid progress from Inspect and Adapt and faster improvements in effectiveness from Develop a Growth Mindset. (Page 89)

Fix the System, Not the Individual. Most software professionals want to do good work. If they aren't doing good work—and especially if it seems like they're trying not to do good work—understand what dynamics are contributing to that. Look for the system problem that's frustrating the person. (Page 98)

Increase Team Capacity by Building Individual Capacity. Teams exhibit attributes that are a combination of the team members' individual attributes and of their interactions. Strengthen your teams by strengthening the individuals on the teams. (Page 103)

Keep Projects Small. Small projects are easier and more often successful. Not all work can be structured into small projects, but the work that can be structured that way should be. (Page 120)

Keep Sprints Short. Short sprints support a frequent Inspect and Adapt feedback loop. They expose problems quickly, making it easy to nip small problems in the bud before they become large problems. (Page 123)

Deliver in Vertical Slices. Feedback is important in Agile. Teams get better feedback on their technology and design choices—both from customers and the business—when they deliver in vertical slices rather than horizontal slices. (Page 128)

Manage Technical Debt. A consistent focus on quality is part of an effective Agile implementation. Managing technical debt supports higher team morale, faster progress, and higher quality products. (Page 131)

Support Large Agile Projects Through Architecture. Good architecture can support portioned work on a project and minimize large-project overhead. Great architecture can make a large project feel like a smaller one. (Page 144)

Minimize the Defect Detection Gap. The cost to fix a defect tends to grow the longer it stays in process. A benefit of Agile's focus on continuous quality work is detecting more defects closer to the source. (Page 155)

Create and Use a Definition of Done. A good Definition of Done helps catch incomplete or faulty work early, minimizing the gap between defect insertion and detection. (Page 157)

Maintain a Releasable Level of Quality. Maintaining a releasable level of quality helps catch additional defects that slip through an earlier DoD. (Page 160)

Use Automated Tests, Created by the Development Team. Automated tests help to minimize the defect detection gap. Making everyone on the team responsible for the tests reinforces the idea that quality is everyone's responsibility. (Page 168)

Refine the Product Backlog. Backlog refinement ensures the team is working on the highest priority items, is not filling in gaps in requirements on its own, and is not starved for work (Page 187)

Create and Use a Definition of Ready. Part of backlog refinement is ensuring that requirements are truly ready before the team begins implementing them. (Page 188)

Automate Repetitive Activities. No one likes repetitive activities, and many of the activities that can be automated in software development provide more benefit when they're automated than when they aren't. (Page 208)

Manage to Outcomes, Not Details. Support your team's Autonomy by clearly communicating desired outcomes while leaving the team free to define the detailed means by which it completes its work. (Page 219)

Express Clear Purpose with Commander's Intent. Support your teams' ability to make timely, local decisions by clearly communicating your objectives for the desired end state. (Page 220)

Focus on Throughput, Not Activity. Similar to managing to outcomes, adding the nuance that busyness is not the objective—getting valuable work done is the objective. (Page 223)

Model Key Agile Behaviors. Effective leaders model the behaviors they want to see in others. (Page 224)

Decriminalize Mistakes. Decriminalize mistakes so that teams surface them without hesitation and you can learn from them. A mistake you don't learn from penalizes your organization twice. (Page 227)

Plan Based on Measured Team Capacity. Agile is an empirical approach; teams and organizations should plan their work based on their measured performance. (Page 232)

Bibliography

⌒

AAMI. 2012. *Guidance on the use of AGILE practices in the development of medical device software.* 2012. AAMI TIR45 2012.

Adolph, Steve. 2006. What Lessons Can the Agile Community Learn from a Maverick Fighter Pilot? *Proceedings of the Agile 2006 Conference.*

Adzic, Gojko and David Evans. 2014. *Fifty Quick Ideas to Improve Your User Stories.* Neuri Consulting LLP.

Aghina, Wouter, et al. 2019. *How to select and develop individuals for successful agile teams: A practical guide.* McKinsey & Company.

Bass, Len, et al. 2012. *Software Architecture in Practice, 3rd Ed.* Addison-Wesley Professional.

Beck, Kent and Cynthia Andres. 2005. *Extreme Programming Explained: Embrace Change, 2nd Ed.* Addison-Wesley.

Beck, Kent. 2000. *Extreme Programming Explained: Embrace Change.* Addison-Wesley.

Belbute, John. 2019. *Continuous Improvement in the Age of Agile Development.*

Boehm, Barry and Richard Turner. 2004. *Balancing Agility and Discipline: A Guide for the Perplexed.* Addison-Wesley.

Boehm, Barry. 1981. *Software Engineering Economics.* Prentice-Hall.

Boehm, Barry W. 1988. A Spiral Model of Software Development and Enhancement. *Computer.* May 1988.

Boehm, Barry, et al. 2000. *Software Cost Estimation with Cocomo II.* Prentice Hall PTR.

Boyd, John R. 2007. *Patterns of Conflict.* January 2007.

Brooks, Fred. 1975. *Mythical Man-Month.* Addison-Wesley.

Carnegie, Dale. 1936. *How to Win Friends and Influence People.* Simon & Schuster.

Cherniss, Cary, Ph.D. 1999. The business case for emotional intelligence. [Online] 1999. [Cited: January 25, 2019.]

Cohn, Mike. 2010. *Succeeding with Agile: Software Development Using Scrum.* Addison-Wesley.

—. 2004. *User Stories Applied: For Agile Software Development.* Addison-Wesley, 2004.

Collyer, Keith and Jordi Manzano. 2013. Being agile while still being compliant: A practical approach for medical device manufacturers. [Online] March 5, 2013. [Cited: January 20, 2019.]

Conway, Melvin E. 1968. How do Committees Invent? *Datamation.* April 1968.

Coram, Robert. 2002. *Boyd: The Fighter Pilot Who Changed the Art of War.* Back Bay Books.

Crispin, Lisa and Janet Gregory. 2009. *Agile Testing: A Practical Guide for Testers and Agile Teams.* Addison-Wesley Professional.

Curtis, Bill, et al. 2009. *People Capability Maturity Model (P-CMM) Version 2.0, 2nd Ed.* Software Engineering Institute.

DeMarco, Tom. 2002. *Slack: Getting Past Burnout, Busywork, and the Myth of Total Efficiency.* Broadway Books.

Derby, Esther and Diana Larsen. 2006. *Agile Retrospectives: Making Good Teams Great.* Pragmatic Bookshelf.

DORA. 2018. *2018 Accelerate: State of Devops.* DevOps Research and Assessment.

Doyle, Michael and David Strauss. 1993. *How to Make Meetings Work!* Jove Books.

Dweck, Carol S. 2006. *Mindset: The New Psychology of Success.* Ballantine Books.

DZone Research. 2015. *The Guide to Continuous Delivery.* Sauce Labs.

Feathers, Michael. 2004. *Working Effectively with Legacy Code.* Prentice Hall PTR.

Fisher, Roger and William Ury. 2011. *Getting to Yes: Negotiating Agreement Without Giving In, 3rd Ed.* Penguin Books.

Forsgren, Nicole, et al. 2018. *Accelerate: The Science of Lean Software and DevOps: Building and Scaling High Performing Technology Organizations.* IT Revolution.

Gilb, Tom. 1988. *Principles of Software Engineering Management.* Addison-Wesley.

Goleman, Daniel. 2004. What Makes a Leader? *Harvard Business Review.* January 2004.

Gould, Stephen Jay. 1977. *Ever Since Darwin.* WW Norton & Co Inc.

Grenning, James. 2001. Launching Extreme Programming at a Process-Intensive Company. *IEEE Software.* November/December 2001.

Hammarberg, Marcus and Joakim Sundén. 2014. *Kanban in Action.* Manning Publications.

Heifetz, Ronald A. and Marty Linsky. 2017. *Leadership on the Line: Staying Alive Through the Dangers of Change, Revised Ed.* Harvard Business Review Press.

Hooker, John, 2003. *Working Across Cultures.* Stanford University Press.

Humble, Jez, et al. 2015. *Lean Enterprise: How High Performance Organizations Innovate at Scale.* O'Reilly Media.

Humble, Jez. 2018. *Building and Scaling High Performing Technology Organizations.* October 26, 2018. Construx Software Leadership Summit.

James, Geoffrey. 2018. It's Official: Open-Plan Offices Are Now the Dumbest Management Fad of All Time. *Inc.* July 16, 2018.

Jarrett, Christian. 2018. Open-plan offices drive down face-to-face interactions and increase use of email. *BPS Research.* July 5, 2018.

—. 2013. The supposed benefits of open-plan offices do not outweigh the costs. *BPS Research.* August 19, 2013.

Jones, Capers and Olivier Bonsignour. 2012. *The Economics of Software Quality.* Addison-Wesley.

Jones, Capers. 1991. *Applied Software Measurement: Assuring Productivity and Quality.* McGraw-Hill.

Konnikova, Maria. 2014. The Open-Office Trap. *New Yorker.* January 7, 2014.

Kotter, John and Holger Rathgeber. 2017. *Our Iceberg is Melting, 10th Anniversary Edition.* Portfolio/Penguin.

Kotter, John P. 2012. *Leading Change.* Harvard Business Review Press.

Kruchten, Philippe, et al. 2019. *Managing Technical Debt.* Software Engineering Institute.

Kurtz, C.F., and D. J. Snowden. 2003. The new dynamics of strategy: Sense-making in a complex and complicated world. *IBM Systems Journal.* 2003, Vol. 42, 3.

Lacey, Mitch. 2016. *The Scrum Field Guide: Agile Advice for Your First Year and Beyond, 2d Ed.* Addison-Wesley.

Leffingwell, Dean. 2011. *Agile Software Requirements: Lean Requirements Practices for Teams, Programs, and the Enterprise.* Pearson Education.

Lencioni, Patrick. 2002. *The Five Dysfunctions of a Team.* Jossey-Bass.

Lipmanowicz, Henri and Keith McCandless. 2013. *The Surprising Power of Liberating Structures.* Liberating Structures Press.

Martin, Robert C. 2017. *Clean Architecture: A Craftsman's Guide to Software Structure and Design.* Prentice Hall.

Maxwell, John C. 2007. *The 21 Irrefutable Laws of Leadership.* Thomas Nelson.

McConnell, Steve and Jenny Stuart. 2018. Agile Technical Coach Career Path. [Online] 2018.

—. **2018.** Career Pathing for Software Professionals. [Online] 2018. https://www.construx.com/whitepapers.

—. **2018.** Software Architect Career Path. [Online] 2018. https://www.construx.com/whitepapers.

—. **2018.** Software Product Owner Career Path. [Online] 2018. https://www.construx.com/whitepapers.

—. **2018.** Software Quality Manager Career Path. [Online] 2018. https://www.construx.com/whitepapers.

—. **2018.** Software Technical Manager Career Path. [Online] 2018. https://www.construx.com/whitepapers.

McConnell, Steve. 2004. *Code Complete, 2nd Ed.* Microsoft Press.

—. **2016.** Measuring Software Development Productivity. [Online] 2016. [Cited: January 19, 2019].

—. **2016.** Measuring Software Development Productivity. *Construx Software.* [Online] Construx Sofware, 2016. [Cited: June 26, 2019].

—. **2004.** *Professional Software Development.* Addison-Wesley.

—. **1996.** *Rapid Development: Taming Wild Software Schedules.* Microsoft Press.

—. **2000.** Sitting on the Suitcase. *IEEE Software.* May/June 2000.

—. **2006.** *Software Estimation: Demystifying the Black Art.* Microsoft Press.

—. **2019.** Understanding Software Projects Lecture Series. *Construx OnDemand.* [Online]

—. **2011.** What does 10x mean? Measuring Variations in Programmer Productivity. [book auth.] Andy and Greg Wilson, Eds Oram. *Making Software: What Really Works, and Why We Believe It.* O'Reilly.

Meyer, Bertrand. 2014. *Agile! The Good, They Hype and the Ugly.* Springer.

—. **1992.** Applying "Design by Contract". *IEEE Computer.* October 1992.

Moore, Geoffrey. 1991. *Crossing the Chasm, Revised Ed.* Harper Business.

Mulqueen, Casey and David Collins. 2014. *Social Style & Versatility Facilitator Handbook.* TRACOM Press.

Nygard, Michael T. 2018. *Release It!: Design and Deploy Production-Ready Software, 2nd Ed.* Pragmatic Bookshelf.

Oosterwal, Dantar P. 2010. *The Lean Machine: How Harley-Davidson Drove Top-Line Growth and Profitability with Revolutionary Lean Product Development.* AMACOM.

Patterson, Kerry, et al. 2002. *Crucial Conversations: Tools for talking when the stakes are high.* McGraw-Hill.

Patton, Jeff. 2014. *User Story Mapping: Discover the Whole Story, Build the Right Product.* O'Reilly Media.

Pink, Daniel H. 2009. *Drive: The Surprising Truth About What Motivates Us.* Riverhead Books.

Poole, Charles and Jan Willem Huisman. 2001. Using Extreme Programming in a Maintenance Environment. *IEEE Software.* November/December 2001.

Poppendieck, Mary and Tom. 2006. *Implementing Lean Software Development.* Addison-Wesley Professional.

Puppet Labs. 2014. *2014 State of DevOps Report.* 2014.

Putnam, Lawrence H., and and Ware Myers. 1992. *Measures for Excellence: Reliable Software On Time, Within Budget.* Yourdon Press.

Reinertsen, Donald G. 2009. *The Principles of Product Development Flow: Second Generation Lean Product Development.* Celeritas Publishing.

Richards, Chet. 2004. *Certain to Win: The Strategy of John Boyd, Applied to Business.* Xlibris Corporation.

Rico, Dr. David F. 2009. *The Business Value of Agile Software Methods.* J. Ross Publishing.

Robertson, Robertson Suzanne and James. 2013. *Mastering the Requirements Process: Getting Requirements Right, 3rd Ed.* Addison-Wesley.

Rogers, Everett M. 1995. *Diffusion of Innovation, 4th Ed.* The Free Press.

Rotary International. The Four-Way Test. *Wikipedia.* [Online] [Cited: June 23, 2019.]

Rozovsky, Julia. 2015. The five keys to a successful Google team. [Online] November 17, 2015. [Cited: November 25, 2018.]

Rubin, Kenneth. 2012. *Essential Scrum: A Practical Guide to the Most Popular Agile Process.* Addison-Wesley.

Scaled Agile, Inc. 2017. Achieving Regulatory and Industry Standards Compliance with the Scaled Agile Framework. *Scaled Agile Framework.* [Online] August 2017. [Cited: June 25, 2019.]

Schuh, Peter. 2001. Recovery, Redemption, and Extreme Programming. *IEEE Software.* November/December 2001.

Schwaber, Ken and Jeff Sutherland. 2017. *The Scrum Guide: The Definitive Guide to Scrum: The Rules of the Game.* 2017. [Online]

Schwaber, Ken. 1995. SCRUM Development Process. *Proceedings of the 10th Annual ACM Conference on Object Oriented Programming Systems, Languages, and Applications (OOPSLA)*. 1995.

Scrum Alliance. 2017. *State of Scrum 2017-2018.*

Snowden, David J. and Mary E. Boone. 2007. A Leader's Framework for Decision Making. *Harvard Business Review.* November 2007.

Standish Group. 2013. *Chaos Manifesto 2013: Think Big, Act Small.*

Stellman, Andrew and Jennifer Green. 2013. *Learning Agile: Understanding Scrum, XP, Lean, and Kanban.* O'Reilly Media.

Stuart, Jenny and Melvin Perez. 2018. Retrofitting Legacy Systems with Unit Tests. [Online] July 2018.

Stuart, Jenny, et al. 2018. Six Things Every Software Executive Should Know About Scrum. [Online] 2018.

—. 2017. Staffing Scrum Roles. [Online] 2017.

—. 2018. Succeeding with Geographically Distributed Scrum. [Online]

—. 2018. Ten Keys to Successful Scrum Adoption. [Online] 2018.

—. 2018. Ten Pitfalls of Enterprise Agile Adoption. [Online] 2018.

Sutherland, Jeff. 2014. *Scrum: The Art of Doing Twice the Work in Half the Time.* Crown Business.

Tockey, Steve. 2005. *Return on Software: Maximizing the Return on Your Software Investment.* Addison-Wesley.

Twardochleb, Michal. 2017. Optimal selection of team members according to Belbin's theory. *Scientific Journals of the Maritime University of Szczecin.* September 15, 2017.

U.S. Marine Corps Staff. 1989. *Warfighting: The U.S. Marine Corp Book of Strategy.* Currency Doubleday.

Velocity Culture (The Unmet Challenge in Ops). Jenkins, Jon. June 16, 2011. June 16, 2011. O'Reilly Velocity Conference.

Westrum, Ron. 2005. A Typology of Organisational Cultures. January 2005, pp. 22-27.

Wiegers, Karl and Joy Beatty. 2013. *Software Requirements, 3rd Ed.* Microsoft Press.

Williams, Laurie and Robert Kessler. 2002. *Pair Programming Illuminated.* Addison-Wesley.

Yale Center for Emotional Intelligence. 2019. The RULER Model. [Online]. [Cited: January 19, 2019.] http://ei.yale.edu/ruler/.

Acknowledgments

⁓

Thanks first and foremost to my technical colleagues at Construx Software. I have the good fortune to work with a remarkably intelligent, talented, and experienced staff, and this book—largely a summary of our collective experiences—would not be possible without their contributions. Thanks to **Jenny Stuart**, VP of Consulting, for her incredible experience and insights working on large-scale Agile adoptions. I appreciate her comments on navigating organizational issues in large organizations. Thanks to **Matt Peloquin**, CTO, for his expertise, unrivaled worldwide after leading more than 500 architecture reviews, in software architecture and the role it plays in Agile implementations. Thanks to **Earl Beede**, Senior Fellow, consultant and instructor extraordinaire, for his insights into the clearest ways of presenting Agile concepts so that teams understand them and can implement them effectively. Thanks to **Melvin Pérez-Cedano**, Senior Fellow, for his combination of worldwide experience and capacious book knowledge. Thank you, Melvin, for being my walking reference resource for this project and a key guide to the practices that work most effectively. Thanks to

Erik Simmons, Senior Fellow, for being a bottomless well of knowledge about research in uncertainty and complexity and for his expert guidance in implementing Agile practices in large-scale, traditional companies. Thanks to **Steve Tockey**, Principal Consultant, for his deep insight and unmatched foundational knowledge about traditional, rigorous software practices and how they interplay with Agile practices. Thanks to **Bob Webber**, Senior Fellow, for his insights into Agile product management—his decades of leadership experience have helped focus this book on what leaders need. And, finally, thanks to **John Clifford**, Agile Practices Lead, for his track record of encouraging, coaching, exhorting, and occasionally compelling organizations to realize all the value they should from their Agile adoptions. What an incredible group! I have been so fortunate to work with these people.

More than 300 software leaders read earlier drafts of this book and provided review comments. The book is immeasurably better because of their generous contributions.

Special thanks to Chris Alexander for his thorough explanation and terrific examples of OODA. Special thanks to Bernie Anger for extensive commentary on succeeding in the Product Owner role. Special thanks to John Belbute for insightful comments on measurement and process improvement. Special thanks to Bill Curtis and Mike Russell for taking me to task on some misconceptions about PDCA (no longer in the book). Special thanks to Rob Daigneau for his commentary on architecture and CI/CD. Special thanks to Brian Donaldson for the in-depth estimation review. Special thanks to Lars Marowsky-Bree and Ed Sullivan for comprehensive comments on factors needed for success with distributed teams. Special thanks to Marion Miller for describing how emergency response teams are organized and how that relates to Agile organizations. Special thanks to Bryan Pflug for extensive commentary about software development under aerospace regulations.

I appreciate the following reviewers who returned comments on selected portions of the draft: Mark Abermoske, Anant Adke, Haytham Alzeini, Prashant Ambe, Vidyha Anand, Royce Ausburn, Joseph Balistrieri, Erika Barber, Ed Bateman, Mark Beardall, Greg Bertoni, Diana Bittle, Margaret Bohn, Terry Bretz, Darwin Castillo, Jason Cole, Jenson Crawford, Bruce Cronquist, Peter Daly, Brian Daugherty, Matt Davey, Paul David, Tim Dawson, Ritesh Desai, Anthony Diaz, Randy Dojutrek, Adam Dray, Eric Evans, Ron Farrington, Claudio Fayad, Geoff Flamank, Lisa Forsyth, Jim Forsythe, Robin Franko, Jane Fraser, Fazeel Gareeboo, Inbar Gazit, David Geving, Paul Gower, Ashish Gupta, Chris Halton, Ram Hariharan, Jason Hills, Gary Hinkle, Mike Hoffmann, Chris Holl, Peter Horadan, Sandra Howlett, Fred Hugand, Scott Jensen, Steve Karmesin, Peter Kretzman, David Leib, Andrew Levine, Andrew Lichey, Eric Lind, Howard Look, Zhi Cong (Chong) Luo, Dale Lutz, Marianne Marck, Keith B. Marcos, David McTavish, J.D. Meier, Suneel Mendiratta, Henry Meuret, Bertrand Meyer, Rob Muir, Chris Murphy, Pete Nathan, Michael Nassirian, Scott Norton, Daniel Rensilot Okine, Ganesh Palave, Peter Paznokas, Jim Pyles, Mark Ronan, Roshanak Roshandel, Hiranya Samarasekera, Nalin Savara, Tom Schaffernoth, Senthi Senthilmurugan, Charles Seybold, Andrew Sinclair, Tom Spitzer, Dave Spokane, Michael Sprick, Tina Strand, Nancy Sutherland, Jason Tanner, Chris Thompson, Bruce Thorne, Leanne Trevorrow, John Ward, Wendy Wells, Gavian Whishaw, and Howard Wu.

Thanks to the following reviewers who returned comments on the entire manuscript: Edwin Adriaansen, Carlos Amselem, John Anderson, Mehdi Aouadi, Mark Apgar, Brad Appleton, Giovanni Asproni, Joseph Bangs, Alex Barros, Jared Bellows,

John M. Bemis, Robert Binder, Mike Blackstock, Dr. Zarik Boghossian, Gabriel Boiciuc, Greg Borchers, Xander Botha, Melvin Brandman, Kevin Brune, Timothy Byrne, Dale Campbell, Mike Cargal, Mark Cassidy, Mike Cheng, George Chow, Ronda Cilsick, Peter Clark, Michelle K. Cole, John Connolly, Sarah Cooper, John Coster, Alan Crouch, James Cusick, David Daly, Trent Davies, Dan DeLapp, Steve Dienstbier, Ilhan Dilber, Nicholas DiLisi, Jason Domask, David Draffin, Dr. Ryan J. Durante, Jim Durrell, Alex Elentukh, Paul Elia, Robert A. Ensink, Earl Everett, Mark Famous, Craig Fisher, Jamie Forgan, Iain Forsyth, John R Fox, Steven D. Fraser, Steve Freeman, Reeve Fritchman, Krisztian Gaspar, Manny Gatlin, Rege George, Glenn Goodrich, Lee Grant, Kirk Gray, Matthew Grulke, Mir Hajmiragha, Matt Hall, Colin Hammond, Jeff Hanson, Paul Harding, Joshua Harmon, Graham Haythornthwaite, Jim Henley, Ned Henson, Neal Herman, Samuel Hon, Dewey Hou, Bill Humphrey, Lise Hvatum, Nathan Itskovitch, Rob Jasper, Kurian John, James Judd, Mark Karen, Tom Kerr, Yogesh Khambia, Timo Kissel, Katie Knobbs, Mark Kochanski, Hannu Kokko, Sunil Kripalani, Mukesh Kumar, Sumant Kumar, Matt Kuznicki, Stefan Landvogt, Michael Lange, Andrew Lavers, Robert Lee, Anthony Letts, Gilbert Lévesque, Ron Lichty, Ken Liu, Jon Loftin, Sergio Lopes, Arnie Lund, Jeff Malek, Koen Mannaerts, Risto Matikainen, Chris Matts, Kevin McEachern, Ernst Menet, Karl Métivier, Scott Miller, Praveen Minumula, Brad Moore, David Moore, Sean Morley, Steven Mullins, Ben Nguyen, Ryan North, Louis Ormond, Patrick O'Rourke, Uma Palepu, Steve Perrin, Daniel Petersen, Brad Porter, Terri Potts, Jon Price, John Purdy, Mladen Radovic, Venkat Ramamurthy, Vinu Ramasamy, Derek Reading, Barbara Robbins, Tim Roden, Neil Roodyn, Dennis Rubsam, John Santamaria, Pablo Santos Luaces, Barry Saylor, Matt Schouten, Dan Schreiber, Jeff Schroeder, John Sellars, Don Shafer, Desh Sharma, David

Sholan, Creig R. Smith, Dave B Smith, Howie Smith, Steve Snider, Mitch Sonnen, Erik Sowa, Sebastian Speck, Kurk Spendlove, Tim Stauffer, Chris Sterling, Peter Stevens, Lorraine Steyn, Joakim Sundén, Kevin Taylor, Mark Thristan, Bill Tucker, Scot Tutkovics, Christian P. Valcke, PhD, Paul van Hagen, Mark H. Waldron, Bob Wambach, Evan Wang, Phil White, Tim White, Jon Whitney, Matthew Willis, Bob Wilmes, David Wood, Ronnie Yates, Tom Yosick, and Barry Young.

In a large set of reviews, several stood out as especially thorough and useful. Special thanks for these reviews to John Aukshunas, Santanu Banerjee, Jim Bird, Alastair Blakey, Michelle Canfield, Ger Cloudt, Terry Coatta, Charles Davies, Rob Dull, Rik Essenius, Ryan E. Fleming, Tom Greene, Owain Griffiths, Chris Haverkate, Dr Arne Hoffmann, Bradey Honsinger, Philippe Kruchten, Steve Lane, Ashlyn Leahy, Kamil Litman, Steve Maraspin, Jason McCartney, Mike Morton, Shaheeda Nizar, Andrew Park, Jammy Pate, John Reynders, André Sintzoff, Pete Stuntz, Barbara Talley, Eric Upchurch, Maxas Volodin, Ryland Wallace, Matt Warner, Wayne Washburn, and David Wight.

I also want to acknowledge the excellent work of our production team, including Rob Nance for the graphics, Tonya Rimbey for spearheading our review initiative, and Joanne Sprott for indexing. Thanks also to Jesse Bronson, Paul Donovan, Jeff Ehlers, Melissa Feroe, Mark Griffin, and Mark Nygren for recruiting reviewers. Thanks to Cody Madison for the terrific supplemental videos.

Finally, extra special thanks to Devon Musgrave, project editor. This is my third book project with Devon. His editorial judgment improved this book in countless ways, and his steady interest in my various writing projects was instrumental in making this book possible.

Index

W

About the Author

STEVE MCCONNELL is best-known as the author of *Code Complete*, a software industry classic that is often described as the best-reviewed, best-selling software development book of all time. Steve's books have been translated into 20 languages and sold more than one million copies worldwide.

Steve's company, Construx Software, has been helping software organizations improve their capabilities for more than 20 years. Construx's vision is *to make every software project successful by advancing the professional effectiveness of individuals, teams, and organizations.*

For more information, see www.stevemcconnell.com or email Steve at stevemcc@construx.com.

Software Leadership SUMMIT

MORE
More Effective
Agile

Visit the *More Effective Agile* website. You'll find:

> ➤ Suggested Leadership Actions workbook

> ➤ Bibliography with links to online references

> ➤ An interview with Steve McConnell

> ➤ The white papers described in this book

> ➤ Professional development support for your teams

> ➤ Extensive Agile resources

> ➤ Discounts on Construx Agile training, including online and in-person training

Check out the site today, and sign up to become a *More Effective Agile* insider!

Made in the USA
Monee, IL
07 November 2019

16467526R10208